FEELING THE HEAT

A DECADE AS A
FOREIGN CORRESPONDENT IN SPAIN

The Cañada Blanch / Sussex Academic Studies on Contemporary Spain

General Editor: Professor Paul Preston, London School of Economics

A list of all published titles in the series is available on the Press website. More recently published works are presented below.

Concha Alborg, *My Mother, That Stranger: Letters from the Spanish Civil War.*

Peter Anderson, *Friend or Foe?: Occupation, Collaboration and Selective Violence in the Spanish Civil War.*

Germà Bel, *Disdain, Distrust, and Dissolution: The Surge of Support for Independence in Catalonia.*

Carl-Henrik Bjerström, *Josep Renau and the Politics of Culture in Republican Spain, 1931–1939: Re-imagining the Nation.*

Darryl Burrowes, *Historians at War: Cold War Influences on Anglo-American Representations of the Spanish Civil War.*

Andrew Canessa (ed.), *Barrier and Bridge: Spanish and Gibraltarian Perspectives on Their Border.*

Kathryn Crameri, *'Goodbye, Spain?': The Question of Independence for Catalonia.*

Pol Dalmau, *Press, Politics and National Identities in Catalonia: The Transformation of La Vanguardia, 1881–1931.*

Mark Derby, *Petals and Bullets: Dorothy Morris — A New Zealand Nurse in the Spanish Civil War.*

Francisco Espinosa-Maestre, *Shoot the Messenger?: Spanish Democracy and the Crimes of Francoism — From the Pact of Silence to the Trial of Baltasar Garzón.*

María Jesús González, *Raymond Carr: The Curiosity of the Fox.*

Helen Graham, *The War and its Shadow: Spain's Civil War in Europe's Long Twentieth Century.*

Arnau Gonzàlez i Vilalta (ed.), *The Illusion of Statehood: Perceptions of Catalan Independence up to the End of the Spanish Civil War.*

Xabier A. Irujo, *GERNIKA: Genealogy of a Lie.*

Mandie Iveson, *Language Attitudes, National Identity and Migration in Catalonia: 'What the Women Have to Say'*

Angela Jackson, *'For us it was Heaven': The Passion, Grief and Fortitude of Patience Darton — From the Spanish Civil War to Mao's China.*

Gabriel Jackson, *Juan Negrín: Physiologist, Socialist, and Spanish Republican War Leader.*

Nathan Jones, *The Adoption of a Pro-US Foreign Policy by Spain and the United Kingdom: José María Aznar and Tony Blair's Personal Motivations and their Global Impact.*

Xavier Moreno Juliá, *The Blue Division: Spanish Blood in Russia, 1941–1945.*

David Lethbridge, *Norman Bethune in Spain: Commitment, Crisis, and Conspiracy.*

Antonio Miguez Macho, *The Genocidal Genealogy of Francoism: Violence, Memory and Impunity.*

Carles Manera, *The Great Recession: A Subversive View.*

Nicholas Manganas, *Las dos Españas: Terror and Crisis in Contemporary Spain.*

Jorge Marco, *Guerrilleros and Neighbours in Arms: Identities and Cultures of Antifascist Resistance in Spain.*

Emily Mason, *Democracy, Deeds and Dilemmas: Support for the Spanish Republic within British Civil Society, 1936–1939.*

Soledad Fox Maura, *Jorge Semprún: The Spaniard who Survived the Nazis and Conquered Paris.*

Martin Minchom, *Spain's Martyred Cities: From the Battle of Madrid to Picasso's Guernica.*

Olivia Muñoz-Rojas, *Ashes and Granite: Destruction and Reconstruction in the Spanish Civil War and Its Aftermath.*

Linda Palfreeman, *Spain Bleeds: The Development of Battlefield Blood Transfusion during the Civil War.*

Fernando Puell de la Villa and David García Hernán (eds.), *War and Population Displacement: Lessons of History.*

Rúben Serém, *Conspiracy, Coup d'état and Civil War in Seville, 1936–1939: History and Myth in Francoist Spain.*

Gareth Stockey, *Gibraltar: "A Dagger in the Spine of Spain?"*

Maggie Torres, *Anarchism and Political Change in Spain: Schism, Polarisation and Reconstruction of the* Confederación Nacional del Trabajo, *1939–1979.*

Dacia Viejo-Rose, *Reconstructing Spain: Cultural Heritage and Memory after Civil War.*

Antoni Vives, *SMART City Barcelona: The Catalan Quest to Improve Future Urban Living.*

In memory of my father

FEELING THE HEAT

A DECADE AS A
FOREIGN CORRESPONDENT IN SPAIN

From the Financial Crisis to the Pandemic

RAPHAEL MINDER

sussex
ACADEMIC
PRESS
Brighton • Chicago • Toronto

Cañada Blanch Centre
for Contemporary
Spanish Studies

2 4 6 8 10 9 7 5 3 1

First published in Spanish under the title ¿*Esto es España?*:
Una década de corresponsalía, by Ediciones Península, 2019.

Published in English in 2021 in Great Britain by
SUSSEX ACADEMIC PRESS
PO Box 139
Eastbourne BN24 9BP

Distributed in North America by
SUSSEX ACADEMIC PRESS
Independent Publishers Group
814 N. Franklin Street
Chicago, IL 60610

Published in collaboration with the Cañada Blanch Centre for Contemporary Spanish Studies, London School of Economics.

British Library Cataloguing in Publication Data
A CIP catalogue record for this book is available from the British Library.

Library of Congress Cataloging-in-Publication Data
To be applied for.

Paperback ISBN 978-1-78976-149-8

Typeset and designed by Sussex Academic Press, Brighton & Eastbourne.
Printed and bound by CPI Group (UK) Ltd, Croydon, CR0 4YY

Contents

Cañada Blanch Centre for Contemporary Spanish Studies   ix
Series Editor's Preface by Paul Preston   xi

Introducing the Job of Foreign Correspondent   1
A turbulent decade in a country of contrasts   3

Politics
The path of justice: The ups-and-down of Baltasar Garzón   11
The Catalan controversy: The many facets of independence   18
A hot autumn: Chaos and conflict in the Catalan referendum   28
Speaking to all sides: The sharp edges of secessionism   41
A European love: Spain's relationship with the European   48
      Union
The generation of 2015: The end of the two-party system   56

Economy
The gods of money: The bank bailouts   69
Duel in the sun: The rise and fall of Abengoa   77
Brand Spain: The concerns over the country's image   84
The business of the land: The potential of marmalade,   95
      wine and truffles
A more or less global world: Selling sex and colonialism   102

Society
Drugs without violence: Barbate's escape route in the midst   113
      of crisis
The alms of the wealthy: The flimsy culture of Spanish   120
      philanthropy
Jumping fences: The gates of immigration are south   131
Coming out of coma: The fight for justice following a   141
      medical error

Contents

An American omission: Decades of nuclear waste in Palomares   147

Franco's long shadow: Historical memory on the to-do list   152

Small but feisty: How Little Nicolás tricked those in power   164

The fourth estate: The shenanigans within Spanish media at a time of crisis   172

The presumption of innocence: The pedophilia charges filed against a Granada priest   181

Recovering a heritage: The peninsula's Sephardic past   187

The value of the fiesta: A mosaic of unique celebrations   194

The whistle-blower's protection: The dangers of uncovering corruption   201

Epilogue

Covid-19 and other crises: Rising to the challenge   215

About the Author   219

The Cañada Blanch Centre for Contemporary Spanish Studies

In the 1960s, the most important initiative in the cultural and academic relations between Spain and the United Kingdom was launched by a Valencian fruit importer in London. The creation by Vicente Cañada Blanch of the Anglo-Spanish Cultural Foundation has subsequently benefited large numbers of Spanish and British scholars at various levels. Thanks to the generosity of Vicente Cañada Blanch, thousands of Spanish schoolchildren have been educated at the secondary school in West London that bears his name. At the same time, many British and Spanish university students have benefited from the exchange scholarships which fostered cultural and scientific exchanges between the two countries. Some of the most important historical, artistic and literary work on Spanish topics to be produced in Great Britain was initially made possible by Cañada Blanch scholarships.

Vicente Cañada Blanch was, by inclination, a conservative. When his Foundation was created, the Franco regime was still in the plenitude of its power. Nevertheless, the keynote of the Foundation's activities was always a complete open-mindedness on political issues. This was reflected in the diversity of research projects supported by the Foundation, many of which, in Francoist Spain, would have been regarded as subversive. When the Dictator died, Don Vicente was in his seventy-fifth year. In the two decades following the death of the Dictator, although apparently indestructible, Don Vicente was obliged to husband his energies. Increasingly, the work of the Foundation was carried forward by Miguel Dols whose tireless and imaginative work in London was matched in Spain by that of José María Coll Comín. They were united in the Foundation's spirit of open-minded commitment to fostering research of high quality in pursuit of better Anglo-Spanish

ix

cultural relations. Throughout the 1990s, thanks to them, the role of the Foundation grew considerably.

In 1994, in collaboration with the London School of Economics, the Foundation established the Príncipe de Asturias Chair of Contemporary Spanish History and the Cañada Blanch Centre for Contemporary Spanish Studies. It is the particular task of the Cañada Blanch Centre for Contemporary Spanish Studies to promote the understanding of twentieth-century Spain through research and teaching of contemporary Spanish history, politics, economy, sociology and culture. The Centre possesses a valuable library and archival centre for specialists in contemporary Spain. This work is carried on through the publications of the doctoral and post-doctoral researchers at the Centre itself and through the many seminars and lectures held at the London School of Economics. While the seminars are the province of the researchers, the lecture cycles have been the forum in which Spanish politicians have been able to address audiences in the United Kingdom.

The series has ranged widely over Spain's twentieth-century history, with emphasis on many aspects of the civil war, particularly anarchism and both Francoist and Republican repression, on post-war reconstruction and on the Franco dictatorship and opposition to it. Titles on the subsequent democratic regime have tended to be quite specific, with considerable emphasis on the ongoing Catalan issue, on corruption and on the status of Gibraltar. The recent volume edited by Borja de Riquer, Lluís Ferran Toledano and Gemma Rubí on the burning question of corruption in Spain brought us from the nineteenth century to the present day. It is now complemented by the perceptive survey of Spanish economics, politics and society, in *Feeling the Heat* by the *New York Times* correspondent in Spain, Raphael Minder. His tour d'horizon of more than a decade observing a society in turmoil is a worthy addition to the series.

Series Editor's Preface by Paul Preston

Feeling the Heat, Raphael Minder's multi-faceted book on the recent history and politics of Spain, has two complementary dimensions. On the one hand, it deals with a tumultuous period that ranges from the catastrophic economic crash of 2008, via the abdication of the country's hitherto admired monarch Juan Carlos, through a mire of eye-watering corruption that brought down a seemingly impregnable conservative government and the division of the country in October 2017 when the Catalan cabinet defied the central government and Spain's Constitution to hold an illegal referendum on independence. On the other hand, it is not simply a lively recital of those dramatic events but also an account of the day-to-day travails of a foreign correspondent fighting for space on the pages of the *New York Times*. There is also a disturbing litany of the discomfort that can be generated by an inappropriate headline or photo which, more often than not, are the work of others.

In welding together these two aspects of his book, Raphael Minder produces not a chronological survey of this dramatic period – a period somewhat inevitably affected by Brexit and Covid – but something rather more resembling an old-fashioned collection of insightful essays of the sort that a nineteenth-century traveller might have produced. This wide-ranging volume assembles what he calls 'a set of chapter vignettes that can be read separately'. Without making comparisons as far back as Richard Ford or Gerald Brenan, it would not be unreasonable to say that his collection of chapters is, in that sense, rather reminiscent of such distinguished pioneers of the interpretation of post-Franco Spain as John Hooper's *The Spaniards* or Giles Tremlett's *Ghosts of Spain* to both of which it has claims to be a worthy successor. At times, as well as chronicling contemporary Spain, Minder is writing his own autobiography.

The author's acute and perceptive observations about Spanish politics are accompanied by insights into the personal experience of being a foreign correspondent. His personal running commentary reminded me at times of the works that I studied when I was writing my book about war correspondents during the Spanish Civil War or indeed of my own experiences when interviewing politicians. He writes, 'I have sometimes been happy to play the role of devil's advocate, which I believe is an important component of journalism, as it forms part of the right and obligation to question everything.' I assume that he means that he stops short of the confrontation which might well mute his interlocutor. Others, myself included, often think that there is a lot to be said for letting the politician give free rein to his or her opinions. Where Minder differs from some of his illustrious wartime predecessors is in his references to his multilingualism. Not many of them could match this Swiss writer for command of French, German, Spanish and English. He rightly comments on how speaking a language makes a difference in terms of establishing rapport with an informant. Writing in the age of social media, he cannot resist mentioning how hurtful Twitter trolls can be. He adds pertinent comments about his doubts regarding whether to file a story when more dramatic events elsewhere mean that it might get spiked. In that sense, this work is not just a chronicle of what happened but also an account of the difficulties of trying to acquire the information that would permit a fully rounded account of what happened.

One chapter on the Catalan crisis is as much about how he was treated and the reception to his book, while another is devoted the actual crisis. The central government's use of riot police led him to see how 'the story of a heroic act of defiance by ordinary Catalan voters against a powerful Spanish state and its riot police officers has continued to be told among those who believe in Catalonia's right to self-determination'. At the same time he acknowledges that 'While the police intervention remains open to questioning, the referendum was conducted in violation of the Spanish constitution and was not a blank check for the separatist leaders of Catalonia to push ahead with a unilateral declaration of independence.' He provides an eye-witness account of the event on October 27 once the opposition had abandoned the assembly chamber. His acerbic account is personal: 'From the top of the imposing staircase of the Catalan Parliament, I watched as the separatist lawmakers cheered alongside dozens of mayors of Catalan towns, who had come to Barcelona for the celebration. Of course, it proved one of the shortest celebrations in political history. By late evening, the politicians did not join the street party on the square of Sant Jaume. Some of them, in fact, were probably already busy packing up their suitcases for Brussels.' One of the self-exiled politicians that he interviewed was Clara Ponsatí, the Minister of Education in the government that declared independence in October 2017. Although his portrait is sympathetic, he is not the first commentator to be struck by the fact that she was reluctant to concede that any decisions taken then had been mistaken.

While never forgetting the major political dramas of the day, the book teems with fascinating aperçus: whether it be about the wine industry or Spain's endlessly creative cuisine; the sex industry (mechanical and human) or the drug culture and its links with unemployment; tax avoidance and contrasting attitudes to immigration; and, inevitably, the endlessly creative world of fiestas. At the same time, as an ex-journalist of both Bloomberg and the *Financial Times*, his economic comments are never less than insightful. The book abounds in lifelike character sketches of contemporary politicians, whether it be the inscrutable Gallego Prime Minister Mariano Rajoy or the left-wing firebrand Pablo Iglesias, of whom Minder comments very perceptively: 'In retrospect, I feel Iglesias proved a good speaker and charismatic candidate but a poor party leader and flawed negotiator, less open to others than he had suggested to me, as well as increasingly out of touch with the grassroots whom he sought to represent.' The present King, Juan Carlos's son, Felipe VI, does not fare well. Minder repeats a lapidary quote from the journalist John Carlin – which led to his dismissal from *El País*. In the midst of the Catalan crisis when many looked to the King's speech for an exemplar of moderation and conciliation, Felipe, in the words of Carlin, was 'Stiff in his bearing, coldly commanding in his tone, he did not build bridges, he dug trenches.'

More sympathetic is the portrait of the present Socialist Prime Minister Pedro Sánchez, for whom a useful explanation is provided as to how he got ousted from his own party in October 2016 in bitter inner-party wrangling and yet managed to fight back eight months later. Altogether more distressing is the author's insight into the process whereby the ultra-rightist Vox party overtook the more moderate centre-right party, Ciudadanos, by bringing 'to national politics a level of xenophobia, misogyny and ultranationalism that I had not seen since arriving in Spain'. Raphael Minder presents an alarming picture of the toxic nature of political discourse in post-2017 Spain. At the same time, he reminds us of the strength of general Spanish loyalty to the EU. In this regard, he makes a compelling argument as to why Brussels will remain on the side of Madrid in terms of the future of Catalonia. He is perceptive too on one of the mysteries of Spanish local administration, the Diputaciónes Provinciales, a kind of provincial council which he describes pithily as 'a layer of bureaucracy that everybody knows to cost some money but nobody seems able to say exactly what function it has to fulfil, except to pay lip service to the idea of territorial power redistribution and to provide some jobs for the boys'.

Along the way, there are some worthy reminders of issues that have fallen from popular consciousness. Quite remarkable is an astonishing account of an incident long since forgotten by most of Spain. As Minder puts it, at Palomares in the province of Almería, on 17 January 1966, one of the bleakest moments in the relationship between the United States and Spain took place. A U.S. Air Force bomber came within an ace of producing a monumental nuclear tragedy when it collided with a refuelling tanker while flying over the village and dropped four hydrogen bombs. Although two of the bombs released plutonium into the atmosphere, no warheads were detonated. Following the crash, there was a botched attempt to clean the site, as well as a political cover-up operation, which included the sight of the Minister of Information, Manuel Fraga, taking a risky swim with the American Ambassador. In one memorable image, we see local looters falling on the scene, one of whom, unaware of what had fallen, tried to prise open a nuclear bomb with a screwdriver.

Inevitably, the legacy of Franco and the whole issue of 'historical memory' looms large. En passant, we are reminded of how the charismatic investigating magistrate, Baltasar Garzón, had his career destroyed for his temerity – albeit unlawful temerity – in investigating the crimes of Francoism. The issue of the dictator's exhumation is despatched sensibly with a quotation from a one-hundred-year-old Basque: 'Franco didn't forgive, so don't ask us not only to forgive but also to forget now.' He quotes the veteran Catalan historian, Joan Baptista Culla, who compares the restitution of material plundered from Republicans to returning paintings seized from Jews by the Nazis. Not all readers will concur with Minder's rejection of comparisons between Hitler and Mussolini on the one hand and Franco on the other on the grounds that the Axis dictators died a violent death whereas the Caudillo died in a Madrid hospital, aged 82, with thousands of ordinary citizens apparently paying their respects or perhaps exercising their curiosity if not actually just checking that he was dead. If anything, the fact that the Franco regime did not end in foreign invasion and violence is a comment on international relations after the Second World War, which permitted Franco to remain in power for another thirty years and implement a repressive process of national brain-washing that affected mass perceptions of the dictator. Overall, this is a highly recommendable portrait of a nation facing its greatest period of political upheaval since the death of Franco and the transition to democracy. Minder rightly expresses pride in being part of the Fourth Estate. This book justifies the conclusion at which I arrived in my book about foreign correspondents during the Spanish Civil War, *We Saw Spain Die*: Good journalism can be the first draft of history.

INTRODUCING THE JOB OF FOREIGN CORRESPONDENT

Una década turbulenta en un país de contrastes

I landed in Madrid on 1 April 2010, which is celebrated as Fools' Day in the United States and much of Europe. I soon got the impression that some officials in Spain were verging on delusion, somehow believing that they could prolong Spain's decade in the economic sunshine even as the dark clouds of the financial crisis were gathering all around them.

Two weeks after my arrival, I covered a meeting of European finance ministers, which took place in Madrid because Spain then held the rotating presidency of the European Union. The fate of Greece was at the top of the agenda, but some officials also voiced doubts about Spain's ability to meet its budgetary targets. Elena Salgado, who was Spain's finance minister, dismissed their concerns. She apparently remained convinced that the "green shoots" of economic growth (*"brotes verdes"*) that she had forecast could still sprout and sustain Spain.

But in May, Greece won approval for an international bailout and that same month the government of José Luis Rodríguez Zapatero made its first budgetary cuts. Spain's bubble had burst, even though it took another two years for another government, led by Mariano Rajoy, to find itself forced to negotiate a European banking bailout.

As Spain was sinking deeper into crisis, my American editors wanted to discuss the bigger picture, which was whether Spain's derailment would also destroy Europe's financial stability. The idea was that the European Union did not have the resources to save a Spanish economy that was larger than the combination of the three countries — Greece, Ireland and Portugal — that international creditors had already been forced to rescue.

In the end, Spain used less European rescue money than it had requested to survive the financial crisis and managed to pull out of recession only a year later. Soon enough, Spain was starting to win instead plaudits for the cleaning of its banking sector, the rise in its exports, the lowering of its massive unemployment — all of which ensured that the country once more converted itself into one of the economic engines of Europe.

3

But social discontent was still rife and other forces started to strain the fabric of Spain. Having spent my first three years writing almost exclusively for my business editors, I found that my reporting was now shifting heavily toward political and social stories. In any case, Spain remained in the news, from the abdication of King Juan Carlos in 2014 to the end of Spain's two-party system in 2015 and the secession challenge in Catalonia, which reached boiling point during the autumn of 2017.

By that stage, it was clear that I had been a frontline observer of probably the most impactful decade in Spain since the country's return to democracy, even though it fell short of "the second transition" that Pablo Iglesias, the leader of Podemos, forecast when I interviewed him in 2015, shortly before his party won its first seats in Congress.

While Podemos and Ciudadanos were preparing to enter Congress for the first time, I was starting to work on my first book, which was about Catalonia, an issue that I will discuss later. This book was released by my British publishing house in September 2017, in the same week when separatist lawmakers defied the Spanish government and the country's constitutional court by pushing through their Catalan laws to hold an independence referendum.

When my book on Catalonia got published, Ramon Perelló, the then editor of Peninsula, offered to follow up with another book, about my experience as a foreign correspondent in Spain. I was at the time deeply immersed in my newspaper reporting about the turmoil of Spanish politics, so I told him that I was unfortunately too busy. But we started to meet occasionally, either in Madrid or Barcelona, building up a friendship during which I have also learnt much from Perelló's great anecdotes and insightful views on Spain. And as I got closer to completing a decade as a correspondent in Spain, we agreed to revive the generous book proposal that he had already made me in 2017.

This is the result. I have structured the book as a set of 'chapter vignettes' that can be read separately, but I also hope give an overall picture of how I have perceived Spain and written about the country during this past decade. Several chapters are based on reporting that I did for *The New York Times*. But some come from material that I never published, or are more about my personal experiences and candid musings about Spain and the work of a correspondent.

In fact, I hope this book will shed some light on what makes my job exciting, challenging, rewarding and at times also frustrating. It is a huge privilege to work as a foreign correspondent, especially in as diverse, open and fascinating a country as Spain. I hope to take the reader on my journey through Spain, but also on a walk through the kitchen of journalism, to see why some ingredients get added to the mix of news and feature stories that I have written about Spain, while others got kept out.

When it is well practiced, journalism is a public service, long recognized as such in the Anglo-Saxon world under the concept of The Fourth Estate. I love this idea that I form part of The Fourth Estate, which can help inform and steer society, while also defending democracy and human rights by acting as a watchdog against political misdeeds and other economic or social abuses. But for me, the best thing about being a journalist is the opportunity to ask questions and get answers (at least most of the time.) A journalist can learn something new every day, and hence get educated for free while earning a living (of course I believe journalism should get paid decently.) There is no such thing as a stupid question, especially not when you are a foreign correspondent who can always plead ignorance about the structures and customs of a society, or about the history of a country.

Working as a correspondent is therefore a steep and extremely enriching learning curving, sometimes even involving an attempt to master a new language.

The correspondent is a student and observer of a country, but the job is not a constant attempt to reinvent the wheel. Very often, my work has been based on news that was well covered by Spanish journalists and where most of the hard investigative work had already been done. But the challenge has been to explain to a broader and international readership the significance of a story that might be known to people in Spain, but could still be revisited and looked at from a different and broader angle.

This task requires honing in on the elements of the story that could be important or exciting for a reader who has not followed Spain regularly, or who might even struggle to place Spain on the map. I like to compare this with the challenge faced by a photographer who has a great camera, but perhaps finds herself looking at something slightly out of focus. The camera's zoom is perfect to capture details, but not so helpful to get a feel for the overall landscape. A small change in aperture can make a picture look very different. Like a photographer, the correspondent sometimes needs to do some tweaking to help his readership distinguish the wood from the trees.

While thinking about the readership, I must start by convincing my most important reader, who is the editor who will have to invest time and energy in working on a story about Spain. The editors at *The New York Times* are extremely talented and have incredible knowledge of world affairs, but the world is a big and busy place, in which Spain only occupies part of the southwestern corner of Europe.

The job of the correspondent is therefore to understand the details of a story, but then focus only on the most important ones, while archiving the rest of the material. I have also had to think carefully about my timing. It is important not to arrive too late onto a story, especially in this online age in which people can read news instantly and have the idea that they should achieve complete knowledge immediately. But sometimes it is best to set out late rather than to get caught in a news traffic jam. Unless it is a major breaking story, there is little point calling my European news editor with a proposal from Spain on the day when terrorists are attacking Paris or Prime Minister Theresa May is resigning, in the midst of the Brexit chaos.

Working for *The New York Times*, I have also increasingly become a port of call for people in Spain who wish to share their stories, something that I will discuss at more length in this book. Often, the people who reach out to me want to gain international recognition for their work or for an issue. Sometimes, however, they contact me out of sheer frustration, claiming that they could not get a fair hearing in Spain. Some have told me that I should be able to understand them better than Spanish officials or journalists who have been ignoring their problem — or sometimes even helping to cover it up — because I do not have vested interests in Spain.

I certainly do not believe that such a claim is always right. There is a lively and open debate in Spain about myriad issues. As I already mentioned, Spanish journalists conduct important investigations and I often rely on their great work. Prosecutors keep opening up new cases. The functioning of the Spanish judiciary has sometimes been questioned, but it has delivered some very important rulings and has helped reduce the mountain of corruption that accompanied Spain's property boom. I have written about Rodrigo Rato and a few other bankers who were sentenced for fraud. I also covered the imprisonment of Iñaki Urdangarin, a member of the Spanish royal family, as well as that of a handful of politicians, like Jaume Matas, the former president of the Balearic Islands. Not many countries can claim to have put behind bars as many members of their elite as Spain.

But it is true that, as a foreign correspondent, I do not feel that I owe anything on a personal level to Spain, beyond the privilege of being allowed to live and work here. I can marvel at the beauty and complexity of the country, admire its people, make very good friends, love its food and music, but all of this makes me a very happy resident rather than a citizen who flies the Spanish flag. And for the sake of my job, this is a good situation to be in. It allows me to be critical, without feeling that I am betraying anybody or showing disloyalty to this country and its institutions. It also allows me to praise, without letting this turn into adoration or devotion. I have followed football matches in both Madrid and Barcelona, sitting in the press gallery of the Santiago Bernabéu stadium or the Camp Nou, next to local journalists who seem to be getting close to a heart attack while doing their job. Sometimes they even slap the desk or shout out loud before typing the next sentence on their laptop. I have often wondered how these journalists can write an objective report on the match, when so much personal passion is involved.

I got my first job in journalism in 1993 in my native country, Switzerland, reporting for Bloomberg News. I have since worked as a foreign correspondent in five other countries, including a decade spent with the *Financial Times*. In each of these countries, including my own, I have identified issues that were very sensitive and highly emotional, and hence certain to generate some criticism whatever I was going to write about them. In Spain, football is one of them. But my list also includes bullfighting, Catholicism, the civil war and Franco, the monarchy, Basque terrorism and more recently Catalan secessionism.

In this era of social media and online news, some critics have lashed out even before reading my actual article, based on what another person mentioned on Twitter or elsewhere (and whether or not they later read themselves the article is anybody's guess.) This notably happened with the book that I wrote about Catalonia, presenting a challenge that I will discuss in this book. It has also occurred with some articles that upset people not because of my own writing and its content, but because of the headline or the photos accompanying the article.

As a foreign correspondent, I accept that I have to stand on the frontline and sometimes have to dodge the first bullets. No reader cares for the fact that an editor writes my headlines or a photographer takes pictures that are then selected by a separate group of photo editors, and which I normally only see once they are printed. In fact, relatively few people in Spain seem to understand that a newspaper like *The New York Times* has different departments and relies on maintaining internal barriers to keep its impartiality, especially between the people who run the news pages and those who handle the opinion pieces or editorial comments. In 2016, another layer was added when *The New York Times* started a Spanish-language edition, with its own and small editorial team, based in Mexico City, which translated many articles (including my own), but also commissioned opinion pieces from some Spanish-speaking writers for its own online section. In summary, *The New York Times* is a broad church, in which many different people get published, sometimes even in different languages, and editorial decisions have always been taken far above my level of competence and responsibility.

This book is not about American journalism, but it is the chronicle of a Swiss correspondent working for an American newspaper. It is also not an attempt to recount blow-by-blow the momentous events of the last decade. In fact, many of the most memorable stories that I have reported had nothing to do with what what was dominating Spanish news at time. They simply came about because I read or heard something that seemed to me unusual. I met fascinating people in some of the most remote parts of Spain, as well as sometimes almost on my doorstep. For me, one of the most heartbreaking stories, which I feature in this book, is that of a family who built a tent on a Madrid square to protest the medical error that left their son in a coma.

I hope to take the reader along what has been an extraordinary journey of discovery, during which I have been able to test and revise many of my initial assumptions about Spain. If anything, I have stayed in Spain far longer than I had anticipated because there is still so much left for me to learn here.

POLITICS

El camino de la justicia
Los altibajos de Baltasar Garzón

In April 2010, I arrived in Madrid hoping to devote my first week to apartment-hunting rather than reporting. But my house search was almost immediately interrupted by the indictment of Baltasar Garzón, the country's most prominent judge. Having canceled a meeting with a real estate agent, I got instead to inaugurate my new job by writing about why Gárzon stood accused of abusing his own powers as a judge to try to unearth — literally, from mass graves — some of the atrocities committed during the Spanish Civil War.

Gárzon was also facing two other separate lawsuits. One of them concerned a payment he had received from Banco Santander for lecturing at New York University. The other related to whether he had been eavesdropping illegally to secure evidence against defendants in what later turned into one of Spain's biggest political corruption trials, the Gürtel case.

I knew about Garzón because he had made the front pages of newspapers for over a decade. But I knew him as an international defender of human rights, rather than in relation to his investigations within Spain. By making extensive use of Spain's doctrine of universal jurisdiction, he had managed to turn Madrid into a hub for the prosecution of crimes that had been committed on the other side of the world.

Garzón became an international celebrity after his investigation of the killing of Spaniards during the Chilean dictatorship led him to demand the extradition of General Augusto Pinochet, the former Chilean ruler, from Britain in 1998. Rather than extraditing Pinochet, the British government eventually allowed him to return instead to Santiago, citing his poor health.

But Garzón still seized his Chilean moment of fame to investigate other world leaders, stretching his work at times far beyond issues of human rights. He unsuccessfully tried to lift the political immunity of Silvio Berlusconi, who was then prime minister of Italy, in order to investigate whether Berlusconi's television deals breached Spanish antitrust legislation.

In 2009, Garzón also targeted the American administration of President George W. Bush, by launching an investigation into what

11

Garzón described as "an approved systematic plan of torture and ill-treatment" at the Guantánamo prison.

Neither Berlusconi nor Bush ended up in a Madrid courtroom. But Garzón had ruffled feathers and moved important and controversial issues higher up the international agenda, earning along the way plaudits from leading legal experts and human rights advocates around the world. Within Spain, however, it was clear that many people did not support Garzón's work, making him instead one of the country's most polarizing figures.

Between my apartment visits, I read about Garzón's main investigations and important role in the country's fight against terrorism, both against the Basque militants of ETA (*Euskadi Ta Askatasuna* – an armed nationalist movement) and Islamic militants, following the train bombings at Atocha in March 2004. His efforts to combat terrorism had won him much praise and esteem. But I also understood that the way he had handled some cases had generated major controversy and that he had accumulated many enemies and detractors along the way, including within the judiciary, notably after Garzón sided with PRISA, a leading media company, against a fellow judge, Javier Gómez de Liaño, who had launched in 1997 a fraud investigation focused on Sogecable and the group's pay-per-view television earnings. Separately, I also heard some unflattering accounts of Garzón's brief stint in politics in the 1990s, and the personal ambitions he had harbored within the Socialist government. Almost everybody I spoke to about Garzón had a very strong opinion about him, whether favorable or disdainful.

In fact, shortly after my arrival in Madrid in April 2010, I got to see first-hand just how much Garzón divided Spanish society. I followed a large weekend protest on the Puerta del Sol in Madrid, in which thousands of people gathered in support of Garzón. The protest ended with a manifesto that was read out by major figures from the arts world, including Pedro Almodóvar, the film director, the writer Almudena Grandes and the poet Marcos Ana, who had been imprisoned during Franco's dictatorship.

But not far from the Puerta del Sol, I also ran into another smaller, rival march. The protesters were much fewer in numbers, but almost as noisy as the supporters of Gárzon. They included flag-waving sympathizers of the far-right Falange, who were accusing Garzón of committing a crime by violating the 1977 general amnesty law and trying to reopen old wounds by investigating the atrocities of the civil war. So it was with some trepidation that I finally met Garzón a month later, in an office on Madrid's Gran Vía. The meeting had proved very difficult to organize, with Garzón sounding worried about himself being subject to eavesdropping. It was the first interview that he gave to a major newspaper in over one year. Rather than discussing his past international work, I mostly wanted to talk to him about why he had become such a polemic and divisive figure within Spain.

During our interview, Garzón sounded defiant, describing the anger that his work had generated as a mirror reflection of how Spanish society had failed to come to terms with the legacy of its recent and tragic history. He was unrepentant and told me that, whatever the final verdict, his efforts to promote international justice could not be undone.

One of the strangest and deplorable features of Spain, he said, was that its judiciary had managed to lead the way in terms of tracking down criminals across the world, including dictators like Pinochet, but Spain could not confront its own dictatorial past, nor root out its political corruption.

"I believe the seeds have been sown, despite the possible contra-dictions of a country that investigates outside but cannot now investigate inside," Garzón said. The path of justice, he added, is about taking "two steps forward, then one step back, then one forward and then two back — so we advance with a lot of difficul-ties. Why? Because there are a lot of interests at play — judicial as well as political and diplomatic."

In 2010, *The New York Times* was one of the newspapers that led the international chorus of support for him. Shortly after his indictment, it published an editorial, headlined "An injustice in Spain," in which it warned that an expulsion of Garzón from the courts would amount to "a travesty of justice."

The editorial (in whose writing I was not involved) focused on Garzón's attempt to investigate Civil War crimes and stressed the need for Spain to probe its history. "Spain needs an honest accounting of its troubled past, not prosecution of those who have the courage to demand it," the editorial argued. But the *New York Times* editorial also acknowledged some chinks in Garzón's armor, probably tied to his personal ambition.

"High-profile cases, like his bid to try the former Chilean dictator Augusto Pinochet, appeal to him, and sometimes he overreaches," the editorial said. "But his consistent goal has been to deny impunity to the powerful and expand the scope of international human rights law."

Meeting Garzón, I certainly felt that I was talking to somebody with a high sense of his own worth and mission. He told me about how he had never aspired to become a star judge, but had simply taken on important work that other judges on the national court would not touch. "My own experience has been that my colleagues in the national court did nothing on terrorism issues," he said.

Garzón held scant hope that, in his absence, Spain could have a functioning judiciary. He was particularly dismissive about how politicians could manipulate judges — apart from himself — to ensure that corruption would not be punished in Spain. "Impunity is the sister, or perhaps the mother, of corruption," he told me.

In early 2012, I followed Garzón's travails once more, as he took to the stand at his own trial. Garzón told the judges of the Supreme Court that he investigated civil war crimes because "I did what I thought I had to do, beyond any question of ideology." But in February 2012, the Supreme Court suspended Garzón from the courts for eleven years. The ruling risked ending his career as a judge, since he was 54 at the time. After leaving the courthouse, Gárzon issued a statement, calling the decision "unfair and predetermined." He warned that his suspension "cancels any possibility of investigating corruption and related crimes" in Spain.

Shortly after Garzón was sentenced, I interviewed separately two of the most veteran politicians of Spain, who had been on the frontline of its transition from dictatorship to democracy: Manuel Fraga, the former information minister in Franco's regime and Santiago Carrillo, the former leader of Spain's Communist party. I wanted their views on how Spain had evolved since Franco, but I also asked them about Garzón. As one of the writers of the Spanish Constitution, Fraga did not hide his disdain for Garzón and presented him as a threat to the new Spain that Fraga proudly told me he had himself crafted. "He should be kept as far away from Spain as possible," Fraga told me.

Carrillo took a more nuanced view, perhaps because I had also asked him about his own civil war involvement, tainted by the massacre of thousands of prisoners at Paracuellos, outside Madrid, when Carrillo was in charge of security in the city. "Crimes were committed on both sides in the war but not on any comparable scale," Carrillo said, in defense of Garzón's work. "And Franco then jailed or shot any opponent after the war, as well as rehabilitating his dead. That is yet to happen for his victims." (I return to this issue later in the book.)

Star judges like Garzón have run into trouble in many other countries. In 2017, I attended a fascinating debate between Garzón, Antonio Di Pietro, the Italian prosecutor who had led the "Mani pulite," or "Clean hands," investigation against corrupt politicians, and Sergio Moro, the Brazilian judge whose own political corruption investigation, known as "Operation Lava Jato," helped send the country's former president, Lula da Silva, to prison. During the debate, which took place in the Portuguese resort of Estoril, Garzón recalled a discussion he had with Di Pietro in July 1993, at a time when he was running as a candidate in a Spanish general election. "My dear friend Baltasar, you're making a mistake," Di Pietro told him. "A judge should not get into politics."

Four years later, however, Di Pietro did not follow his own advice and also entered politics. "The coincidence is that neither of us gave up our principles," Garzón told the audience. After joining the Socialist government, he said, "I resigned because President Felipe González, who had promised to fight corruption, did not do it. I denounced it and I walked off to the tribunal. With that, what I want to say is that it is not bad for a judge or prosecutor to get into politics: it is public service. The question is how the rotating doors work. Not all politicians are corrupt. This is an easy discourse. There is also corruption among the judges and in the highest spheres of the judiciary and there are also political interests."

As I listened to Garzón talk about his political past, I found it hard to share his view that there was nothing risky about a judge becoming a politician, and then also using the rotating doors of power to return to his courtroom. His removal as a judge in 2012 may have been politically motivated, as he alleged. The decision was also later tainted by the fact that one of his main accusers, the Manos Limpias group, ran into its own legal problems.

But Garzón had entered politics of his own free will and should have known that he would thereafter struggle to regain an image of complete independence. As he himself later told me, "There is a very Spanish view of justice, which consists in suspecting that if you have been in politics, you will for sure prove to be corrupt."

Incidentally, Moro's own political foray also proved controversial and short-lived. He became justice minister in the right-wing government of President Jair Bolsonaro, but was forced to take a leave of absence in July 2019, after the leaking of past phone recordings that suggested Moro violated his duty to remain impartial as a judge by actively collaborating with prosecutors who were chasing corrupt politicians.

In a functioning democracy based on checks and balances, politicians and judges should be kept as far apart as possible. In Spain, the distance has not always been sufficient. Judges have also not always taken responsibility for their own mistakes.

In 2012, I followed the downfall of Carlos Dívar, a judge who was the president of the Supreme Court. But Dívar ran into serious problems outside the courtroom, after the media reported that he had been using public money to enjoy lavish trips and holidays. For weeks, Dívar refused to discuss his luxury weekends in the southern resort of Puerto Banús, at the expense of taxpayers. He also resisted calls to appear before Congress, with the help of the Popular Party and Spain's then justice minister, Alberto Ruiz-Gallardón. But the facts of the scandal were indefensible and Dívar was eventually forced to resign.

The good news for Spain is that the judiciary is a large community in which one bad apple need not rot the entire basket. Other judges also stepped into Garzón's big boots to pursue political corruption, often slowly, but surely. Garzón's own replacement, Pablo Ruz, was a dynamic representative of a new generation of investigative judges. In his limited time as a substitute appointee, Ruz was instrumental in driving forward the investigation into the illegal financing of the Popular Party, orchestrated by its former treasurer, Luis Bárcenas.

Looking back over this past decade, it is in fact striking how many of Garzón's fellow judges have made the headlines, sometimes by making themselves less visible and controversial in terms of their investigative methods. In 2018, Judge Ángel Hurtado handed down an unprecedented sentence against the Popular Party of Mariano Rajoy, which became the first political force in Spain to be found guilty of operating a slush fund.

Within days, the opposition Socialists, led by Pedro Sánchez, used this corruption ruling to oust Rajoy in an unexpected parliamentary vote of no confidence. After surviving two decades at the top of Spanish politics, Rajoy left through the back door, as the first Spanish leader in modern history to get kicked out by lawmakers rather than voters.

The Gürtel ruling vindicated Garzón's efforts, but it was also proof that Spain's judiciary did not stop functioning once he was removed, whatever some leading legal experts argued at the time, like Dolores Delgado, a prosecutor who had worked closely with Garzón. In 2010, she told me Garzón's ouster would deal a lasting blow for Spain's judiciary. "He was a pioneer who managed, from a small state, to ignite a concept of international justice that was dead until he started," she said. "What happens now? He has left and it is very unlikely that another figure like him can emerge."

With the benefit of hindsight, Delgado was probably right to forecast that no other Spanish judge would stretch an investigation so far beyond Spain's borders and even target foreign heads of state, as Garzón had done. The doctrine of universal jurisdiction has been relegated to the history books, it seems. But it seems that she was wrong to think Spain's judiciary would somehow become less efficient and forceful without him. Since Garzón left, other judges have dug deep into the corruption of the Spanish establishment, taking on not only executives and politicians, but also members of the royal family.

In some cases, justice has been handed down, despite serious delays and perhaps even political efforts to obstruct it. In 2014, Judge Mercedes Ayala was removed from her investigation into how Socialist politicians diverted money earmarked for the unemployed. She later publicly denounced how "the system" had pushed her aside, including politicians and some fellow judges. But as in Garzón's case, her departure did not close the case. In November 2019, a court in Seville sentenced José Antonio Griñán, former leader of Andalusia, and 18 others for one of the most costly political fraud cases in Spanish history, involving almost 680 million euros of misused public money.

In late 2019, I interviewed Garzón again, this time to talk about his new life as a lawyer, working on several prominent cases, including as part of the defense team of Julian Assange, the founder of WikiLeaks, who was then fighting Washington's attempt to extradite him from Britain. When I asked him also about his career and whether he regretted having become a lightning rod in the debate over Spain's judiciary, Garzón stuck to his defiant line. Looking back, he still felt that that there had been nothing wrong with his foray into politics in the 1990s. He also denied that he ever sought the limelight as a judge.

While he remained very critical of institutional Spain, he said that, with the passing of time, he had acquired "a more complete view of justice." Among the bright spots, he said, was the fact that the politicization of the judicial system in Spain had not prevented some other judges from pursuing effectively corruption, notably completing the Gürtel case that partly cost him his own job. "Those who thought that they would send a warning by removing me did not take into account that judges, whether they are conservatives or not, have a sense of independence that forms part of their DNA," he said. "This is an achievement: justice has consolidated itself in terms of investigating corruption."

Justice in Spain remains slow, imperfect and unpredictable. But it has still taken more steps forward than backward.

La polémica catalana
Las múltiples caras de la independencia

In November 2015, I received an email from an editor at Hurst, a British publisher, who had read some of my articles and asked whether I would be interested in writing a book about Catalonia. I was flattered by this offer, but I tried to convince him that I should write a broader book about Spain, in which Catalonia would be an important topic, rather than the standalone subject.

However, the Hurst editor specifically wanted to look at Catalonia, a subject that had received relatively little attention from English-speaking authors. There was also a chance that such a book would now attract British readers who had been captivated by the debate in Scotland, which resulted in an independence referendum that voters rejected in 2014. He explained that Hurst's idea was to take an in-depth look at the history, culture and society of Catalonia and its shifting politics, also in the context of a European Union that was being confronted by new political challenges, including the growth of nationalist movements. He convinced me. I also felt that writing a book was an important milestone for a journalist and that it was a luxury to get offered such a valuable experience without having to seek it.

Truth be told, I had not been fascinated by the changing political landscape in Catalonia, although it had interested me. I knew that it was also a subject matter that would require a steep learning curve, as I felt that I had only a superficial understanding of Catalonia and its inhabitants. After all, like many foreigners, I grew up thinking of nationalism in Spain as an issue that was most relevant in the Basque Country, rather than in Catalonia. Although I had been reporting on-and-off about Catalonia since 2010, it had been a struggle at times. I felt that I had not been able to understand exactly how an issue like the Catalan statute of autonomy had stirred so much passion and controversy. Before getting down to my own reporting and interviewing, I started going through the writings of Vicens Vives and other important authors that I had been recommended. To my despair, every time I asked anybody for advice, I was given the name of yet another historian or writer to add to my list, with the warning that this author was essential reading if I wanted to understand anything about Catalonia.

While I was struggling to read more about Catalonia, I had another discussion with Hurst, whose editors wanted to select as quickly as possible the title for my forthcoming book. They came up with three different proposals, each of which sounded catchy, but also not entirely suitable. I got worried that the wording of their choices could generate controversy in Spain, as might the decision to put the Estelada flag on the cover. But I was new to the world of books and of course I understood that a publisher wanted a book to catch the attention of possible readers amid the vast offering of a bookshop.

In the end, we agreed that "The Struggle for Catalonia" should be the title, fine-tuning their original idea, which was to call the book "The Fight for Catalonia." I had managed to convince them that fight, as a term, sounded too belligerent.

In retrospect, I feel that this choice had been premonitory, and certainly not too strong. There has been and continues to be a struggle for Catalonia. The book was released on 4 September 2017, only days before pro-independence lawmakers managed to push through the Catalan Parliament new laws that they drafted in order to hold an independence referendum and ignore the rulings of the Spanish Constitutional Court.

I did not have a crystal ball to help me predict the future while writing my book, and what unfolded next in Catalonia went far beyond my expectations. I also believe that very few of the more than 150 people whom I interviewed for this book could have predicted what happened in the autumn of 2017. The only certainty was that the book's publication was very timely, just as Catalan secessionism was reaching boiling point.

In fact, my book unleashed some fierce criticism even before it was released, especially once people saw online a preview of the book's cover. I received insults and all sorts of other unfounded comments by email and on social media, including defamatory claims that the book had been commissioned and financed by the Generalitat, the regional government of Catalonia. Some of these attacks even came from people whom I knew personally and held in high regard. I had thanked Martin Ortega Carcelén, a former official in the Spanish foreign ministry, for sending me a copy of his book.

But two months before my own book was published, Ortega Carcelén wrote on Twitter that I would soon be trying to "sell an anti-Spanish pamphlet." Disappointed and surprised, I asked him by email what had prompted such a public attack and suggested to him that he should at least have had the intellectual rigor to first read the book before dismissing it as a pamphlet. By this time, he was teaching at different universities while working as a senior research fellow at the Elcano Royal Institute, a think tank based in Madrid. I never got an answer from Ortega Carcelén. But I am thankful to him and others for having helped me prepare for some of the even more vitriolic criticism that soon came my way. His attack also helped me understand that the timing of my book was a two-edged sword. On the one hand, it was great to have spent so much energy working on a topic that had once seemed to me to be too obscure to attract an international readership, but that was now suddenly reaching the top of the world news agenda, including for *The New York Times*.

On the other hand, however, I understood that whatever plaudits I might receive for my book from outside Spain, they risked getting outweighed by the attacks from within, including from people who decided to cast me as some kind of villainous secret agent, involved in an international conspiracy to build up more turmoil in Catalonia. After all, as one dubious Spanish official told me, why would a foreigner take the time to write a whole book about Catalonia if this effort was not also meant to form part of the secessionist propaganda?

In the conflict over Catalonia, each side has accused the other of brainwashing their supporters. What is certain is that, in Catalonia, the brain has often been clouded by emotion, which tends in any case to be stronger than reason. This emotional dimension is not always correlated to how much or how little people actually know about an issue. Some of the most emotion-driven statements about Catalonia have come from highly accomplished professionals, ranging from historians to economists, who have sometimes also ignored facts in order to fit their own version of the story.

In a column published in April 2018 in *El País*, the writer Javier Cercas talked about the criticism that he received from an "old American friend" for writing too often about the politics of Catalonia. "Catalonia is now a question of faith, not reasons," the American tells Cercas. Cercas ends up agreeing with him, and I also feel a lot of understanding for his American friend. In my book, I tried to highlight many of the grey areas in the Catalan debate, after talking to people who had other much more important preoccupations than politics or whose political interest was confined to a very specific issue, like the safeguard of the waters of the Ebro river.

But that was of course before the turmoil of October 2017. Since then, I think that it has become very difficult for anybody in Catalonia to remain on the sidelines of a debate that has split Catalan society in two. Most people also know somebody who has at some stage lost the plot over Catalonia, allowing their nerves and emotions to get the better of them, sometimes out of sheer frustration.

As the Catalan conflict intensified, Josep Borrell returned to the forefront of public life in Spain as one of the flag bearers of the anti-secession movement. As a respected economist, he co-authored a book aimed at debunking many of the financial arguments that had been made by the pro-independence movement, which has been arguing that Catalonia could afford economically to split from Spain. A week after the independence referendum, he was one the main speakers at a giant demonstration in Barcelona to defend the unity of Spain. In June 2018, Pedro Sánchez appointed him as foreign minister in his new Socialist government.

Borrell knows about the relationship between Madrid and Barcelona like few other politicians. Which made it weird to watch him walk out during an interview with Deutsche Welle in March 2019, a small incident that highlighted for me how easily emotions can boil over when discussing Catalonia.

The British interviewer, Tim Sebastian, irritated Borrell from the start with his aggressive and loaded style of questioning. He first asked Borrell to explain why Catalan separatists were kept in jail when "convicted of nothing." "Why do you say convicted of nothing?" Borrell fired back. "I am starting to think that you don't know anything about it." Sebastian then told Borrell that there was a difference between being charged and getting convicted, but Borrell did not retract. Later on, Borrell accused Sebastian of lying.

Borrell is of course not the only politician to lose his cool over Catalonia. Several separatist leaders have overheated, or played with the emotions of others. A Judas reference made by Gabriel Rufián, in a Tweet that read "155 pieces of silver," hit a very raw nerve in Carles Puigdemont, just as the Catalan leader was deciding whether to risk declaring unilateral independence, in late October 2017.

I have also watched some friendships break down over Catalonia, even between some of Spain's most brilliant minds. As academics, Luis Garicano and Carles Boix conducted research together at the University of Chicago in the early 2000s. They became friends and would enjoy evenings together at the cinema. Garicano then became a professor at the London School of Economics, where he also established his reputation as somebody who could make difficult topics understandable to a wide audience, a skill that he later used to jump into politics with the Ciudadanos party. In 2008, he even explained to Queen Elizabeth II the origins of the credit crisis when she visited his London university. The Queen was reportedly impressed by the chart that he drew on a blackboard. After Chicago, Boix became a professor at Princeton University. He has written award-winning books and is a leading researcher on economic inequality.

The two academics ended up in different places, but it was Catalan politics that drove them apart. In September 2017, the editor of the *Jot Down* magazine asked me whether I would be willing to moderate a conversation between Boix and Garicano, which would be their first encounter in several years. But the night before, Boix pulled out. He later explained to me that his U-turn had been provoked by a parliamentary proposal tabled by Ciudadanos, the party of Garicano. Boix apologized profusely for his last-minute withdrawal, but maintained that it would have been "absurd" to debate with his former friend in such circumstances. I had instead a coffee with Garicano the following day. He regretted the situation, but made it sound almost inevitable. As Garicano put it, "the independence movement pulled us apart." Thus, a long-standing friendship was sacrificed on the altar of Catalan politics.

I have found myself under fire over my writings about Catalonia, but I have sometimes been happy to play the role of devil's advocate, which I believe is an important component of journalism, as it forms part of the right and obligation to question everything. A foreign correspondent observes the lay of the land not only from the hilltop, but also sometimes by plunging into dangerous territory. In a conflict, the correspondent must occasionally stick his head above the parapet, get out of the trenches and cross the lines, in the search for different opinions and facts that can be contrasted with what some people accept as their only truth. In over 25 years of work as a correspondent, I have sometimes sat patiently through interviews with people who inspired nothing positive in me. This effort is required in order to form an understanding that can be turned into a balanced newspaper article.

To continue the military analogy, the risk is that the correspondent can get stranded in a no man's land, becoming an easy target from both sides. I have sometimes joked that the success of my articles on Catalonia can best be measured in terms of whether they trigger an equal amount of discontent and frustration. For some readers in Madrid, I have been the correspondent who has joined a crusade to undermine Spain, stretching this effort as far as writing a book about Catalonia. For other readers in Catalonia, however, I have always lived in Madrid and befriended the Spanish establishment, without ever reading their local media in Catalan.

I once got an email from a reader who asked why I had joined a debate on Catalan television knowing that everybody would be speaking Catalan, when clearly I could not speak the language. I replied that, when it came to languages, I did my best to adjust whenever possible.

Thanks to my French and Spanish, I can manage to follow a debate in Catalan, and respond in Spanish. Basque, unfortunately, is a step too far. I have also been covering Portugal for *The New York Times*, but I have unfortunately not spent enough time in Portugal to learn the language. I took a few Portuguese lessons after arriving in Madrid in 2010, but I soon got too busy covering the financial crisis and abandoned the classes. Luckily, I have survived in Portugal by switching mostly between English and my own pathetic version of "Portuñol," which is how some people call the attempt to blend Portuguese and Spanish. I have conducted some interviews in Spanish, while listening to the answers in Portuguese and asking the person to take pity on me, by speaking slowly. I then used the recording to help clear up any possible confusion.

Thankfully, the Portuguese mostly like to speak other languages. But I still believe that my inability to speak Portuguese to them has put me at a disadvantage while reporting in Portugal. It makes a difference to be able to communicate with people in their native tongue. The exchange of stories and opinions not only becomes more humane and colorful but also far more insightful, even if the other person speaks great English.

As a Swiss who grew up in a family of polyglots, I value languages and welcome linguistic diversity in a country. But I was not entirely surprised to get the reader's complaint about my attempt to join a debate in Catalan, because the language issue has become part of the political feuding over Catalonia. Almost every week, I have followed a story on social media about somebody getting told not to speak Spanish in Catalonia, or instead somebody getting stopped from speaking Catalan by Spanish officialdom. Personally, I have not met a Catalan who has refused to speak Spanish to me. On the other hand, I have met a few Catalans who clearly welcomed my efforts to understand them in Catalan, just as people in Madrid or Seville have congratulated me on my Spanish.

Spain is one of the most diverse countries that I know, even though many people struggle to recognize the value of this asset. In my view, languages enrich a society, even if at times they can complicate communication. Castilian Spanish has produced an extraordinary literary heritage that obviously includes Don Quixote, the world's first modern novel. It should be promoted and defended as a world language, now also spoken by more people in the United States than in Spain. But I also believe that younger Spaniards would benefit from better language training, which should include making them watch movies with subtitles rather than dubbed (as is the case in neighbouring Portugal.) Aged 14, Princess Leonor set an example for her generation by delivering a speech in Barcelona in November 2019 in Spanish, Catalan, English and Arabic.

Spanish politics could also gain if national lawmakers were given the choice to debate not only in Spanish but also to switch to their own Catalan, Basque or Galician languages and rely on simultaneous interpretation, as is done in several other national parliaments, from Belgium and Finland to Canada and Singapore which, like Switzerland, has four official languages.

Reporting on Catalonia has at times required growing a thick skin. At one stage, I received repeated messages on Twitter from an unidentifiable account, asking me threateningly whether I had set a date for leaving the country. For the sake of my own mental sanity, I decided that it was best to have my morning shower before looking at my Twitter account.

At times, I have been attacked based on completely mistaken perceptions. A publication called es.diario wrote in 2018 an article claiming that I had been "humiliated" by my own newspaper, because another writer, Daniel Gascón, published an opinion piece in the Spanish version of *The New York Times* that criticized Quim Torra, the president of Catalonia. Es.diario suggested that Gascón had taken over my job, even though I never write opinion pieces. The truth is that the more interesting opinion pieces get published about Spain, by Gascón or anybody else, the better. Like probably for any other correspondent, it is in my interest to have people worldwide debate and read about a country that I cover.

I have been lucky enough to get full support from my editors at *The New York Times*, who have sometimes followed with bewilderment the story unfold in Catalonia. On a few occasions, readers who have been unhappy with my work have complained directly to New York, asking my bosses to correct information that they claimed was inaccurate. My editors want to correct quickly any mistake, but, sometimes, I have had to argue that the complaint was motivated by political bias. My list of such bias correction claims has unfortunately been getting longer since the conflict over Catalonia heated up.

No journalist is happy to make a mistake, particularly not at a newspaper like *The New York Times* that has a corrections editor who keeps track of mistakes. But I believe it is essential for the credibility of any media to correct well and clearly, a practice that needs improvement in Spain. I have read several articles in Spanish media in which changes were made online without acknowledging an earlier mistake, as if editors treat the Web as a blackboard that can be wiped entirely clean. Instead, the Internet leaves a trail, particularly on social media, that often extends very far and fast.

Sometimes, mistakes are provoked by the protagonists of the story, rather than attributable to a journalist. In November 2017, *The New York Times* published an opinion piece written by Oriol Junqueras, which he signed off as vice president of Catalonia, even though he had been removed from office by the Spanish government a few weeks earlier. As the newspaper purposefully separates departments, I did not know that Junqueras was publishing an opinion piece, and nobody in New York questioned how Junqueras had represented himself. His job description provoked outrage in Madrid, while Pedro Morenes, then Spain's ambassador in Washington, sent a letter of protest to the newspaper. The piece was obviously corrected. This incident also probably helped show some New York editors just how important it was to tread particularly carefully through the information minefield of Catalonia.

Given the timing of my book, I found myself in late 2017 in the awkward and difficult position of getting invitations to talk about the book while separately reporting on a fast-evolving story. Sometimes those who invited me had apparently not read the book and simply fed upon some of the hearsay comments about it.

Two weeks after the referendum, I spoke at a lunch event in Barcelona, organized by Sobirania i Justicia, a pro-independence association. The opening remarks were delivered Antoni Bassas, a veteran Catalan journalist who had been the correspondent of TV3 in Washington. Bassas spoke clearly but also emotionally about the situation in Catalonia and was warmly applauded. He introduced me with some kind words, but when I suggested that the separatist politicians had been going too far and too fast, some people left their table even before their main course had been served. As he got up, one guest mumbled a complaint about why his association had bothered inviting me in the first place. The organizer of the event later apologized to me, but I said that I had been very happy to speak to the rest of the audience.

Because, after all, I am convinced that no conflict can be properly resolved without having a dialogue. Sadly, in the debate over Catalonia, the lines of communication have broken down, also leaving people to preach loud and clear, but only to the faithful. The Catalan crisis has therefore unfolded in parallel universes, relayed by competing media groups that often tell the same story, but only part of it. They pick out specific events that fit into their broader rhetoric. I found interesting to look at the contrasting newspaper headlines after the referendum, highlighting either the illegality of the vote or the police violence. I have also followed with dismay the dispute over whether those who stood trial before the Supreme Court for sedition should have been called imprisoned politicians or political prisoners (imprisoned politicians is correct, in my view.) Choosing to highlight certain elements of the story, while mostly ignoring the rest, is no different to how the media has split over other divisive issues, from President Donald Trump's clampdown on migration to Brexit.

In late October 2017, the Spanish government used its emergency constitutional powers, granted by Article 155, to take charge in Catalonia. One of the most debated aspects of this intervention was whether to take control over TV3, the publicly-owned television in Catalonia, which stood accused of sectarianism in Madrid. This debate gave me an opportunity to write an article for *The New York Times* about the media split in Spain, including the development of regional broadcasters like TV3, which Jordi Pujol promoted as a way of anchoring Catalonia's political autonomy and promoting the Catalan language.

I talked to many people about what had gone wrong. But perhaps my most emotionally charged conversation was with Susanna Griso, who had left her native Barcelona to work instead as a television presenter in Madrid. Shortly before we talked, she had choked back tears on live television while arguing with a Catalan mayor about the stationing of Spanish policemen in the mayor's town. "These are extreme circumstances when you are giving opinions about an issue that affects your family and those you love," Griso told me. "From the media coverage, it often now looks as if we are already living in different states, but real life is a lot more complicated than that."

The dispute over Catalonia has not only touched personal issues, but it has also stretched to other areas like sports. Pep Guardiola, the Catalan coach of Manchester City, has arguably done more than any politician to raise the profile of the pro-independence movement in Britain.

In Spain, like elsewhere, social media has mostly helped raise rather than ease tensions. It has created silos in which fake news and conspiracy theories spread fast. They also get accelerated by algorithms and poisoned by bots. Readers seem unable to differentiate between the quality and the intensity of the debate.

A Catalan politician once proudly told me about how he was blocking on Twitter people who disagreed with his support for the independence movement. I told him that I could not see any benefit in vetoing opposing views, as long as they were not expressed as personal insults. In fact, every politician has a duty to hear all points of view within his community, even if this listening exercise might at times prove unpleasant. Similarly, I have rarely met in Madrid a hardline opponent of Catalan independence who has actually watched the Diada demonstration held on Catalonia's national day. A few have instead suggested it was shameful to report on a rally that was an act of disloyalty toward Spain. But the Diada gatherings have also been some of the largest protests in Europe of the past decade. And without at least trying to understand the feelings expressed by hundreds of thousands of Catalans every September 11, National Day of Catalonia, any attempt to reunite the peoples of Spain is likely to go nowhere.

Un octubre caliente
Caos y conflicto en el referéndum catalán

Everybody living in Spain knows what happened on 1 October 2017, when the government in Catalonia staged an independence referendum in defiance of the constitutional court and the government in Madrid.

Or at least everybody thinks they know. But my memories of this event are mostly those of a day in which Catalonia was engulfed in a thick cloud of chaos and confusion. A tense dawn was followed by several hours of violent clashes between police officers and voters. The evening yielded competing claims of victory, made by feuding politicians who all knew that their speeches were filled with half-truths, at best. It was a day that oscillated between the normal and the surreal.

Of course, this Catalan referendum was never going to be like any other normal voting day, following a very volatile and tense month. After the hiatus of their summer vacation, the governing separatist politicians of Catalonia returned to work in September and immediately escalated the tensions within their regional parliament, pushing through a series of laws that contravened and ignored Spain's national legislation.

When visiting Barcelona, I had normally accepted the hospitality of a friend, Joan, who lived in a small apartment in the Barcelona neighborhood of Gracia. But as my reporting workload grew, I realized that I was overstaying his welcome, working late at night and making phone calls to editors in New York while he was trying to sleep on the other side of a flimsy wall partition. I switched to a hotel near Plaza Catalunya, where all the staff soon got to know me by name, as I kept traveling back-and-forth between Madrid and Barcelona. When I would check in, the concierge would invariably greet me by saying: "It's good to see you again, but does your return to Barcelona mean anything really bad is going to happen now?"

I had no good answer for him. But as the date of the promised referendum got nearer, I felt like I was watching a slow-motion train crash. On September 11, in his Diada speech to celebrate Catalonia's national day, President Carles Puigdemont had insisted that citizens would take part in a referendum that would be celebrated like any other normal voting occasion. But at the same time in Madrid, President Mariano Rajoy repeated his pledge that the Spanish government would ensure that no such referendum would happen. The politicians had created an impossible situation in which at least one of them was going to be proven wrong. Having worked in Asia before, I knew how important it can be for people not to be seen losing face in an argument. In this case, there seemed to be no way for everybody to at least save appearances and come out unscathed from this standoff.

I felt in a good position to follow the events unfolding in Catalonia. After all, as discussed in the previous chapter, I had spent about 18 months crisscrossing Catalonia, as well as the Basque Country, Galicia and Madrid to speak to people about regional tensions and nationalism in Spain, in order to write my book about Catalonia. In fact, some of the people whom I had interviewed for my book had in the meantime become lead characters in this Catalan conflict.

I knew that I was covering an important and unpredictable story that could have wider repercussions for the European Union, and my editors shared this view. A year after the Brexit referendum, it seemed that the EU could ill afford a new crisis in Spain. With no sign of a possible settlement, or even a return to dialogue between the governing politicians in Madrid and Barcelona, my most senior editors decided to send reinforcements to Catalonia.

The New York Times has significant resources at its disposal. Using another military analogy, it can deploy talented investigative reporters to almost any country, who then operate swiftly and efficiently on the ground, as if they formed part of an elite commando. But on some occasions, *The New York Times* uses its significant resources to cover every possible angle of a major news story, bringing enough ammunition and big guns to ensure that it will not miss the target. Over the next two months, *The New York Times* sent five reporters to cover the Catalan story, backed by a few talented Spanish freelance journalists, who helped our correspondents in Barcelona and other cities, by organizing interviews and sometimes also serving as their interpreters. I think it is safe to claim that *The New York Times* assigned more of its foreign newsroom resources to Catalonia in the autumn of 2017 than any other international newspaper. The risk, it seemed to me, was not that we would miss the story but that it would be hard to maintain good coordination among all our reporters and editors while covering such a confusing situation. Too many cooks can spoil the broth.

Aware of this risk, we split the workload and focused on different aspects of the story ahead of the referendum, including reporting in detail on the deployment of thousands of Spanish police officers in Catalonia and their tense relationship with the Mossos, the name given to members of the Catalan police force. One of our correspondents also traveled to the Basque Country and Madrid to take a fresh look at nationalism in other parts of the country.

I spent the afternoon before the referendum in one of the polling stations of the Raval neighborhood of Barcelona, located within a school. The building was filled with people playing scrabble and other board games, listening to guitar music and arguing over whether Ada Colau, the mayor, was doing a good job for Barcelona. It felt like a festive gathering where the only moments of tension came from the fact that too many people were crammed into a tight space.

As I made my way back to the hotel, I was still unclear about whether and how people would vote the next day. Around midnight, I received a message from the mayor of Arenys de Munt, the town that had organized the first and symbolic independence consultation in Catalonia, in September 2009. The mayor sent me a photo of the plastic ballot box that had just been set up in the polling station of Arenys. "Believe me, we are absolutely ready," he wrote underneath.

The Spanish government had given instructions for the Mossos to force the closing of the polling stations by 8 a.m., when Puigdemont's government had instead scheduled the voting to start. I returned to the Raval's polling station around 6 a.m. It was still packed. Near the columns that adorned the school's entrance door, a group of Mossos had gathered, talking among themselves and sharing cigarettes while waiting for further orders. I went up to the officer who looked like their commander and told him that I was a journalist who wanted to know what the Mossos plan was. How could a dozen officers force a large crowd to abandon a polling station? "There is absolutely no plan," he said. "So you will not force their evacuation?" I asked. "Would you force them out?" he responded.

I reminded him that, as a journalist, I was meant to ask the questions and not respond to them, nor of course take over the role of police coordinator. It was clear that the commander was not enjoying my questions, nor his assignment at this early hour of the morning. He ended our conversation by telling me that "if the people at the top really want to do something about this, they should come here and try to do it themselves." I asked him whether I could quote him by name, but he just turned his back on me and started to regroup his men.

Just before the voting was due to start, the commander and his Mossos gently pushed their way past the people who were blocking the entrance. Inside, they took down the DNI identification details of a few people and they then walked out, to loud cheers and applauses. I was trying to remember the last time that I had seen such crowd enthusiasm for the police. I knew that this would not be the last strange scene of the day, but I had no idea that the situation would get so far out of control.

A hot autumn

Once I had watched the first people voting in the Raval, I made my way to the radio studio of Cadena Ser, just off Plaza Catalunya, to join Javier Del Pino, the moderator of the "A vivir" weekend program. I was there to take part in a brief radio conversation with a few correspondents at 9 a.m., but just as we were about to go on air, we saw on television the first images of Spanish police bursting into Catalan polling stations. The sound on the television was switched off, which made it almost look like a science fiction movie. Was this really happening on Spanish soil? I left immediately the radio studio for my next-door hotel, while Del Pino scrambled to reorganize his radio show.

For the next hour or so, a group of *New York Times* correspondents watched on a hotel television screen the unlikely images that were getting beamed from Catalonia to the rest of Spain and the world. I called local officials to try to understand how widespread the police intervention was. It soon became clear that, while police officers were forcing the closure of some polling stations, in several other places the voting was going ahead as Puigdemont had predicted, with people queuing outside as they waited to cast their ballot paper. I had no idea when and how this could end. But I knew that the maths did not add up. Catalonia has a census of more than five million voters. Without help from the Mossos, the Spanish government could rely on about 10,000 officers spread across a vast territory dotted with 2,600 polling stations.

Who had decided in Madrid that the riot police should intervene, and what was the plan of action? What would the Mossos do if the situation worsened? Which politicians and police commanders would be held accountable if people got seriously injured?

More than three years later, I still do not have the definite answers, but neither unfortunately does any citizen of Spain. The Spanish Parliament, which has the power to order a special investigation after momentous events, decided that the referendum of 1 October 2017 was not worth such an effort. The task of understanding what had happened was shifted from the Congress to the courtrooms, while the political recriminations have continued and ill feelings have been allowed to fester. And whatever the judges have decided, the story of a heroic act of defiance by ordinary Catalan voters against a powerful Spanish state and its riot police officers has continued to be told among those who believe in Catalonia's right to self-determination.

Chaos and conflict in the Catalan referendum

In early 2019, I followed the Supreme Court trial of the dozen former leaders of the independence movement. I attended personally three sessions during the four months of the trial, but also watched on television some of the other 422 witnesses who appeared before the Supreme Court trial, among them Mariano Rajoy and Juan Ignacio Zoido, his former interior minister. I expected little from Rajoy, a man of few words in public at the best of times. But I expected more from Zoido, a warm-blooded politician whom I had first met on the day that he was elected mayor of Seville.

However, in February 2019, Zoido told seven judges who were trying to determine acts of rebellion and sedition that he knew nothing about anything. It was as if tens of millions of Spanish had been glued to their television set on the morning of October 1, but Zoido had been out of the country that day. Asked about the police intervention during the referendum, Zoido answered the following: "My habit has been neither to design nor judge security arrangements, I don't know many ministers who have dared do this, unless they had specific knowledge in this kind of matter. I didn't design or do anything."

I was left wondering exactly why some elected politicians did not understand that accountability was part of their job description, and why they were allowed to get away with it. It is question that can apply worldwide, but one that certainly seems relevant in Spain.

In the most tragic and momentous of occasions, including accidents like the Prestige oil spill, the Valencia metro derailment or the Santiago de Compostela train crash, the politicians and senior executives somehow vanish from the scene, or are never made to answer for their inadequate decisions and explanations. A lone ship captain or a train conductor end up bearing the full blame for the catastrophe.

But unlike a train tragedy, the political collision in Catalonia was one for which politicians had plenty of time to prepare. The referendum, if nothing else, was a huge slap in the face for Rajoy and his government because it showed an inability to plan and handle properly law and order, which is one of the cornerstones of a functioning democracy. The tensions and standoff between the Mossos and other Spanish police officers were something that the country had not witnessed since the failed coup of February 1981.

It also gave an image of conflict and violence that was anathema for the millions of tourists and other visitors who have made Spain one of the world's most popular tourist destinations, delighting in its beauty, sunshine and also relaxed pace of life. Soon enough, I got emails from readers of *The New York Times* asking me whether they should cancel their trip to Barcelona.

While the police intervention remains open to questioning, the referendum was conducted in violation of the Spanish constitution and was not a blank check for the separatist leaders of Catalonia to push ahead with a unilateral declaration of independence. Its result was in any case not verifiable, without a proper recount and without an agreed census. The Catalan government invited a few sympathetic international observers to Barcelona to monitor the referendum, including a few members of the European Parliament, but their presence did not amount to proper international scrutiny. Half of the voters had followed Madrid's instructions and stayed away from the polling stations, ensuring that the referendum would be approved by an overwhelming majority. In the end, the Catalan government announced that the referendum turnout was 42 percent, in a region where elections have regularly drawn more than 70 percent of voters during this past decade.

In fact, every number used in relation to this referendum continues to be debated. As a correspondent, I try to rely on official data, rather than hearsay, assuming that this official data can be considered reliable. But in the conflict over Catalonia, part of the data has occasionally lost its required objectivity.

I first drew this conclusion on 11 September 2012, when I joined the huge crowd in Barcelona that transformed the Diada into the largest pro-independence march since Spain's return to democracy. By the end of the demonstration, however, I was forced to include three sets of figures into my report, which ranged from 600,000 to 1.5 million people.

How could it be that, in an age of drones and satellite imagery, official estimates of crowd participation in Barcelona differed so widely? Unfortunately, of course, similar efforts to distort the data have occurred almost everywhere else since. A few years later, I could only smile while listening to President Trump claim that a record crowd had come to Washington for his inauguration address, in January 2017. When then asked to defend the idea that more people listened to Trump than Barack Obama when he took office, Trump's counselor, Kellyanne Conway, coined the "alternative facts" phrase that has come to define this phenomenon. The past decade in Catalonia has been filled with such alternative facts. Unfortunately, it makes the job of any correspondent a lot more complicated, particularly when it comes to verifying information in the heat of the moment.

During the referendum, my colleagues and I could simply not witness first-hand all that was happening, particularly outside Barcelona. Meanwhile, we were getting flooded with conflicting (supposedly official) data, from the number of voters to the number of injured. The main piece that we wrote that day was read by more than one million people and headlined "Catalonia's Independence Vote Descends Into Chaos and Clashes." It did not aim to draw any firm conclusion about what had happened and what could happen next. "By the day's end, both sides were claiming victory," I wrote in a joint piece with Ellen Barry, one of the most experienced and talented correspondents of *The New York Times*. "The day's events left nothing clear except that the clashes over the status of the region had left supporters on both sides more hardened and polarized than before."

In the following days, we tried to sift through this wreckage of information to understand better what had occurred and where this left Catalonia, while listening to politicians who were drawing their own divergent conclusions. The tension was ebbing and flowing, as if nobody had really planned for the day after a referendum. The politicians engaged in a standoff that resembled a game of poker in which each player not only tries to guess the other's cards, but is also struggling to find value in the cards that he holds in his hand. As a correspondent, it felt at times very difficult to simplify and explain the unexplainable.

Shortly after the referendum, Puigdemont announced that the vote's result gave him a mandate to declare independence. On October 10, over 1,000 journalists got accredited to hear him address the Catalan Parliament and fulfill the promise that he had made to his supporters that this would be a historic moment for Catalonia. Instead, we found ourselves drowned in a sea of rumors and tense arguments, watching nervous lawmakers run around the corridors of their assembly. After much waiting, we heard Puigdemont say nothing and everything. I later wrote a personal account of this surreal parliamentary session for *The New York Times*, which produced every kind of emotion possible. Outside the building, my colleague Jason Horowitz reported on how he watched the supporters of independence "kicking beer cans in frustration," because they had not heard the magic words they had expected from Puigdemont. Late that night, Horowitz, Patrick Kingsley and I shared our own beers in a bar near our hotel, exhausted by another very confusing reporting day. We were too tired to laugh, except when Horowitz, with his dry sense of humor, posted a goodnight Tweet summing his view of Puigdemont. At least, he wrote, we had discovered that the Catalan leader could also be "Fudgemont."

It was one of the few light-hearted moments in what turned out to be one of my toughest months as a correspondent. The story was full of unexpected twists and turns and the tensions kept mounting — not only on the streets but also inside the halls of powers and within the newsrooms. Eventually, the political turmoil culminated in another surreal moment, when separatist lawmakers declared unilateral independence on October 27, after their opponents had abandoned the assembly chamber. From the top of the imposing staircase of the Catalan Parliament, I watched as the separatist lawmakers cheered alongside dozens of mayors of Catalan towns, who had come to Barcelona for the celebration. Of course, it proved one of the shortest celebrations in political history. By late evening, the politicians did not join the street party on the square of Sant Jaume. Some of them, in fact, were probably already busy packing up their suitcases for Brussels.

In this book, my aim has not been to recount every moment of this extraordinary month, nor its aftermath. But I do want to close this chapter by mentioning how I feel that the referendum also marked a turning point for correspondents working in Spain, who found themselves caught in an intense cross fire. Politicians in Barcelona had long understood the importance of public opinion and international support for their cause. But until October 2017, Rajoy and the other politicians in Madrid mostly seemed to believe that it was enough to talk about Catalonia in terms of the rule of law. That changed after the referendum. The government in Madrid realized that its handling of Catalonia needed to be defended not only within Spain, but also outside, as this conflict was now worrying people in Brussels and beyond. Both sides then engaged in a battle for world public opinion and seemed to call on their respective domestic media to back them.

It was as if disagreement, let alone dissent, were no longer possible. A week after the referendum, two Spanish journalists who had regularly taken part in debates on public television and radio in Catalonia quit, writing a column in *El País* headlined "Farewell to the circus of hatred." One of the two journalists, Joan López Alegre, later told me about how he had endured "unbelievable, destructive and exhausting harassment" whenever he had tried to be the lone voice of dissent on the set of TV3.

It was clear, however, that this virulent propaganda battle was also being fought in Madrid. Two weeks after *El País* published the piece denouncing TV3's handling of unionist journalists, *El País* itself fired one of its most prominent columnists, John Carlin, who had written for the newspaper for two decades and is also an international bestselling author. I had read Carlin's work since arriving in Spain, exchanged some emails, but never met him in person. *El País* ended Carlin's contract after he wrote a column for *The Times* of London in which he was particularly critical of King Felipe's intervention in the Catalan crisis (which I discuss elsewhere in the book.) "Stiff in his bearing, coldly commanding in his tone, he did not build bridges, he dug trenches," Carlin wrote about the king's speech, which was broadcast to the nation two days after the referendum.

Carlin's removal provoked some debate on Spanish social media about freedom of expression, but it was mostly cheered by the defenders of Spanish sovereignty and seemed to fit the mood of intolerance building up at the time. During an interview with newspaper *El Español*, Josep Borrell talked at length about the propaganda battle which secessionism had been winning, arguing that "the first victim in such a battle is always the truth." He then spontaneously mentioned Carlin's ouster, concluding that it was "well deserved." I found it hard to understand how a politician (who is now the current leader of the European Union's foreign policy) could applaud the loss of a columnist, over what he had written for a British newspaper. Whatever the merits or shortcomings of Carlin's column, it seems to me that he is in a special position to understand Spain and overcome the "guiri' (foreigner) label that is attached to most correspondents, as a writer born in London to a Scottish father and Spanish mother.

For those of us correspondents without any privileged family connection to Spain, it was clear that, after the referendum, the message from Borrell and others was that we should not be trusted. Things had become too tense and emotional, and the so-called Anglo-Saxon perspective of Spain was no longer flavor of the month in Spain. This view was summed up by José Ignacio Torreblanca, whom I befriended as the head of the Madrid office of the European Council of Foreign Affairs, a research institute, but who had by then switched to one of the most powerful jobs in Spanish media, as the opinion pages editor of *El País*.

In a column headlined "Anglocondescendence," Torreblanca talked about "this insufferable feeling of Anglo-Saxon superiority that we have been suffering" since the referendum. He listed all the cliches and features of Spain, from its flamenco to its paella, which had made Spain condescendingly endearing to foreigners, at least until the images of the referendum were broadcast worldwide. Torreblanca was a staunch opponent of the independence movement, which had now also spilled over into distrust and frustration with foreign correspondents. Still, some of his arguments seemed justified. For instance, I have long felt unease about how my newspaper and most of the English-speaking media maintain the description of ETA as "a separatist group." As a consequence, I have added references to ETA's terrorism as often as possible, noting also that ETA was officially labeled as terrorist by both the European Union and the United States.

It seems to me obvious that distance makes it easier to forget the real harm, shock and violence that terrorism brings to a society. Just as proximity makes it hard to see the broader picture. I lived in New York the year after the 9/11 attack during which planes crashed into the World Trade Center, as the United States was engaged in a war in Afghanistan and preparing for another in Iraq. I soon gave up trying to convince anybody that removing Saddam Hussein would probably do nothing to help reduce the chances of another terrorist attack on New York.

In my view, a foreign correspondent, unlike perhaps an opinion writer, is in the business of explaining as many aspects of the story as possible for a foreign audience, without joining the ranks of the domestic media that positions itself more forcefully. Catalonia is simply not a black-and-white story, in which one side is the force of good fighting against the evil of the other. Political and social tensions have ebbed and flowed not only in 2017, but for much of the history of Spain and Catalonia, making it necessary to scratch below the surface. That was fundamental to my book research and continues to be my approach as a correspondent.

But in terms of the propaganda battle, it seems relatively clear to me that some episodes have been won by one side, while others by the other. The Spanish police handling of the referendum was an own goal scored by the authorities in Madrid, because it shifted the focus from the ballot boxes to the police truncheons and rubber bullets fired by officers in a region where the use of such bullets had been banned, following past excesses from the Mossos. It gave the independence movement the perfect opportunity to stop talking only about their referendum and instead engage in a broader and more emotional debate over whether Spain respected democracy and human rights. I remember being struck by a huge banner that floated from one of the buildings on Plaza Catalunya, which I could read every day when I walked out of my hotel. It had read *"Independencia."* But then, one morning shortly before the referendum, it was changed for a new banner that read *"Democracia."*

Two years later, the Catalan independence movement scored an own goal of its own when street violence overshadowed the peaceful daytime demonstrators that followed the Supreme Court's ruling against the 12 former Catalan leaders.

In October 2019, Barcelona did not turn into Aleppo or Baghdad, despite the claim made at the time by Albert Rivera, the leader of Ciudadanos, who also talked about "a tsunami of violence." Still, what I witnessed on the streets of Barcelona was certainly unlike anything that I had seen before. I saw people cut off streets by lighting bonfires, smash down sign posts and other public infrastructure, throw flares and rocks at the police. This was not the Barcelona that built itself into one of Europe's main investment and tourism hubs. And as had happened after the referendum, I started receiving a few messages from American readers, who wanted to know whether they should cancel a visit to Barcelona, after watching the street violence on American television.

Some separatist leaders were quick to condemn this outburst of violence, starting with the politician who had just received the toughest prison sentence of 13 years, Oriol Junqueras. Others, like Quim Torra, sounded far more ambivalent. And some seemed to fail completely to understand how damaging it could be for the rhetoric of the independence movement if it stopped claiming to be entirely peaceful. The president of the ANC, Elisenda Paluzie, told Catalan television that the violent clashes between protesters and the police "make the conflict visible," suggesting that what was happening in Catalonia was understandable given that "the world is the way it is." She then sugarcoated her comment by insisting that "ultimately, the main responsibility for the violence lies with the state" of Spain.

Paluzie lost an opportunity to at least stay quiet. I remembered her words a few days later, when I met Ian Gibson, the historian, who told me about how he always carried a notebook with him to his meetings, to jot down any interesting point or piece of advice. In contrast, Gibson said, he could not remember any Spaniard noting down any recommendation that he had made. "The Spanish mostly do not understand conversation as an opportunity to listen and learn, but instead as a chance to compete for the limelight," Gibson said. He referred me back to Domingo García-Sabell, the Galician writer and politician, who had looked at why in Spain "even secret confidences get shouted out." García-Sabell's conclusion was that "we are looking to amaze others," so that "we raise our voices looking to the front rows, waiting for the tacit ovation of the public. We are showmen."

There are of course many thoughtful and good public speakers in Spain, some of whom are also capable of adjusting their views as events unfold, or depending on what their audience is. What is said in private is not always what is written or spoken out in public.

Several months after Torreblanca published his column, he invited me to have lunch near his office. We had not met for a long time and I got somewhat anxious because Torreblanca had told me that he wanted to discuss my book and my articles about Catalonia. I hoped that his feelings about Catalonia would not ruin our lunch.

I eased back as soon as I saw that he had brought with him a copy of my book that was filled with underlined sentences and penciled-in annotations. At least I was going to get more than just blunt criticism from the bully pulpit. Two hours later, I left feeling that we had an intense but constructive discussion, in which two people took the time to listen to each other.

Over Catalonia, however, there has been a lot of the shouting and showmanship deplored by García-Sabell, and nowadays echoed forcefully by the modern showroom that is social media. Much more can be achieved by learning how to listen, perhaps agree to disagree over precise issues, while finding some points of consensus. At the same time, everybody, from voters to the media, must make clear to the politicians on all sides that it is time to stop the shouting, behave responsibly and realize how much damage this has already caused.

Hablar con todos
Las aristas del procés

Covering Spain for a leading international newspaper, I inevitably got caught in the crossfire over Catalonia. Even my exact location became an issue. The independence movement got upset that I was living and mostly writing from Madrid, while some readers in the rest of Spain felt I had already overspent time in Barcelona by writing a book about Catalonia, as discussed earlier.

Personally, I consider that Spain's incredible high-speed train network makes it possible to crisscross this vast and arid land like almost no other country of the world. I have sometimes worked better inside a silent carriage traveling between Madrid and Barcelona than at home or in a press room. In the end, what matters is to be able to discover new places and hear from different people as often as possible. But some of the criticism went further, focusing not only on what and where I wrote, but who I spoke to.

I believe reporting requires hearing things straight from the horse's mouth, whenever possible. If a society accepts that a sound justice system should give a defendant a fair hearing in a courtroom, surely this principle should extend to the media, whose job is to inform on different points of view. That does not mean necessarily publishing all that is said. If a person shares blatantly false or defamatory information, it should obviously not be parlayed.

In March 2016, I wrote an article a few days before the release from prison of Arnaldo Otegi, based partly on an interview that I had conducted with him by writing, while he was in his cell. A Spanish politician phoned me to say that it was shameful that *The New York Times* should speak with an ETA terrorist. This politician had however no specific complaint about the content of the article, which explained Otegi's background and what he had been sentenced for. I told the politician that, whether he liked it or not, Otegi was a person of public interest, whose release would also no doubt be covered by every Spanish media.

Two years later, some people also got upset that correspondents were speaking to Catalan politicians who then stood accused of crimes including sedition or rebellion. I talked to some of them, both in jail and outside, which does not mean I always wrote about our meetings. One such unpublished meeting took place in April 2018, when I met Clara Ponsatí, while staying with a friend of mine and his family in Edinburgh. He drove me to the university town of St Andrews, where Ponsatí is a professor of economics. We found the legendary golf course of St Andrews windswept, but also shimmering in the bright green light of its grass, sunlit after a lengthy period of rain. As we then walked around the historic courtyards of the university, it struck me that the grass of their lawns was just as immaculately cut as the greens of the golf course. This was a beautiful and open space that had little to do with the gloom of a prison cell.

Ponsatí's office also offered a stunning view onto the North Sea. Only a defiant tree stood between her desk and the waves crashing onto the rocks below. "There's no need to mention how beautiful this place gets when the weather is good, because then nobody is going to believe how tough my situation is," Ponsatí told me jokingly, as she led the way upstairs to a lounge and then disappeared into the pantry to prepare coffee.

During my stay in Edinburgh, I had already met some people who were interested in the Catalan conflict. I visited the Scottish Parliament and also the University of Edinburgh, where I talked to some of its professors. I had planned to go to St Andrews to give a lecture, but it was canceled by a teachers' strike, so I got instead in touch with Ponsatí, who had coincidentally returned recently to St Andrews from Brussels. I had been monitoring her whereabouts since Spain's attorney general put her on the list of prosecuted separatist politicians, after their failed attempt to declare unilateral independence in October 2017. But once summoned to court, Ponsatí was among the politicians who instead fled to Brussels, led by Catalonia's ousted president, Carles Puigdemont.

Ponsatí was now back in her prestigious British university, specifically in its school of economics and finance, which she had led for two years before plunging into Catalan politics instead and accepting Puigdemont's offer to join his administration. As we waited for the coffee to cool down, Ponsatí looked strangely relaxed for somebody under an international arrest warrant, issued by Judge Pablo Llarena from the Supreme Court. I asked her whether that was because she had long known that her political involvement would land her into hot waters.

"I knew that I was getting intro trouble — but not so much trouble," she said. "Getting into trouble is always a question of degree." Still, Ponsatí was determined to avoid the trouble of a Spanish courtroom. She had engaged in a cat-and-mouse chase with Judge Llarena, who now wanted her to appear in court in Scotland to face extradition proceedings.

Born in 1957, Ponsatí explained to me that she didn't wait to turn 60 to decide that she was ready to defy Spain's judiciary. "I was the oldest person in our government, so I certainly remember Franco and I have friends and relatives who went to prison during his time — and I wasn't going to follow them," she said. When Spain returned to democracy after Franco's death, "there was no cleaning out of the judges" who served during the dictatorship, she claimed. "I'm not saying that everybody is a Fascist but there is of course the tendency toward self-reproduction in the judiciary."

Ponsatí was not the only person to make such a complaint to me. Manuela Carmena, who was a judge before serving as a far-left mayor of Madrid, once told me about her own experience of the judiciary, including when she was twice detained during Franco's regime for her involvement in the underground Communist party. "When I became a judge, I found among my new colleagues the same judges who had detained me under Franco," she told me. "We made a transition to democracy during which we tried to avoid any kind of confrontation, but we didn't close the cycle by giving homage to those who deserved it and by censoring those who were responsible for the dictatorship."

I discuss both Franco's legacy and Spain's legal system elsewhere in the book. But I want to stress again that I do not believe democratic Spain has a dysfunctional judiciary. It sometimes falters, as happens elsewhere. My own sister has been a judge in Switzerland and her list of complaints about the the Swiss legal system is lengthy. Even if some Spanish judges perhaps remain steeped in the past, I have no evidence to support Ponsatí's claim that those who become judges are mostly "the children of judges." It seems obvious to me that a new generation of judges has emerged in Spain, just as there has been a major overhaul in the country's political leadership.

Still, Ponsatí told me that she faced political persecution in Spain, and she was particularly scathing about the role played by King Felipe VI in the Catalan conflict. "The presumption of innocence was thrown out from the beginning, even before any trial could start," she said. "After all, we had already been condemned by the king," she added, in reference to King Felipe's speech, delivered two days after the Catalan referendum of 1 October 2017, in which he castigated Catalan politicians for staging an unconstitutional referendum on independence. The King's intervention thrilled opponents of secessionism while enraging the pro-independence movement. Personally, I had been surprised that the monarch made the bold decision to jump into a political minefield rather than force the ultra-cautious Rajoy to sort things out. But once he decided to act, King Felipe had mostly said what was expected of him, as the highest defender of Spanish sovereignty.

What was less understandable to me was why the king had not used his speech to deliver not only strong condemnation but also a clear message of conciliation. After all, the images of the riot police intervention during the referendum had shocked many people who had a positive perception of modern Spain, independent of their political leanings. Many of these shocked viewers were not in Barcelona but had instead watched the referendum television footage from Madrid, Valencia, Bilbao or any other city worldwide.

King Felipe spoke on the evening of a general strike in Catalonia and amid worsening recriminations from both sides. While Puigdemont was accusing Rajoy of returning Spain to the darks days of Franco's dictatorship, Rafael Hernando, the parliamentary spokesman for Rajoy's Popular Party, claimed that the Catalan strike was "clearly political, with Nazi" connotations in terms of indoctrinating Catalans into following a separatist ideology. Hernando told Spanish national radio that separatist politicians "are hoping to provoke deaths in Catalonia." Watching from the sidelines, it felt like a situation spinning dangerously out of control, in which politicians were pouring oil on the fire rather than helping reduce tensions. After the King spoke, I remember talking to an editor in London about his speech. "Did the king not also say that he was simply sorry to see the chaos in Catalonia?" my editor asked.

Mediation is a skill that Ponsatí has studied at length, since she wrote her doctoral thesis on this topic and is a recognized expert of game theory, which uses mathematical models to analyze conflict and cooperation between rational decision-makers. I asked her why mediation had not been used between the politicians in Madrid and Barcelona. "I don't think the current politicians of Spain believe that the status of Catalonia is something that should be negotiated," she said. "If one of the parties doesn't want to negotiate, it's not a viable situation."

Whether in Spain or elsewhere in the world, she said, "politics is always about negotiations and you can always use force as part of your negotiations, but of course your capability to use force then conditions your negotiating stance." In Spain, she argued, "we're not in a situation of civilized negotiation." But exactly what room for negotiation did Puigdemont offer Rajoy's government over his claim to independence? "If you want negotiations, you also have to keep your position, you have to respect yourself if you want others to respect you," Ponsatí replied.

In Scotland, Ponsatí enjoyed more support than many of her Madrid detractors seem to believe. Her legal defense team was led by a lawyer, Aamer Anwar, who gained fame for working on important cases involving racism and asylum seekers. I didn't meet Anwar during my visit, but instead admired his framed family photo, which hangs in the Scottish National Portrait Gallery.

Ponsatí had also quickly raised 200,000 British Pounds in a crowd funding campaign to help pay for her legal defense. "Scotland is a good place from the point of view of political and popular support because people here understand that putting someone in prison for organizing a referendum sounds very extreme — independent of whether these same people in Scotland support the idea of independence or not," she said.

Despite the setback of October 2017, Ponsatí maintained that "Catalonia is getting nearer to independence. The question is whether the strategy of Puigdemont made things more difficult or easier, but when you have a popular mandate, obeying that mandate is what you have to do."

As an economist, I also asked Ponsatí for her assessment of the financial impact on Catalonia of its secessionist conflict. As the crisis boiled over in the autumn of 2017, more than 3,000 companies had relocated their legal headquarters from Catalonia to other parts of Spain. The relocations, according to Ponsatí, were mostly symbolic gestures that had not altered Catalonia's economy in any significant way. "We've seen that all these claims that there would be catastrophic events hitting the economy were totally false and politically motivated," she said.

Whatever would happen next for the economy and in Spanish politics, she dismissed the idea that support for independence could evaporate if the conflict dragged on, or if Madrid took tougher measures against separatist politicians. "Many believe this in Spain but this is totally mistaken," she said. "You certainly don't stop pursuing a cause because you're facing repression."

Ponsatí took her time to choose her words. But what intrigued me was that, as an expert on game theory and mediation, she still sounded absolutely convinced that she and her fellow separatists would emerge as the winners in their struggle over independence. She barely conceded that any mistake had been made in 2017, although she admitted that "Catalan politics is always very complicated and it would probably do ourselves good to be more straight-forward." I was interested in listening to Ponsatí, as an academic turned politician, but I didn't try to turn this interview into an article. After several months of intense coverage of Catalonia, I felt the international readers of the *New York Times* were probably satiated.

On the drive back from St Andrews, I thought again about how politics are shaped by very personal decisions, like those that split the former Catalan government between a group that faced Spanish justice and another that escaped prosecution, led by Puigdemont. Six months later, I got a chance to return to this issue during a visit to the Lledoners prison, a secluded spot in the midst of the Catalan countryside whose access road was covered with pro-independence graffiti and felt a world away from the beautiful lawns of Scotland. I had come to speak to Oriol Junqueras, the former deputy president of Catalonia, and Raül Romeva, who had been in charge of foreign affairs. They had then already spent a year in jail, ahead of their Supreme Court trial.

I was not their only visitor that day. As I put my cellphone and other belongings in a locker before being allowed to enter the main compound, a man with narrow eyes and a familiar face stepped out. It was Juan José Ibarretxe, the former Basque nationalist leader, whose own plan to loosen his region's ties with Madrid had been dismissed by an overwhelming majority in Congress in 2005. I remember wondering how Ibarretxe felt about his departure from the hot waters of nationalist politics.

Ahead of my visit, I had heard complaints about the special VIP treatment received by Junqueras and his fellow inmates since the incoming Socialist government had allowed them to switch from a Madrid prison to one in Catalonia. Some Spanish publications even compared Junqueras to Pablo Escobar, the Colombian drug lord who was allowed to turn his prison almost into a hotel, from where he could also continue to run his cocaine business. Junqueras told me that the only real privilege he got since being transferred to Catalonia was being allowed to return to his academic roots as a university professor. He taught astronomy, history, mathematics and other subjects to fellow inmates. "I care about politics," he said. "But I also like people to know about our discovery of UY Scuti, the biggest star in our universe."

I could not corroborate the VIP complaints made in Madrid. But speaking to him and Romeva using an old-style telephone, through the glass pane of the visitation booth, it was clear to me that a prison is a prison, whether near Madrid or in Catalonia.

When I asked Junqueras his views about Puigdemont, Ponsatí and others enjoying freedom rather than incarceration, he hesitated before answering. "I'm not interested in evaluating the actions of other leaders," he said. "My own goal has always been to stay close to my people, to show them that I am willing to make every effort and sacrifice possible to defend what I believe in." It was a diplomatic reply, but one that still revealed the simmering tensions between politicians who had once agreed to share control over Catalonia's government.

In late 2019, Judge Llarena reissued international arrest warrants for Puigdemont, Ponsatí and other politicians who had avoided conviction in Madrid, after the Supreme Court sentenced nine other separatists to prison for sedition. Junqueras got 13 years, the toughest conviction. But then in June 2021, Prime Minister Pedro Sánchez issued pardons to release the nine separatists from jail. The gesture was designed to restore "concord" in Catalonia, he said, but it was also fiercely opposed by Spain's right-wing opposition politicians.

At the time of writing, the final outcome of this long judicial and political battle remained unclear. The tensions also stayed high, and just a single comment has at times been enough to put a politician back in the headlines, often for the wrong reasons. At the start of the coronavirus crisis, for instance, Ponsatí had to apologize over the outcry that she provoked in Spain with a sarcastic Tweet about how Madrid's political management of the epidemic was sending people "from Madrid to Heaven." It was just the kind of inflammatory comment that is likely to guarantee that Catalonia's conflict will continue to simmer. In the meantime, I and other foreign correspondents will no doubt keep a watchful eye on Catalonia, while knowing that we are writing for an international readership that is not interested in each and every detail of the story.

Un amor europeo
La relación entre España y la Unión Europea

Whenever I hear about the Brexit referendum, I think back to the European flags of my English youth, or more precisely the lack thereof. I spent the 1980s studying in England and I was often struck by the fact that there was almost never an EU flag floating on a public building, next to the Union Jack. It was as if Britain felt ashamed about forming part of the wider European family. It therefore came to me only as a mild surprise to see how easily some British politicians then managed to turn Brussels into a scapegoat and present the EU institutions as an unaccountable and over-reaching bureaucracy.

In contrast, modern Spain has struck me as enjoying a maturing love affair with the European Union. Spanish society has embraced the idea of stronger European integration and flies the EU flag proudly whenever it can be raised.

In Luis García Berlanga's 1953 classic comedy movie, *Welcome Mr. Marshall!* the long-awaited American donors never come to visit the inhabitants of the Castilian village that have prepared a special welcome for them. But instead Spain did receive billions in subsidies after it joined the European Union in 1986, and continues to show gratitude for the help that it got from its European partners to modernize an economy that had suffered from political and financial isolation for much of Franco's dictatorship. Traveling across Spain on the lookout for the EU logo that adorns its roads, railway lines and bridges, it sometimes feels as if almost none of the modern infrastructure of Spain was built without EU money.

Many other European countries were transformed by EU subsidies. But not all have maintained the same allegiance to Brussels. In fact, some have developed significant anti-EU feelings since the 2008 financial crisis, allowing politicians to make progress by defying Brussels, in countries ranging from Hungary and Poland to Italy and Greece. But in Spain, even at the height of the banking crisis in 2012, anti-EU sentiment only went as far as pointing an accusatory finger toward "the men in black," the disparaging and dark term coined to refer to the officials from Brussels, Frankfurt and Washington, who forced budget cuts on some European governments in return for rescue money.

If anything, the crisis was presented as a plot by Germany to use its financial muscle to take fully charge of the EU. In private during the crisis, some Spanish bankers and officials spoke to me negatively about Angela Merkel and her finance minister, Wolfgang Schäuble, who were accused of putting undue pressure on Spain. But such views were very rarely expressed in public. And I never heard anybody blame Spain's other EU partners, led by France, even though French president François Hollande was doing his best to safeguard French banks that had also participated heavily in the reckless lending in Greece and the rest of southern Europe.

Where were the Spaniards who had once been skeptical about European integration or openly opposed to American interventionism in Europe? If anything, it sometimes seemed to me as if Spain had created a new generation of *conversos* as part of its transition, with politicians who had understood that their future advancement also required changing ideology. When I first worked as a correspondent in Brussels, the most prominent Spaniard in town was Javier Solana, who was elected secretary general of NATO in late 1995. I was surprised to find out that Solana had once fervently opposed American militarism and had written a manifesto detailing as many as 50 reasons why Spain should not join NATO.

Political radicalism returned to Spain around the time of the financial crisis, as a new generation of politicians tapped into growing discontent among voters about corruption and economic inequality. But none of these newcomers stuck to a decidedly anti-EU message, with the notable exception of the CUP (Popular Unity Party) in Catalonia. Pablo Iglesias and his Podemos party started out on an anti-EU trajectory, partly inspired by the success of Alexis Tsipras and his Syriza party in Greece. But by the time Podemos won its first seats in Congress in 2015, Iglesias and his fellow party leaders had taken out of the Podemos program any suggestion that Spain should leave the EU, or even drop the euro. In the case of the far-right Vox, which entered Congress in early 2019, the party's campaign message was that power should be recentralized in Madrid and that the EU should become more efficient and less wasteful, but not that Brussels should be closed down. Vox's emergence was therefore less of a preoccupation for the safeguard of the EU than the rise of far-right parties elsewhere in Europe with a much more aggressive approach to Brussels, including that of Marine Le Pen in France, who campaigned for the presidency — albeit unsuccessfully — against Emmanuel Macron by arguing that France should abandon the euro.

After every Spanish election, the media urges the incoming government to work harder to raise Spain's presence in Brussels. The message is always that Spain should aim to have more seats at the EU table. Unlike in some other European countries, there are no publications in Spain that suggest that the time has come for Spain to bite the Brussels hand that once fed it and free itself from the pressure of EU legislation. Whenever there is a tussle between Madrid and Brussels over the Spanish budget, the Spanish media puts the onus on the government to comply with the deficit targets set in Brussels. Spain is clearly not Italy, whose government openly defied Brussels in 2018 when it was told to revise its budget and squeeze spending. Italy's deputy prime minister at the time, Luigi Di Maio, fired back by sending a letter to the European Commission to say that Italy would not alter its budget and the Commission should instead show more "respect" for Italians.

Do some politicians in Italy believe that their country is due special respect as an original signatory of the Treaty of Rome that helped create today's EU? Do Spanish politicians feel that they are relative newcomers to the EU table? Or is it that Spanish politicians are under pressure from their voters to show respect for Brussels because Spanish voters trust them less than the bureaucrats in Brussels to help keep Spain's house on a sound financial footing?

Of course, there have been times when many people in Spain

have felt hurt or miscomprehension because of a decision taken by a European institution. I attended a dinner in Madrid on the day of November 2018 when the European Court of Human Rights ruled that Spain had not granted a fair trial to Arnaldo Otegi, who spent six years in prison for crimes related to ETA. When I asked the other invitees what they thought about Europe's highest court finding Spain's judiciary guilty of mishandling Otegi's trial, there was a deafening silence around the table, as if I had mentioned the Devil. Finally, somebody reminded me that Otegi was a vile terrorist, but nobody questioned the judgement of the Strasbourg court. Pablo Casado, as leader of the opposition Popular Party, also took aim that day at Otegi rather than debating the sentence itself and why European judges should have the final say. "Everybody knows what Otegi has done: he should be the one asking for forgiveness," Casado said that day.

Perhaps inevitably, the European ruling in favor of Otegi rather than Spain drew applause among the Catalan independence movement. Quim Torra, the president of Catalonia, said that the ruling was "good news, and reminds us that their higher courts where we can appeal against the arbitrariness and injustice" in Spain.

Perhaps nothing has highlighted more the political importance of the EU for Spain than the conflict over Catalonia, in which both sides maintained the firm belief that the EU would support them, even though it seemed at times that Brussels was instead doing everything possible to stay out of the Catalan quagmire.

In fact, while the government of Mariano Rajoy is often accused of doing too little to solve the Catalan conflict, I watched it shift gradually in terms of trying to use the EU as a buffer against the Catalan independence drive. Initially, Rajoy treated any possible foreign meddling as a challenge to Spanish sovereignty, because Catalonia was a purely domestic issue. But as the Catalan conflict deepened, Rajoy started to welcome any comment from a European leader that could be interpreted as a warning against secessionism.

When David Cameron, the then British prime minister, visited Madrid in September 2015, Rajoy smiled broadly as Cameron told a joint news conference that "if one part of a state secedes from that state, it is no longer part of the European Union and it has to take its place at the back of the queue, behind those other countries that are applying to become members of the European Union." Angela

Merkel, the German chancellor, also provided sweet music to Rajoy's ears at another joint press conference, when she said that it was important to respect "the European treaties that guarantee the sovereignty and territorial integrity of each state."

In October 2017, a week before separatist lawmakers proclaimed Catalonia's unilateral independence, Rajoy joined the royal couple in Oviedo for the ceremony of the Principe de Asturias prizes, which gave Spain an opportunity to host and honor the heads of the three main EU institutions and hear in return Jean-Claude Juncker, Donald Tusk and Antonio Tajani wax lyrical about Spain. Having long limited his obligations to rub shoulders with EU dignitaries, Rajoy had suddenly become instead the first leader of the Spanish government to attend the Asturias ceremony since Leopoldo Calvo-Sotelo in 1981.

At the same time, the Spanish government did not hesitate to translate its own preoccupations about Catalonia into strong interventions to avoid the break-up of any other European state that could not set a precedent for Catalan secession. After the British voted in June 2016 to leave the European Union, Rajoy tried to dash any hope among Scots that they could somehow remain within the EU. Scotland's first minister, Nicola Sturgeon, rushed to Brussels to claim the right to hold her own negotiations on behalf of Scotland. But when Rajoy himself visited Brussels, he made clear that "Scotland has no competencies to negotiate with the EU." As a word of warning, he told a news conference that "the Spanish government rejects any negotiation with anyone other than the United Kingdom."

This position, of course, predated the turmoil in Catalonia in 2017. Following the Yugoslavia war of the 1990s, the sovereignty claim of Kosovo already set a very worrying precedent for many Spanish politicians. Spain took part in Nato air bombings on Serbia and later joined the international military force deployed in Kosovo. But in February 2008, when the Republic of Kosovo declared independence from Serbia, Spain did not join the United States and others in recognizing it, even after George W. Bush, the American president, said that an independent Kosovo would "bring peace to a region scarred by war." Spain's rejection of Kosovo was not initially motivated by Catalan separatism alone. But as Francisco de Borja Lasheras, a Spanish expert on the Balkans, once told me, "Catalonia makes it hard to imagine Spain ever recognising

Kosovo." Overall, he said, "Spain has a direct interest in putting a brake on any internationalisation of the Catalan problem."

The worries in Madrid about maintaining the EU's unflinching allegiance to Spain as one of its member states mounted once the governing separatists in Catalonia started to boost their own diplomatic campaign to garner more international support.

Initially, Rajoy's government seemed happy to downplay the diplomatic efforts of the Catalan independence movement. Eventually, however, the Spanish government took legal action to prevent Catalonia from setting up a full-fledged foreign ministry and other institutions. Raül Romeva, who was at the time in charge of foreign affairs within Catalonia's regional ministry, once asked me: "If Catalonia's diplomacy is toothless, then why does Madrid bother deploying Spain's considerable diplomatic arsenal to counter it?"

As a former correspondent in Brussels, I felt that I knew enough about how the EU worked to feel certain that Brussels would always remain on the side of Madrid. After all, what had been created was a European Union of member states rather than member regions, one in which no state had any interest in watching another state break up, let alone create a domino effect and fuel sovereignty claims in other regions of the continent.

In fact, anybody who has ever visited the Committee of the Regions in Brussels will understand how toothless it is. If anything, it reminds me of the so-called "deputations" in Spain, a layer of bureaucracy that everybody knows to cost some money but nobody seems able to say exactly what function it has to fulfill, except to pay lip service to the idea of territorial power redistribution and to provide some jobs for the boys. (It is worth looking back at how many different Spanish politicians have promised to close down the deputations, without later doing anything about them.)

Why then have some Catalan separatist politicians maintained a blind faith in their ability to convince the EU? Perhaps it is because they believe that the EU is like a massive cruise ship that only tries to change course once it realizes that it has hit an iceberg that could result in a modern version of the Titanic tragedy. When I first met Oriol Junqueras, he recalled the independence referendum that was held in Lithuania and other Baltic states in 1991. Junqueras was particularly struck by how Helmut Kohl, the German chancellor, advised against such a referendum, warning that Germany would not endanger its relationship with Moscow by stepping into a sover-eignty issue. But after Lithuanians voted overwhelmingly for independence, Kohl was among the first leaders to offer his congrat-ulations and welcome Lithuania's landmark step toward full democracy. "Kohl was pragmatic enough to understand the time had come to change," he said.

I got another interesting Catalan perspective on the European Union from Jordi Pujol, whom I interviewed in 2016, shortly after his fall from grace after he admitted tax evasion. While running Catalonia for 23 years, Pujol also spent four of these years as president of another obscure European institutional initiative, called the Assembly of the European Regions. We talked about how EU policy-making could influence the politics of Catalonia, and Pujol acknowledged that the independence movement was bordering a state of delusion if its leaders believed that the EU would ever be willing to side with one its regions against a member state. In 1991, "Estonia, Latvia and Lithuania gained independence because they wanted it, but above all because the Soviet empire was exploding," he said. "Catalonia is like Lithuania, but Spain is not the Soviet Union."

In this sense, the most coherent position in Catalonia regarding the EU has perhaps been that of the CUP, which has never counted on support from Brussels to achieve independence. Instead, the politicians of the CUP believe that a divorce from Spain must also mean abandoning the EU. I do not share the goals of the CUP and I get worried by its revolutionary idealism, but I believe that it is a party that should get some credit for staying loyal to the promises that it has made to its voters.

Upon arriving in Brussels after his botched declaration of inde-pendence in October 2017, Carles Puigdemont told reporters that he had escaped prosecution in Spain in order to put instead the issue of Catalan independence "in the institutional heart of Europe." But Puigdemont soon found that almost every door stayed closed to him, except those of Flemish separatists and some fringe European politicians. Frustrated by his lack of access, Puigdemont briefly proposed that Catalonia should follow Britain's example and hold a referendum on EU membership. In an interview with an Israeli television channel, he also once suggested that not many people would want to form part of an EU that trampled human rights and that was resembling a "club of decadent and obsolete countries." His frontal attack on the EU however, was short-lived and in fact backfired, creating tensions within the independence movement in Catalonia. Soon enough, Puigdemont decided instead to run for office within an EU institution. In 2019, he got elected to the European Parliament. But once more, he found that the door to the Strasbourg assembly remained tightly shut for him.

Puigdemont did not manage to shake or reform the European Union, but he helped awake instead Spanish nationalism. Just as I had once followed the spread of separatist Estelada flags flying on the town halls and roundabouts of Catalonia, I watched the proliferation of Spanish flags floating across Madrid and other cities in late 2017, as the Catalan crisis boiled over. My apartment building faces directly onto another block, which sometimes makes me feel a bit like the photographer in Alfred Hitchcock's great movie, "Rear Window," as I am close enough to see what people on the other side of my street are watching on their large TV screens. But rather than looking at their screens, I started to count instead how many neighbors were hoisting the Spanish flag on their balconies. In the metro, I found myself looking at the wrists of fellow passengers, to see whether they had it wrapped with a yellow-and-red bracelet.

It was fascinating to see a society change so quickly before my eyes, but also a bit disconcerting. I could understand that many people felt almost a sense of relief in being able to display their pride in being Spanish. It was as if the conflict over Catalonia had wiped out during the autumn of 2017 decades of stigma inherited from Franco's Catholic nationalism. One of my tennis partners, José Manuel Villacañas, has always voted for left-wing parties, including recently Podemos. But he once told me that he resented the way some left-wing leaders made him feel bad about showing pride in Spanish. "I don't believe that you should have to vote for the right in order to be able to say that you really love Spain," he insisted.

At the same time, however, I feel that this love of Spain should be built around positive feelings, rather than a counter-reaction to Catalan nationalism. Nobody should insult a flag or show disrespect for the symbols that matter to others. Catalan mayors had no right to take down the flag of Spain, especially not when they are meant to work for cohesion and tolerance and represent all the citizens within the municipalities, not only those who share their beliefs. But I also could not understand why Albert Rivera and Inés

Arrimadas, the party leaders of Ciudadanos, decided to rip off yellow ribbons and throw them into rubbish bags on a tour of the streets of the Catalan town of Alella, in August 2018. Their "cleansing" operation drew applause from their supporters and received widespread media coverage. But throwing a symbol that has become meaningful to someone else into a rubbish bag is at best, it seems to me, an unnecessary act of provocation.

La generación del 2015
El fin del bipartidismo

In October 2013, I traveled from Ronda to Madrid with a little known Socialist member of the Congress: Pedro Sánchez. We were returning from Ronda after a weekend seminar organized by the Spanish branch of the Aspen Institute. The seminar had been enriching as well as intense, spent reading and debating texts from great writers across centuries of political thinking, from the ancient Greece of Plato to the post-Communist Europe of Vaclav Havel. Only two Spanish luminaries featured on our reading list, Ortega y Gasset and Unamuno. The participants in the seminar mostly held conservative views, in part perhaps reflecting the fact that many were executives from large companies. So it was nice to get some left-wing counterbalance from Sánchez, who defended his opinions in fluent English. On one of our two evenings in Ronda, our group headed to a local bar after dinner. We ended up on the dance floor, shuffling along to old hit songs. Sánchez took center stage, almost touching the disco ball with his head because of his height.

During our return journey from Ronda, I joked with Sánchez about his political ambitions. We have the same age and I challenged him to take his career a step further. After all, I argued, Alfredo Pérez Rubalcaba was a savvy Socialist leader, but without the fresh face that could rejuvenate the party following its crushing electoral defeat in November 2011. I suggested to Sánchez that he could lead a generational switch. But Sánchez laughed off my proposal. He told me that he already felt lucky to have scraped into Congress as a substitute candidate. Leading the party, he said, was simply not on the cards.

These were famous last words, of course. A few months later, after the Socialists suffered another humiliating election defeat, Sánchez unexpectedly stood and won the party's primary election. When he became secretary general of the Socialist Party in July 2014, I sent him a congratulatory message, to which he warmly responded. But this pretty much marked the end of our personal communication. Sánchez was now elevated to leader of the opposition, with a communications department whose tasks included trying to filter or block any unwanted journalistic attention.

Instead, I then got to follow from the media gallery the extraordinary rollercoaster career of Sánchez. Sánchez forms part of what I call the generation of 2015, the year that Spain stopped having a two-party system. Sánchez did not break up the system — the artisans of the change were instead Pablo Iglesias and his Podemos party alongside Albert Rivera and his Ciudadanos party. But while neither Iglesias nor Rivera achieved the "*sorpasso*" of the two established parties that they had promised, Sánchez unexpectedly became the first representative of this generation to occupy the Moncloa, the seat of the Spanish government.

When I ask people about Sánchez, some people start talking with passion about his Socialist Party, which also reflects the growing polarization of Spanish politics. Some talk about his good looks, or instead the fact that he has been losing them after a few years spent on the political battleground. Most, however, mention his surprising resilience, or some nastier comment about how he can talk without actually saying anything clearly. Ironically, it is the same kind of answers that I heard for many years when discussing Mariano Rajoy. Like Rajoy before him, Sánchez learnt to exploit the weaknesses and mistakes of others, pushing aside the barons and other rivals who briefly removed him in 2016. Both men, it seems, developed the art of turning the tables on those who underestimated them.

Rarely have I seen a politician sink so fast as Sánchez in 2016, when he went from meeting King Felipe VI to get his royal blessing to form a government to finding himself removed by his own party. If anybody thought that Socialism involved a concept of solidarity, it was clearly lost that year. The campaign to remove Sánchez was at times spiteful, and fueled by the media. Felipe González used his position as the spiritual father of modern Socialism to lambast

Sánchez on the radio of Cadena Ser. In a stinging editorial, *El País* went as far as calling Sánchez "a fool without scruples."

The campaign succeeded — Sánchez was ousted in October 2016 in a party mutiny — but this humiliating defeat also seemed to give Sánchez the kind of resolve he had clearly not displayed when I first talked to him during our Ronda weekend. His comeback was remarkable by any measure. Within seven months of abandoning Congress and starting on a tour of the country in his Peugeot car to reconnect with voters, Sánchez got re-elected as Socialist leader. The mutiny against Sánchez was one of the very few events in 2016 that drew the attention of my editors. For the most part, however, the year of political limbo was a non-event outside of Spain, however much it seemed to grip the nation.

Of course, a year of complete political uncertainty, shaped by two inconclusive general elections, produced its fair share of drama and personal confrontations. But overall, particularly from the perspective of international readers, it never made for a gripping narrative. 2016 was a lost year of Spanish politics. A second election produced almost exactly the same result as the previous one, extending the deadlock.

Disappointingly, Sánchez apparently learnt little from this bitter experience. In 2019, he helped ensure that exactly the same scenario played out, with another year of repeat elections, squabbling among party leaders and near-nothingness in terms of moving forward the social and economic agenda of Spain. Lawmakers spent months away from Congress while their leaders exchanged personal accusations.

If anything, the new generation of politicians who had promised voters to usher in change were instead better at guaranteeing blockage. Their squabbling amounted to what the journalist Luis María Anson called "a depressing show," in a column he wrote for the newspaper *El Mundo* in 2016. Spanish politics, he argued, looked like "a circus ring in which every day acrobatic leaders make ridiculous pirouettes to the stupefaction of citizens."

My American editors certainly had little time for the Spanish circus, however much I tried to make clear the underlying importance of what was at stake. Every time I picked up the phone to discuss the latest twist in the coalition talks, an editor would cut the conversation short by asking: "So does it mean we now know when and who will run the next government?" The best that I could offer in response was an educated guess, while stressing that Spain was sailing uncharted waters. So the editor would sigh and recommend that I call again, but best when I had more concrete news to offer.

It was at times frustrating to watch Spanish journalists fill the pages and screens with the latest political confrontation, while all I could do was listen and read, rather than write. In the ten months of political limbo of 2016, I only managed to write one article that was displayed prominently by *The New York Times*. It included a warning that Spain was getting close to repeating the example of Belgium, which famously spent 589 days without an elected government.

If anything, this year of political sclerosis rapidly made this new generation of 2015 look every bit like the old one, or possibly more inept, as they outdid each other in trading accusations and sometimes even insults. Both Rivera and Iglesias got soiled in the mud fight, which was particularly damaging for Iglesias who had promised his voters that he would offer a new way of handling politics, breaking with the bad practices of what his party called "the caste." Along the way, as would then happen a year later in the Catalan Parliament, politicians forgot that many of their voters had no time for political bickering, and instead cared about improving their highways, universities, hospitals and, above all, the employment situation in Spain.

I remember following one particularly depressing debate in Congress in April 2016, which was supposed to focus on Europe's refugee crisis. Opposition lawmakers had promised to challenge Rajoy on why his government backed a controversial European Union agreement with Turkey to take back refugees from Greece and other countries in Western Europe. But instead of talking about a humanitarian crisis, Iglesias and Rivera spent most of the time accusing each other of cronyism. The refugees became their side issue, even though the fate of suffering Syrians and others actually mattered to many people in Spain, as I will discuss in another chapter.

Still, for all their shortcomings, it was important to note that Spain had achieved a generational switch in its politics. In Iglesias and Rivera, Congress had acquired two new and energetic party leaders in their 30s, who seemed to have all the right credentials to reshape the debate. And I was certainly keen to meet them.

In March 2015, I interviewed Iglesias in his makeshift Madrid party headquarters, next to Plaza España. We sat on an uncomfortable sofa that was part of the eclectic furniture that had been assembled there. The corridors were filled with posters and banners that activists had been preparing for a forthcoming public event. It really felt like I was visiting a political organization in the making.

The interview made the front page of the international edition of *The New York Times*, with a large photo of Iglesias and the headline "New left shakes the politics of Spain." The article put the focus on Iglesias and his seemingly bottomless ambition to reshape Spain, as well as his admiration for the role model set by the Syriza party in Greece. "I really never thought I could become president of the government, but I think we're now in a situation where this could happen," he told me.

At the same time, Iglesias went to great lengths during our interview to make clear that Europe's left-wing politicians had nothing to do with anti-establishment parties on the right that were tapping into fears about migration and the European Union. "We're perhaps all part of a general situation of dissatisfaction with the politics of Europe, but the big difference is that we are democratic, pro-European and clearly not racist," Iglesias said. "Political forces like Podemos and Syriza provide among the last opportunities to convince citizens that something positive can still be achieved within a European Union project," he added.

I ended the article by mentioning how "for a man who has cast himself as an outsider, Iglesias sounded curiously pragmatic about forming possible coalitions, should no party emerge as a clear victor from this year's elections." We had spent part of the interview discussing what would happen if nobody won outright the next general election. In his answers, I found Iglesias unexpectedly open to negotiating with those he had been deriding as members of the caste. "We are not sectarian and our hand is held out to all who want to change," he said. "We will always reach out to any party willing to recognize that what they have been doing until now simply didn't work."

In retrospect, I feel Iglesias proved a good speaker and charismatic candidate but a poor party leader and flawed negotiator, less open to others than he had suggested to me, as well as increasingly out of touch with the grassroots whom he sought to represent. The most emblematic example of this disconnection was the purchase by Iglesias and his partner Irene Montero of a villa in Galapagar, which had become Spain's most wealthy municipality. To put an end to the controversy, Iglesias held an internal party referendum in May 2018. The referendum was won, but I am not certain that the right lesson was learnt. After winning the vote, Iglesias suggested in an interview with Radiocable that he had been treated unfairly, rather than offering a mea culpa. "I have nothing to feel ashamed about, but what I have learnt is that you have to be aware, when you take part in a game, that you are playing with the referee against you," he said,

Both Iglesias and Rivera failed to assume the personal responsibility for not living up to the high expectations that they generated in 2015, when their parties won their first seats in Congress. Neither achieved the long-promised "sorpasso" by overtaking the two established parties. Instead, both watched some close colleagues and friends abandon them along the way in frustration.

One of the images that most Spanish people remember of Albert Rivera was an early one, dating back to 2006, when he provocatively stood naked on an election campaign poster. The first time I interviewed him, I was struck by another picture of him, but one that certainly gave him a more elevated status. As we sat in an underground meeting room in his party headquarters in Barcelona, there was a portrait of Rivera on the wall, hanging framed between those of Victor Hugo and John F. Kennedy.

Ciudadanos was born in 2008, before the financial crisis really hit Spain, as an opposition bulwark against the Catalan independence movement. But as a national opposition party, it then also used the crisis and joined Podemos in calling for a significant overhaul of a political system undermined by corruption and cronyism. In the problems of Spain, it found ample ammunition to become far more than a one-trick pony, focused on stopping Catalan secessionists.

Rivera took his party onto the national stage in part because the rise of Catalan separatism created "a political blockade" that made it harder for him to sell his message in the regional media, according to Iñaki Ellakuria, a journalist who published a book about Ciudadanos. At the same time, Spain's crisis, both financial and institutional, created "a new opportunity to grab all those voters who felt abandoned by the shortcomings of the two big parties," Ellakuria told me.

When I first met him, Rivera talked to me about his own political journey and how, as a young voter, he had switched his votes between different parties, from the Socialists and Convergencia y Unión to the Popular Party, without ever feeling that any one of them truly espoused his views on what constitutionalism should mean in Spain. But once a group of intellectuals wrote in 2005 a manifesto that lay the foundations for the creation of Ciudadanos, "I finally found the political space that I had been looking for," Rivera said. And to his credit, a decade later, so did about 3.5 million voters who cast their ballot in favor of Ciudadanos and its young leader in the party's breakthrough general election in 2015.

The breakup of Spain's two-party system was broadly welcomed after that landmark election. University professors and media columnists waxed lyrical about the fresh air that was sweeping into Congress and the other institutions of Spain. José Ignacio Torreblanca, a politics professor and newspaper columnist, told me at the time that "there has been a big problem of checks and balances in Spain, created by a long history of absolute majorities, which has meant that everything gets decided by those in power, from policies down to who holds all the key jobs, including in public television. May be we can now finally create this system of checks and balances that has been badly missing in Spain."

But in November 2019, after another frustrating and polarizing repeat election, many of those who had welcomed Spain's political fragmentation appeared to regret its outcome. Worse still, the stalemate was fertile ground for another party to emerge, Vox, which also brought to national politics a level of xenophobia, misoginism and ultranationalism that I had not seen since arriving in Spain.

In late 2019, as the Catalan crisis turned violent on the streets of Barcelona, following the prison sentencing by the Supreme Court of the former Catalan leaders, Santiago Abascal and his Vox party upstaged Rivera and his Ciudadanos party as the most strident force against secessionism. In the repeat election of November 2019, Vox doubled its seats while Ciudadanos slumped catastrophically. Rivera resigned. Like Rajoy a year earlier, he abandoned politics. The difference was that Rivera was about to turn 40, while Rajoy had reached retirement age and had been a minister since the 1990s.

As I write these lines, Ciudadanos is a party that is threatening to vanish altogether from the political landscape, also after failing to get a single seat in the regional assembly of Madrid, in an election held in May 2021. While Ciudadanos can still cast pivotal votes in the national Parliament thanks to the support that it got in 2019, there is little evidence that Inés Arrimadas, who replaced Rivera as party leader, will be able to stop more of her party supporters from jumping ship, in particular to the Popular Party, as happened in the Madrid election (whose outcome also got Iglesias to abandon politics). But the pragmatism of Arrimadas at least contrasts with the uncompromising rigidity of Rivera, who turned his back on the idea of forming an alliance with Sánchez in 2019 and instead engaged in a blame game during which he accused Sánchez in Parliament of promoting "sectarian Spain," as part of a plan "to stay forever in power and benefit his friends."

The emergence of Vox has also added to the already acrimonious political debating in Spain. Moderation and restraint were never meant to be on Vox's menu. As Santiago Abascal, the leader of Vox, told his supporters on the night of November 2019 when his party became the third-largest in Spain, "we have managed to open up all the forbidden debates."

To my dismay, Abascal was left unchallenged by his rivals during his first televised election debate, held a few days before the election of November 2019. While he issued xenophobic warnings about the threat of Islamic migration, nobody reminded him that Spain was a state that guaranteed freedom of religion. Instead, Sánchez produced drab statistics to defend his government's track record against illegal immigration.

In my view, the people who are keeping Spanish democracy alive are not the politicians but the voters, who continue to be engaged in politics and cast their ballot, even while often holding their nose. Before every recent election, I have heard from people saying that they felt too frustrated and depressed to vote. In the end, however, it seems that most of them set aside part of their Sunday to line up at a polling station and do just that.

In April 2019, the turnout was almost 76 percent, which was the highest since Felipe González was voted into office in 1980, and which was also 20 percentage points higher than the number of Americans who voted in the election that allowed Donald Trump to become President of the United States. In Madrid's regional election of May 2021, the turnout was also a record 76 percent — even though residents were being called to vote while Spain was still under a coronavirus state of emergency. In my native Switzerland, which is considered by many to be the flagship of direct democracy, it is rare that even half of the voters take part in our referendums and other elections.

The generation of 2015 rejuvenated Spanish politics, but it singularly failed to transform Spain, or even improve its political discourse. At the time of writing, it had produced more theatrics than substance, let alone groundbreaking legislation. Sánchez and Iglesias hugged in front of the cameras in November 2019, two days after the general election, as if a loving partnership photo could somehow wipe out five months of sterile and bitter negotiations. And their reconciliation certainly did not set an example for other party leaders, who instead launched into another round of public mudslinging.

The parliamentary session in January 2020 that paved the way for Sánchez's narrow re-election in Congress was a low point in political debating, filled with scaremongering that bordered on the defamatory. Pablo Casado, as leader of the main opposition Popular Party, managed to add "sociopath" to his already long list of personal insults thrown at Sánchez. Congress looked like a boxing ring inside which fighters are delivering all their blows below the belt and only waiting for the final bell and the judges' voting.

Worse still, the vitriolic and hyperbolic rhetoric used in Congress rapidly poisoned minds beyond its walls. The leader of Teruel Existe, Tomás Guitarte, was forced to seek police protection after receiving thousands of threatening messages, in which he was accused of being a "traitor" for deciding to cast his pivotal vote in favor of Sánchez's investiture. In which modern and healthy democracy does a parliamentarian have to fear for his personal safety because of his voting choices?

Political fragmentation and polarization resulted in four elections in four years, none of which will be remembered for helping make Spain more governable. But in early 2020, Spain at least finally got a government, after spending much of the previous year in limbo. Between 2015 and 2020, I often heard commentators argue that Spain was stuck politically because it had no "culture of coalition." Yet the opposite could be argued, namely that Spain has never lacked such a culture, since there have long been coalitions at every other level of government, from the municipalities to the regions, The problem was at the national level, where it unfortunately took five years for party leaders to understand that, in a four-or-five-party contest, nobody is likely to enter the Moncloa again without having at least one coalition partner on board.

The worry, of course, is how long coalitions can stick together, particularly when politicians seem to prefer to insult rather than talk to each other. There is of course still time for this new generation of party leaders to show a greater sense of statesmanship, but I see little prospect for Sánchez to fulfill the call that he made to Congress just before taking office, in January 2020, for the politicians to rid Spain of "the toxic climate" that they themselves helped create.

ECONOMY

Los dioses del dinero
Los rescates de las cajas

"In the name of Jesus Christ, amen." When I told my business editor that the chairman of a collapsed Spanish bank had been using a religious blessing to open board meetings, it briefly left him speechless. He sent me to Córdoba in May 2010, a month after my arrival in Madrid and shortly after the Bank of Spain announced that it would rescue and take control of CajaSur, Córdoba's emblematic banking institution.

CajaSur was one of the first victims of Spain's financial crisis. Although it was only a regional bank, its demise suggested that the scale of Spain's financial troubles was bigger than what its politicians, regulators and bankers had estimated. It also coincided with the first budgetary cuts of the Socialist government of José Luis Rodríguez Zapatero. Spain's long property boom had come to an abrupt end. The government and central bank could also no longer argue that Spanish banks, boosted by counter-cyclical provisions, were certain to weather the storm of the world financial crisis that had boiled over two years earlier in the United States, with the collapse of Lehman Brothers.

In fact, the abrupt and shocking demise of Lehman Brothers had not only provoked an earthquake on Wall Street and across the world financial system, but it had also helped reshape the thinking in newsrooms, including that of *The New York Times*. For many editors, the takeaway from the Lehman fiasco was that any reassuring statement delivered by a banker, or in fact an official from the economics ministry or the central bank, should be received with a heavy dose of skepticism and should immediately undergo further scrutiny.

In fact, for my American editor, the story of CajaSur had the opaque ingredients of a novel by Dan Brown, the best-selling author of *The Da Vinci Code*. The bank's Church affiliation was certainly not seen in New York as a guarantee of sanctity. After all, colleagues in Rome had also been writing for years about the murky finances of the Vatican, an issue that boiled over in 2019 when the Vatican's chief financial regulator resigned and Pope Francis acknowledged a corruption scandal in the way charitable donations had been used by the Vatican.

Following my boss's instructions, I arrived in Córdoba expecting to discuss more than just finances and balance sheets. Soon enough, I found myself plunged into a convoluted story about the convergence of political, religious and banking activities — and the conflicts of interest that often arise when historic relationships become so intertwined. Here was a bank that local priests had controlled since 1864, originally as a pawn shop but eventually as a major lender to local farmers and entrepreneurs. Over time, the caja had allowed the Church to consolidate significantly its influence over Córdoba and its 325,000 inhabitants. The priests had also fought hard to keep their banking powers, even after a merger with a secular competitor created CajaSur in the mid-1990s.

Along the way, the bankers and priests had not only learnt how to reward and help each other, but they had also understood how to cohabit with the politicians. Remarkably, Córdoba was not a bastion of political conservatism. Instead, since Spain's return to democracy, the city had mostly been run by politicians who expressed distrust, if not aversion, toward the Catholic Church. Some were Communists, who later came to represent Izquierda Unida. But in the "red Córdoba" that emerged from the transition, the Church somehow managed to keep its bank. It seemed that money — and the ability to hand it out — had helped unite divergent ideologies rather than divide them.

This all fitted into what I sometimes call the Bermuda Triangle of Spain's construction boom, formed between politicians, bankers and property developers, in which a lot of money disappeared or got wasted in almost every region of Spain. The city authorities had been happy to subsidize Córdoba's economy with public money, granted through loans provided by a local bank that gave the Church the special status of financial benefactor. Like other cajas, instead of paying dividends, the bank distributed about a third of its earnings to social works. Through such donations, CajaSur supported schools and housing for the elderly and disabled, hospital and university research, as well as museums and cultural events like an annual guitar festival. It was also the main sponsor of Córdoba's football team and a shareholder in the printing works and city newspaper.

By 2010, local political parties in Córdoba had accumulated loans from the bank totaling 87 million euros over five years. With a heavy dose of sarcasm, Luis Martín Luna, a conservative politician who had also once been a CajaSur director, summarized this situation for me: "We've been Spain's only Communist city, a place where everybody, including the Church, seems to believe in relying on subsidies." With CajaSur maintaining its generosity toward borrowers even after construction activity came to a standstill, "it was probably difficult to tell the bank to stop lending when your own party was relying on its loans," Martín Luna added. In return, of course, "CajaSur certainly financed the restoration of churches."

CajaSur had competitors in Córdoba. But none in terms of its social network of influence. By the time I visited, CajaSur required a capital injection of 550 million euros to survive. This extra money would end the Church's control over the bank, but it was not even sure that it would be enough to stop the bank's financial hemorrhage, because the bank was also tied to several other disastrous financial operations, including the construction of an airport in Ciudad Real. The airport was declared insolvent by a judge just as I was visiting Córdoba. CajaSur was one of the airport's largest creditors, holding 18.8 million euros of its outstanding loans.

Some of CajaSur's real estate investments, which were concentrated along the Costa del Sol, were tainted by conflicts of interest and fraud. For instance, there was a separate corruption case against the management of Arenal Sur 21, a property developer in which CajaSur had acted as both creditor and shareholder. Somehow, no regulator questioned how a bank could in effect lend to itself in a construction project. During the boom years, the Bank of Spain and the other regulators somehow took time off, or ignored the warnings of their own inspectors, until it was far too late. (The scale of the regulatory failure only became apparent in 2017, when Spain's national court indicted the former governor of the Bank of Spain, Miguel Ángel Fernández Ordóñez, for ignoring dire warnings issued internally by his own inspectors ahead of the initial public offering of Bankia.)

To understand how priests had controlled a bank like CajaSur that had 3,100 employees and 500 branches, I went looking around Córdoba for Fernando Cruz Conde, who had been CajaSur's third-most senior director until it was taken over by the Bank of Spain. He remained, however, vicar general of Córdoba, which made him second to the bishop of the city.

I eventually found him in the sacristy of a church. It seemed an inappropriate venue to conduct an interview about banking, particularly as he was busy assembling candles and making the final preparations for his next religious celebration. But he kindly agreed to meet that evening in a café next to the stunning mosque-cathedral of Córdoba. I found that Cruz Conde had a dry sense of humor and a sharp mind. He did not wish to discuss specific details about CajaSur's business dealings, particularly as he had just been removed from the bank. He sounded wary about making any comment that could be turned into court evidence, as part of the legal proceedings against former directors, led by the deposed chairman, Santiago Gómez Sierra.

But Cruz Conde gave me plenty of his time to help understand how the intertwining of politics, business and religion in Córdoba had allowed a caja to continue operating unchallenged, even once its losses started to balloon after 2008. He also offered his own explanation for CajaSur's cozy relationship with local politicians, despite the long conflict between the Roman Catholic Church and Communism. "It's been easy to cooperate with Izquierda Unida and other parties," he said, "because everybody knew that if CajaSur was no longer under the authority of Córdoba's diocese, decision-making powers risked moving elsewhere, perhaps to Seville or Málaga." Indeed, CajaSur was rescued a day after merger talks broke off with Unicaja, a larger bank based in Málaga. Their fruitless merger negotiations had lasted ten months, but were tainted by politics. In Córdoba, I heard nobody regret not having CajaSur fall under the control of bankers from Málaga. And almost no-one wanted to blame the priests for mismanagement, let alone question their switch from the sacristy to the boardroom.

"Competence has nothing to do with being a priest or not," said Francisco Tejada, one of Izquierda Unida's representatives in Córdoba's city hall. "Somebody with all the world's economics degrees can prove a disastrous bank manager."

I could relate to Tejada's argument. I had studied in England, where students sometimes spend years at university learning about religion, or classical languages like Latin and Greek, before joining the trading floor of one of the banks of the City of London. But what was more surprising to me was to find the customers of the bank seemingly nonplused by its crisis. My editor had asked me to check whether a bank run was underway. Instead, I found depositors queuing patiently inside a branch and hardly interested in discussing CajaSur's problems.

"I've got faith in the system — and that's not because I'm an ardent Catholic," said Juan Antonio Exposito Pelado, a retired metals factory worker who was then 81 years old and collecting his monthly pension of 550 euros from his CajaSur branch. "I know the bank has problems, but I can't imagine them letting down a wretched old man." CajaSur was a big warning of the troubles ahead but, since it accounted for a tiny share of the banking assets in Spain, its collapse was not enough to sink the whole system. The troubles of the cajas also largely escaped notice in the early stages of the financial crisis because prominent commercial banks like Santander and BBVA, which were subject to more stringent regulation, did not need government rescue money like many other banks in Europe and in the United States.

But CajaSur's collapse did convince the Socialist government to push for a clean-up of the cajas, using an approach that was agreed with the opposition Popular Party. The politicians decided that the best solution would be to force a rapid consolidation of the cajas. Spain's 45 cajas were given an ultimatum to complete merger talks, with the goal of halving their overall number. The bankers got down to work and responded quickly with a flurry of transactions, the most spectacular of which was the seven-way merger that created Bankia. Still, the pressure kept mounting on Spain, as well as the cost of financing its public debt, as Ireland and then Portugal joined Greece on the list of countries forced into a bailout.

The final act of bravado was staged by Bankia, which held an initial public offering in the summer 2011. On the day when trading in Bankia shares started, the bank's president, Rodrigo Rato, rang the stock exchange bell, raised a victory thumb and then drank a celebration glass of champagne alongside some of his fellow executives. It was a birthday party that should have been instead a funeral wake.

In April 2012, I visited the Madrid skyscraper that housed Bankia's headquarters to interview Rato. As I had been told that he would be delayed, I took a walk around the corridors of his upper floor, decorated with beautiful artwork, and enjoyed the spectacular views of the mountains one side and the heavy traffic along the Castellana on the other side of the building. I remember thinking how Madrid would look if it was divided by a meandering river rather than a straight avenue.

When Rato finally showed up, he didn't look to me like a banker under pressure. We settled down in his spacious office and he spent the next hour telling me that, even if his bank was facing strong headwinds, Bankia was solid enough to withstand major turmoil. "I can assure you that there's no reason to question our solvency," Rato told me. "I know many foreigners are getting worried about Spanish banks, but they don't seem to understand how much we have done to avoid getting into really serious problems."

Famous last words, of course. Rato was forced to resign a few weeks later. Once the government took charge of Bankia, it restated the bank's 2011 results, suddenly turning a reported profit of 309 million euros into a loss of almost 3 billion euros, the largest in Spanish banking history.

Shortly after his resignation, I watched Rato sit through a two-hour parliamentary hearing in which he was accused of lying and defrauding investors. Rato this time looked like a naughty schoolboy caught eating sweets in the classroom. But he kept his calm and insisted that Bankia's collapse was a shared responsibility between the bankers who had allowed unchecked loans before his arrival in 2010, the regulators and politicians who had encouraged Bankia's merger and listing, as well as the auditors of Deloitte who had signed off on the accounts.

While investors had reasons to lament a collapse in the share price, he argued, they too should have known better. He also had no regret about his champagne moment at the stock exchange. When Bankia listed, "our prospectus had several pages about risk factors," Rato told the lawmakers. Still, Rato was soon charged with fraud and has since moved between the courtroom and a prison cell, fighting a series of lawsuits. His predecessor at the bank, Miguel Blesa, shot himself with a rifle while visiting his hunting estate.

For the rest of the summer, I spent my time trying to work out whether there were more skeletons in the cupboards of Spanish banks. I also dug deeper into financial corruption. On a visit to Vigo, I met a dozen bankers, politicians and trade unionists to hear about Julio Fernández Gayoso, who joined his bank as a 16-year old and ended up running it for over four decades, turning himself into "Don Julio," another great benefactor to his city.

His life sounded like the perfect rags-to-riches story, in the true spirit of the pawn shop that Caixanova had been when it started out

74

in 1880. Fernández Gayoso joined the bank in 1947, but he was now a disgraced 80-year old former banker. He had finally been ousted after getting indicted in a fraud investigation. He later had a brief stay in prison, although he got an early release because of his age and ill health.

On a walk around Vigo with a former employee of his bank, we stopped in front of all the wonderful buildings that Fernández Gayoso had acquired or renovated using his bank's money. We walked into cultural centers filled with paintings owned by the bank's foundation. We also went to Vigo's first university campus, of course also financed by the bank. "This is a workers' city, but even our Communist painters got so many commissions from him that they portrayed him as a God," Vigo's former mayor, Carlos González Príncipe, told me. Príncipe clearly had his own axe to grind: he claimed that his own political career was brought to end when Fernández Gayoso financed his rival's election campaign.

Fernández Gayoso refused to meet me, but I had listened to his testimony in Congress, in which he presented himself as a chairman kept on a tight leash by his board members. "I didn't take a single personal decision, because I didn't have the power," he told lawmakers.

In Vigo, however, I heard instead one account after the other about the tentacular reach of Fernández Gayoso into almost every business of the city, as well as his overwhelming control over a boardroom filled with his cronies. Whatever Fernández Gayoso asked the board, "there was no debating and never any voting," José Luis Veiga, a former board member told me. "The bank's leadership and strategy were completely in his hands." To be on the board was about "how close the relationship was with the chairman, rather than experience," according to Santiago Lago-Peñas, an economics professor at the University of Vigo.

Eventually, Fernández Gayoso joined the bandwagon of *caja* mergers and tied the knot with his erstwhile rival from La Coruña, José Luis Méndez, who had run his bank, Caixa Galicia, for 29 years. The two men could compete not only in longevity, but also perhaps in lifestyle. Caixa Galicia had bought a luxury yacht, which came with a crew, anchored at the permanent disposal of Méndez. Méndez also enjoyed being a patron of the arts and had even convinced his board to build a cultural center in Vigo, in a historic cinema in the heart of the city.

Fernández Gayoso, Méndez and some of the other top banking executives took more than their just reward for services rendered to their cities and Galicia, even as they plunged their banks into property losses and finally a merger that resulted in another costly bailout for taxpayers. They set up massive pension schemes for themselves, on top of their huge salaries. While Fernández Gayoso and a few other bankers got prison sentences, Méndez was lucky enough to get sidelined from his bank just before its merger, so that he could walk away with his money before getting caught in the final debacle.

If this surreal movie of banking excess was playing out in broad daylight, why did nobody stop it earlier? Miguel Ángel Quinteiro, a former bank employee, gave me some kind of answer. He worked in Caixanova's information technology department in the 1980s and was eventually promoted to become the staff representative on the bank's board. Having heard rumors that the *caja* was writing off the value of bad loans to some local businesses, Quinteiro asked for a list of loan defaults, to no avail. He said that he also requested, again unsuccessfully, details of a cash bonus paid in envelopes to employees each year.

Eventually, Quinteiro said he was fired after being accused of leaking confidential information from board meetings to a trade union. He threatened to sue for unfair dismissal – until, he said, the bank offered him the equivalent of 180,000 euros. Feeling that he had by then already become a pariah within his own bank, Quinteiro threw in the towel. Furthermore, the money that he was being offered was "one of the highest settlements at that time and enough to do what I wanted," which was to set up his own information technology company. As discussed elsewhere, it is hard to blow the whistle in Spain.

Spain can take credit for cleaning up its banks, starting with Bankia, which returned to profit in 2013, after needing about half of the 41 billion euros of European bailout money granted to Spain. The fund for toxic assets set up by the government, to which Bankia transferred 22 billion euros of bad loans, helped take out about 50 billion euros worth of unwanted property assets without undermining the functioning of the rest of the publicly-controlled banking system. Like other banks, Bankia then slimmed down significantly its staff and branch network. It also sought to turn the page on a fraudulent culture symbolized by the scandal of the so-called "black cards," which were the corporate credit cards given to executives and used by them to get their bank (and its shareholders) to pick up the bill for their lavish lifestyle, from restaurant bills to golf club memberships.

Spain's judiciary should get some praise for sending powerful bankers like Rato and Fernández Gayoso to prison. After all, before overseeing the black card system, Rato had once instead been praised as the architect of Spain's economic miracle, the obvious successor to José María Aznar and Spain's most prominent ambassador overseas, as managing director of the International Monetary Fund. Altogether, Spain accounted for 11 of the 47 bankers of Europe and the United States who were sentenced to jail for their role in the financial crisis, according to a study published in September 2018 by the *Financial Times*. Only tiny Iceland punished its fraudulent bankers more harshly, with 25 prison convictions.

But I still think back to my interview with Rato whenever I hear anybody suggest that the foreign media treated Spain unfairly during the crisis. I had sat with Rato for one hour and somehow allowed him to maintain that foreigners should stop worrying about the Spanish banking system. If only I had been tougher with him, perhaps I could have written a more insightful story, forewarning that Rato was instead preparing Spain for the biggest banking disaster in its modern history.

Duelo al sol
Auge y ocaso de Abengoa

From a distance, the towers outside Sanlúcar la Mayor look like giant ocean lighthouses, each of them beaming a ray of light so powerful that it can be seen miles away. But the towers stand in the middle of the Andalusian countryside, rising high above sunflower fields and cattle farms like modern obelisks to solar energy. They form part of the world's first commercial thermal solar power plant, built by Abengoa in 2007.

When I visited this industrial site, a decade after its construction, the towers had lost none of their shiny bright coating of white paint, and they still constituted an extraordinary feat of technology. An engineer took me around the plant, explaining as patiently as he could to a science novice how a thermal solar power plant actually works.

By the end of our tour, I had understood at least the basics about this technology: the plant uses mirrors to reflect the sun's rays toward the top of a tower, concentrating the light and generating high enough temperatures to heat up a transfer fluid. This heat then creates steam to power a turbine, generating electricity. This thermal solar plant allows energy to be stored, unlike that produced by conventional solar power. In other words, after sunset, the turbines of Sánlucar continue to operate and generate additional power overnight.

The reason why I was visiting Sanlúcar, however, was not to understand its engineering prowess. Instead, Abengoa was in the spotlight because investors wanted to know why and how the company had been financially mismanaged, and whether there was any chance of a recovery. A legal battle was underway to determine who should bear the blame for a loss that was the largest in history for a Spanish industrial company.

Although Abengoa was not a household name in the United States, it was one of the Spanish companies that had invested prominently there, building two plants, in Arizona and California, that supplied electricity to more than 160,000 homes. Like in Spain, the company had benefited from favorable political winds, as President Barack Obama had been offering government backing to companies that could make his country's voracious energy consumption a little greener.

To help sell my story proposal, I had mentioned to my business editor that Obama had in fact singled out Abengoa for special praise in 2010, when the company agreed to build its Arizona plant. "It's good news that we've attracted a company to our shores to build a plant and create jobs right here in America," Obama said at the time. But what my American editor most wanted to know was whether Spain had found in Abengoa its homemade version of the scandal of Enron, the energy company that imploded in late 2001.

Enron, of course, had grown during the Internet bubble, as a company that promised to revolutionize the energy sector but instead proved a fraudulent pipe dream. Its collapse, which was at the time the biggest American corporate bankruptcy, also then dragged into bankruptcy Arthur Anderson, Enron's accounting firm, which was at the time one of the five largest audit and accountancy partnerships in the world.

Abengoa was also the story of an energy champion that had turned into a financial disaster. But unlike Enron, which was formed in the 1980s, it was a company with much older roots, whose engineering reputation was established long before Spain embarked on its attempt to dominate solar power. Founded in 1941 by two engineers in Seville, Abengoa initially set out to manufacture a type of electricity meter. Though that project never gained traction, the company then began installing auxiliary panels for power stations and electrical systems for buildings.

By the 1960s, Abengoa was starting to expand overseas, in Central and South America, notably by erecting transmissions lines in Argentina. In the 1980s, it made its first foray into renewables. From then on, its growth was exponential. By the time Abengoa landed into financial trouble, it accounted for more than a quarter of the five gigawatts produced worldwide by thermal solar plants. It had built its two American plants, but had also invested from Latin America to Africa, including desalination plants in countries such as Algeria and Ghana.

As it continued to expand, investors rewarded Abengoa. In 2007, in the same year that the Sanlúcar plant opened, Abengoa's stock price hit a record of 7.39 euros per share. The company's growth helped attract powerful outsiders, like the Socialist politician Josep Borrell, who joined Abengoa's board in 2009. Abengoa's fall from grace, however, was a lot faster than its climb. Saddled with debt from its expansion effort, the company found that the world financial crisis not only increased its cost of borrowing but also made it near-impossible to raise fresh financing. As losses mounted and financial support evaporated, creditors and shareholders began to run for the exit door, while threatening lawsuits if the company ended up insolvent.

The company's switch from industry darling to financial cripple turned into an extreme example of the challenges facing players in the renewable energy business. By the time Abengoa filed for bankruptcy protection, its share price had fallen below 40 euro cents, converting Abengoa into a penny stock. The scramble to offload Abengoa shares in itself yielded some unexpected news. Borrell left the board in 2016, but he was then found guilty of insider trading while selling Abengoa shares and was ordered in 2018 by the stock market regulator to pay a fine of 30,000 euros — a tenth of what he had earned annually as a board member.

Still, I found many people eager to limit the damage that Abengoa could cause to Spain's business reputation. For a start, other executives in the renewables sector maintained that Abengoa's problems should not tarnish the reputation of the sector as a whole, nor cast doubt on its technology. "The problem of Abengoa is not the failure of a sector, far from it," Luis Crespo, the president of Estela, the European solar thermal electricity association, told me. "We really hope policy-makers don't start mixing up cost and value."

The cast of characters was also different to that in the story of Enron, where the main villains became the company's founder, Ken Lay, and a chief executive called Jeff Skilling. Skilling was convicted in 2006 of felony and eventually sentenced to 24 years in prison. Lay died three months before he was due to receive his sentence. The American Senate held a series of commitee hearings about Enron that eventually led to the adoption of the Sarbanes–Oxley Act in 2002, to help avoid similar corporate governance shortcomings and raise auditing standards.

The main player in the Abengoa story, Felipe Benjumea, struck me as a very different kind of person. Benjumea was the company chairman, but he inherited rather than invented his family company. His father, Javier Benjumea Puigcerver, was one of the two engineers who founded Abengoa.

The Abengoa crisis also had an element of family drama. Although Felipe Benjumea has a brother, Javier, who is five years older than him, their father decided to ignore the age hierarchy. After surviving a brain stroke, he handed over the reins to the younger son, Felipe, who was 33 at the time. The decision created serious tensions within the families of Abengoa. Sidelined, Javier in effect stopped talking to his brother, while some other family members also shared his frustration.

But Felipe still maintained majority support among the 300 or so relatives who were shareholders in Abengoa's controlling family holding. From then on, he told me, he learnt how to run a company in which he could count on the backing of about 70 percent of his relatives, while the rest of his family opposed him.

Still, Benjumea attributed his downfall not to any fratricide treason but instead to "blackmail" from his main bank, Banco

Santander, which, he said, refused to underwrite a capital increase in 2015 unless he was removed as chairman. Benjumea was ousted as Abengoa's chairman in September 2015. Two months later, he was ordered by a judge to post bail of 11.5 million euros — equivalent to his payout — ahead of a court case over Abengoa's mismanagement. The company's former chief executive, Manuel Sánchez Ortega, was also ordered to post bail of 4.5 million euros.

Within months, a man who had once been the toast of Andalusian high society found himself instead turned into a pariah. "At first, I would find it hard to get up in the morning," he told me during an interview in June 2018. "I felt treated like a real gangster. I was kicked out of all places. Nobody would let me work anywhere else." As part of the judge's order, Benjumea had to hand in his passport and report to a courthouse every 15 days. His bank accounts were frozen, so that "I lived off my wife," he said.

Enron had been based in Houston, an energy hub within America's oil state, Texas. Abengoa, in contrast, was embedded within a region known for its agriculture, but not for its pioneering technology. Before Abengoa's financial collapse, whenever I had met officials who wanted to talk about Andalusia's future, they would inevitably mention Abengoa as proof that Spain's largest region could do far more than just produce olive oil. While Abengoa was founded shortly after the civil war, its big burst of growth came several decades later, on the back of Prime Minister José Luis Rodríguez Zapatero's bet on renewable energy, at a time when the Socialist party also had a strong grip on the politics of Andalusia.

Shortly after arriving in Spain in 2010, I attended a conference in Madrid in which Miguel Sebastián, Spain's industry and energy minister, waxed lyrical about the virtues of Spain's investment in solar power and the government support that came with it. The minister proudly told his audience that Spain had finally found a sector in which it could claim world leadership. During the question time, I asked Sebastián a question that left him flummoxed: "What is the real benefit of being world number one in solar?" The minister looked incredulous, as if he had misunderstood my question or as if I had asked something self-explanatory, like whether the sun was an important source of energy.

So rather than wait to get his answer, I told him that what I wanted to know is whether the Spanish government was certain that there was a first-mover advantage in solar power. Sebastián gave short thrift to my concerns. He assured me and the rest of the audience that Spain would benefit from its first-mover advantage and that its pioneering solar technology would open up markets worldwide.

I was unconvinced by his answer, however. In other technologies, I had seen examples in which the leadership had changed hands and some of the early competitors had dropped out altogether, unable to foot the bill to upgrade their technology or simply forced to accept that they had invested heftily in the wrong products. Anybody who ever bought a Sony Walkman, spoke with a Nokia phone or used Altavista to browse the Internet could realize that, in technology, there is no guarantee about who will finish as the winner in the race to dominate the sector.

A few years earlier, while working in Hong Kong, I had also had the opportunity to report on how China was changing the rules of the game for renewable energy. In the Shandong province of eastern China, I visited enormous assembly plants that seemed to churn out solar panels and blades for wind turbines as if they were producing biscuits. Would Spain be able to sustain such competition? As it turned out, Sebastián and his Socialist government brushed aside financial caution in a bid to lead the solar power sector. They encouraged companies to invest in solar energy by promising them guaranteed tariff rates, thereby reducing massively their financial risks.

When I asked Benjumea whether the Socialists had got it wrong, he argued that it was instead the Popular Party that sunk Spain's reputation as a sound investment place for renewables, by changing the tariff rules that Zapatero's government had guaranteed. The result was not only a mountain of corporate lawsuits against Spain but also a policy U-turn that "killed an industry," Benjumea said. As president of Spain's largest renewable energy company, Benjumea told me that it was very strange that he had never managed to visit Prime Minister Mariano Rajoy, who had instead rejected several meeting requests. "I think the Popular Party was working for the electricity companies, and not the renewables, and I think it was a mistake," he said.

As I was listening to Benjumea, I kept thinking the safest conclusion to draw was that whoever governed Spain, whether from the right or the left, always sided with corporate interests without taking into account properly some of the longer term risks. And without of course ever thinking about the consequences of changing policy every time a new government steps in. This has created a serious issue for Spain in many areas, but it came to the forefront in the energy sector when Spain was taken to court for reducing its support for renewables in 2011, when the premiums paid to producers of solar energy were cut by 30 percent in order to help reduce the country's massive energy deficit.

I believe in the promotion of renewable energy to help protect our planet from devastating climate change, but no government should use taxpayers' money as a collateral to offer a blank check for risky and large industrial projects. Worse still, Zapatero's government applied the same approach to some other energy projects that presented no obvious benefit except to its promoters, most notably the Castor offshore gas drilling facility backed by ACS (*Actividades de Construcción y Servicios*), the company run by Florentino Pérez. In October 2019, another Socialist government ordered the dismantling of the Castor platform, at a cost of tens of millions of euros, and acknowledged that the project was approved in 2008 even though it was not considered then to be viable. ACS led the building of a platform that later made the earth shake along the eastern coastline of Spain, but without shaking its own corporate balance sheet thanks to the backing of Zapatero's government.

Abengoa did not need government support in the same way, even though Benjumea talked at length about how he had suffered at the hands of his bank, the government and some of his major shareholders, including some family relatives. But he never mentioned the suffering that his company caused to smaller investors, many of whom were ordinary citizens whose had trusted Abengoa without ever trying to work out how one of its thermal plants operated.

I met a handful of upset Abengoa shareholders, most of them pensioners, at a meeting held in 2015 in the headquarters of Cremades & Calvo-Sotelo, a law firm that represented a group of minority shareholders whose money had evaporated like snow in the sun once Abengoa came close to collapse. Cándido Sánchez, a pensioner who was a former employee of Renfe, talked about how he had poured his savings into Abengoa shares only a few months earlier, after hearing on television that Abengoa had attributed a sudden fall in its share price to *"un error informatico"* (computing error). Visibly upset, Sánchez concluded: "These people cheated us in a miserable way."

Many of the complaints from Abengoa's shareholders sounded remarkably like those that I had heard from pensioners who had invested their savings into risky and ultimately worthless banking preference shares, often sold to them by a banker who sat in their local branch. After Bankia's fall snowballed into a Spanish crisis, some of these people spent months gathering regularly in Madrid and other cities demanding justice and their money back.

Elena Gaillard, a widow, said that, during a visit to her local bank in June 2015, her branch agent suggested that she pour part of her liquidity into Abengoa. Following this advice, she bought 100,000 euros of Abengoa shares. "All I knew about Abengoa is that they had some solar energy in the US and where based in Seville," she told me. "For the rest, I have trust in what I am told." In Spain, as elsewhere, ordinary citizens have been paying a heavy price for showing blind faith in those who should know better.

La marca España
La preocupación por la imagen del país

Everybody feels the right to talk badly about their own parents, or even insult their siblings. But if an outsider criticizes the family, then all hell breaks loose. This is a common feature in every society that I have known. Spain is no exception.

Understanding this difference forms part of the job of the foreign correspondent. What makes the task perhaps a bit more complicated in Spain is that this is coupled with a huge degree of interest within the country about any outside praise or criticism that Spain generates, as if the foreign observer was also saying and revealing things that most Spaniards did not know already.

It has fascinated me to see how often people have asked me about how I viewed things "from the outside." I always tell them that, even if I never claim to understand fully a culture and maintain some emotional distance, I am actually "inside," living in the same city and eating at the same table, even if only as a guest and observer rather than a member of their family.

Could it be that some people care less about the foreigner's opinion than others? Is it because they have a more consolidated democracy, or feel more secure about their own worth? I have not studied sociology and I don't know the answer. But I can say that my experience of places like France has been somewhat different to that of Spain. When I worked in Paris as a correspondent for the *Financial Times*, I represented a newspaper from the "Perfidious Albion," the proverbial English enemy of Napoleon. But the French mostly shrugged off articles that they did not like, or attributed them to ignorance rather than malice. Only the few articles that really broke news about France got considerable attention.

I discussed this difference with Ian Gibson, the Irish-born historian, who was granted citizenship by the Spanish government in 1984 in recognition of his breakthrough research about the poet Federico García Lorca. At the same time, Gibson is also a lifetime admirer of France and its language. "I think it's inconceivable for somebody like me to gain real presence on French public television," Gibson told me. "The French don't need a foreign authority on Marcel Proust, because they feel they already have enough of their own."

Perhaps the perception of foreign opinion also changes when the situation of a country becomes more fragile. I arrived in 2010 just as Spain was sinking into its biggest economic crisis since returning to democracy. The crisis hurt ordinary people, but was also a huge slap in the face for a generation of politicians, central bankers and entrepreneurs who had been enjoying a decade-long property boom that they believed would never end, or at least not so painfully. In July 2009, President José Luís Rodríguez Zapatero had even proudly used his first participation in a G-8 meeting to claim that "the hour of Spain has come" (*Ha llegado la hora de España*).

But it turned out not to be the kind of hour that Zapatero had in mind. The country soon found itself in the international media spotlight, but struggling to stay afloat and contain an unemployment rate that reached 27 percent.

As the euro debt crisis deepened, Spain got caught in a terrible spiral, like other countries before. Once investors worry about their money, they pull out and accelerate the risk of insolvency, while raising the country's cost of borrowing. The debt problems that started in Greece had already spread to Ireland and Portugal and foreign investors were fast withdrawing from all the other countries that looked most vulnerable, starting with Spain. By the start of 2012, the Spanish banking sector was on the verge of collapse. There was a battle to be fought to retain the little trust that the world financial markets still had left in Spain. Part of the challenge was to strengthen Spain's brand.

In a way, Spain was also suddenly facing an unwanted rise in international media coverage. For much of the 1990s and the following decade, Spain had provided a second-tier news story, as a country that was politically stable, controlled in turn by two giant parties, and growing steadily. Everywhere, people were building a lot of houses, even in larger quantity than the United States by the time the property bubble burst. But adding more houses and motorways was not a particularly exciting story, and Spain was not at the same time leading the world in terms of revolutionary entrepreneurship and technological innovation (with perhaps the exception of solar power, which I discuss elsewhere in this book.)

Of course, there were some major and sometimes tragic events that also stunned the rest of the world, particularly the Madrid train bombings of 2004. But overall, Spain spent the decade before my arrival mostly away from the front pages of international newspapers. That point was made very clearly to me when I signed my contract in Paris with the *International Herald Tribune*, which was then the international brand of *The New York Times*. Tom Redburn, one of the editors, had told me when we first met that the newspaper had two cities from which correspondents were leaving, Frankfurt and Madrid. I spoke both German and Spanish so that I could perhaps apply for either job. Frankfurt, as the seat of the European Central Bank and the heart of the eurozone, was the most important of the two posts, Redburn said. Madrid rarely produced big news. But it was of course the capital of a fascinating country, which meant that a good and ambitious reporter could find some great feature stories. Redburn also pointed out that I could probably write often for other sections of the newspaper, particularly on Spanish culture, as well as football and other sports.

After listening to him, I had no hesitation in choosing to apply for Madrid over Frankfurt. I felt that Madrid would be a fabulous posting, even if less important than Frankfurt from the newspaper's point of view. However, just like Redburn, I had no way to predict that I would very soon find myself thrown into the eye of a hurricane of news, frantically focused on the shaky finances of Spain, without almost any time to report about football or any other topic that did not relate to the financial meltdown.

The New York Times and the rest of the international media soon presented Spain as an economic story that had implications for the whole of Europe. In response, every foreign opinion piece relating to the debt crisis received heavy scrutiny in Spain. Taxi drivers in Madrid were talking to me for the first time about the premium risk of Spanish bonds, rather than the latest football match. And investors were not only following the bond market, but also reading much more closely the foreign press. In July 2012, I remember meeting with two Spanish bankers, who looked anxious. On the table, they had a copy of *The Economist*, which put Spain on the cover. But the headline read "pain," with the "S" of Spain shown to be falling down, like a banderilla into the head of the wounded bull.

Spain no doubt found itself portrayed in a grim light after June 2012, when the government of Mariano Rajoy was forced to nego-tiate a European banking bailout. But I would argue that journalists should have raised more alarm bells about Spain's economy at an earlier stage in the crisis. Spain was not helped by politicians and central bankers who buried their heads in the sand, hoping that the crisis would sweep past Spain without damaging the country. In November 2011, voters ousted the Socialists from office not only for plunging Spain into crisis, but also for denying for far too long that Spain was vulnerable to an economic shock.

But, in his own way, Rajoy then also did his utmost to minimize the seriousness of the banking meltdown. As I discuss in another chapter, he found himself in the uncomfortable situation of having to handle the near-bankruptcy of a bank, Bankia, that was closely tied to his Popular Party and led by his former government colleague, Rodrigo Rato.

Once Rato was forced to resign, Rajoy repeatedly denied that Bankia's collapse would force Spain to require outside help. He avoided using the word "bailout," as if it were taboo. On the day he finally announced that Spain had negotiated a banking bailout, Rajoy gave a news conference without ever using the dreaded word. In an extraordinary final twist to his uncomfortable encounter with the media, he then cut short the question time, saying that he did not want to miss his flight to Poland to watch Spain's opening match in the European football championships. It was as if the banking crisis was done and dusted, and certainly not sufficiently grave to come in the way of football. "I believe the Spanish national team deserves this. It's always possible to have different views about such things, but I really think that I have to go," he said, before leaving for the airport. I was stunned by his valuation of what was most important for Spain, football success over financial survival.

Not everybody in Spain shared Rajoy's list of priorities. Nor did foreign investors, of course. So Rajoy's government then created a new post with a long title: High Commissioner of Brand Spain. The job was entrusted to Carlos Espinosa de los Monteros y Bernaldo de Quirós, an aristocrat who had an impressive track record as long as his name. In 1982, the Socialist government appointed him to run Iberia and he later worked in the automotive sector, as well as for Inditex, the giant clothing retailer.

Although Espinosa de los Monteros was given the tough task of improving the tarnished reputation of Spain in the midst of a major economic crisis, he was never given the financial resources to respond fully to this challenge. For the following six years, Espinosa de los Monteros kept complaining about his lack of budget, which, he said, amounted to helping instead those who want to hurt Spain. As he told the newspaper *ABC* when he was ousted by the incoming Socialist government of Pedro Sánchez, in 2018, "without funding, we leave the terrain open to those who issue anti-Spain messages."

Espinosa de los Monteros, who took on his job without a salary, later told me that it was worth comparing the significant amount that some other countries spend on promoting their national brand, let alone companies like Iberia or Mercedes-Benz for which he had once worked. At Mercedes, "there were 300 people dedicated exclusively to taking care of the brand," he recalled. "The brand is key, perhaps even more than the car."

In June 2018, the Socialist government rebranded the office, from Marca España to España Global. Espinosa de los Monteros did not mince his words, calling the name change "a stupidity," driven by politics. He added: "To change brand is to go against any guide-book about marketing, because if you have a brand whose fame is rising, you don't get rid of it to choose another. This is the ABC of marketing." But Espinosa de los Monteros also agreed with me that not everybody within Spain had believed in his message of recovery at the height of the banking crisis. Many executives worked hard to distance themselves from their country brand rather than embrace it. "There was a bit of everything," he said. "There were some messages in order not to identify with Spain, but there were also some companies that instead showcased their Spanish roots."

I particularly remember an advertising campaign by Banco Santander, which used a world map to show how its banking activities stretched across several continents, giving the exact percentage of the bank's earnings that came from Spain or elsewhere. And as the Spanish proportion fell, so Santander kept relaunching its advertising campaign to highlight its falling reliance on a troubled home market.

Like many others, the sudden collapse of Bankia in 2012 caught me flat-footed. It also left me with the unpleasant feeling that I let Rato off the hook, having had the chance to interview him a month before he was was forced to leave his bank, as discussed in another chapter. After Spain negotiated its banking bailout, the mandate from my editors shifted slightly. The question became whether, in addition to Bankia, any other major banks had skeletons hidden in the cupboard. Suspicions were also fueled by the fact that, in neighboring Portugal, the end of its bailout program coincided with a sudden banking scandal, centering on the fraudulent activities of the only major financial institution that had claimed no rescue money during the crisis, Banco Espírito Santo. In 2014, the Portuguese government used another 4.9 billion of public money to save Espírito Santo.

In the case of Spain, its next banking fiasco took another two years to come to light, with the near-collapse of Banco Popular in 2016. By that time, luckily for Spain, its economy was firmly back on the growth track and other banks could afford to absorb an ailing competitor. In a swift move, Banco Santander bought Banco Popular for one euro. Santander later told the CNMV (*Comisión Nacional del Mercado de Valores*) regulator that its purchase amounted to an act of public salvation, which had avoided spending about 36 billion of taxpayers' money on another bailout. Whatever Santander's own assessment, the demise of Banco Popular served as a reminder that all was not well in Spain even after it avoided a banking meltdown in 2012. But understandably, nobody in government during these years took kindly to reports that talked about Spain's fragile economy, or articles that highlighted the extent to which the crisis was increasing the wealth gap between the elite and the poor and unemployed.

In September 2012, I received a phone call from the Moncloa. From the icy tone of the voice at the other end of the line, I immediately knew that I needed to brace myself for a furious onslaught. After the banking bailout, tensions were running very high. *The New York Times* had just published a reportage centered on photos by Samuel Aranda. Aranda had been given carte blanche to roam Spain for several weeks to capture how people were dealing with the financial crisis. The newspaper published his photos, in black and white, showing social and economic problems in different parts of the country. They included street protests in Andalusia, people eating at a soup kitchen in Catalonia and the bursting of the construction bubble in the region of Valencia, illustrated by the striking contrast in the skyline of the seaside resort of Benidorm, between its massive skyscrapers and its unfinished buildings. Under a stark headline — "In Spain, austerity and hunger" — the newspaper's international edition ran on its front page one of Aranda's photos, showing a man leaning into a rubbish dump.

The Moncloa official told me that the photos had been reviewed at the highest levels of government and that the conclusion was that they represented an outrageous assault on the dignity and reputation of Spain. Nobody at the Moncloa was challenging the facts mentioned in the story, but I was told that everybody agreed that our newspaper presented Spain as if it was back in 1939, struggling to emerge from its civil war. "Just look at the terrible face of one the protestors you have photographed," the official said. "Nobody else in Spain now has bad and missing teeth like him."

I agreed that Spain had created one of the world's best and most accessible health systems and that it was now very rare to meet people missing several teeth. I also agreed that the photos portrayed a country that was hurting deeply and that the decision to shoot them in black-and-white not only gave more impact to the photography, but also probably added to the sense of gloom and decay. In sunny Spain, everything tends to look a bit less dark.

Yet Aranda had not asked anybody to pause for his photos, nor had he then used Photoshop to make them more impactful, as some people later claimed to me. He was also not a foreigner who had zero understanding of the situation in Spain, but instead somebody with a deep sensitivity for social unrest and human tragedies, which he has photographed around the world. As a result of such work, Aranda is the only Spanish photographer to date to have won the top prize in the prestigious World Press Photo awards. The text that accompanied his photos, which was written by the newspaper's European correspondent, Suzanne Daley, was also based on official studies and statistics, including a report by Caritas, the Catholic charity, which said that it had fed almost one million Spaniards in 2010, more than twice as many as in 2007, and that this number had risen again in 2011 by 65,000.

My own personal feeling was that the set of photos could also have shown more of the paradoxes of a crisis that affected a whole country, but certainly not everybody in the same way. Across Spain, people were still paying significant sums of money to go to the stadium and watch their football team, and not just demonstrating on the streets. As I discuss in another chapter, crime had not risen even as the unemployment data showed that about half of the youth of Spain could not find a job. And while impoverished people had to rely more on Caritas and other charities, many instead got help from their parents and other relatives. The crisis had also sparked an incredible outburst of solidarity, which acted as a cushion to soften the blow and which I believe would be unimaginable in a place like America, where family bonds have weakened significantly.

For me, this situation was an example of how correspondents can find themselves in a difficult situation, under unexpected pressure from different parts. For several months after Aranda's photos were published, it remained a subject of conversation while I continued my own reporting during a difficult time for the country.

The publication of Aranda's photos also coincided with King Juan Carlos visiting the headquarters of *The New York Times*, while Rajoy was also in New York to attend a general assembly of the United Nations. Some critics in Spain told me that the timing was proof that the country was the victim of an American media conspiracy. They also noted that the photos came out two weeks after a Diada manifestation that turned into the largest pro-independence street protest in Barcelona since Spain's return to democracy. Aranda is Catalan, and soon enough people started telling me that his photos formed part of his crusade to break up Spain.

It was not the first time that I had faced Spanish conspiracy theories relating to my newspaper. During the financial crisis, there was much social media speculation that *The New York Times* was working to help investors on Wall Street make more money from the debt problems of Spain, just as the *Financial Times* was accused of backing the interests of the City of London. Only days after Aranda's photos were released, El Confidencial, the online publication, had an article, citing unnamed sources in the Spanish government, saying that Rajoy was trying to find out who was leaking information to the international media in order to seriously hurt Spain's reputation. According to El Confidencial, Rajoy had asked the secret agents of the CNI (Spain's National Intelligence Centre) to lead this investigation. As the alleged targets of this investigation, El Confidencial named *The New York Times*, the *Financial Times* and Reuters.

Following the publication of Aranda's photos, I received some nasty calls, as well as interview requests from Spanish media, which I declined and referred instead to our editorial communications department. I did not want to pour more oil on the fire, nor to discuss a project that was not mine. In fact, part of the aim of the newspaper had precisely been to take a look at the crisis from a different angle and through a fresh pair of eyes. Still, two months later, I found myself standing alongside Miles Johnson, who was then a correspondent in Madrid for the *Financial Times*, for a joint interview as part of the "Comando Actualidad" program produced by RTVE, the broadcasting service. Pablo Fons Alvaro, a journalist from the public broadcaster, had asked me to contribute to a story about "Spain's brand," to help explain how the foreign media presented the country. He convinced me, but only on the condition that I would not be discussing the photos of Aranda.

Unfortunately, as soon as our interview started, the journalist held up in front of the camera a copy of the front page with Aranda's photo of the rubbish container. I responded as best as I could to his questions. But once the interview was finished, I told him that he had violated our agreement, and asked him not to incorporate this segment of our conversation in the final production montage. In the end, RTVE put together a good program, but sadly it did not remove my segment discussing Aranda's photo. I later wrote to Fons Alvaro to tell him that "there are basic rules that must be respected if this journalism profession really wants to have a future." He apologized, stressing that he had not handled the production process. In retrospect, this incident helped me understand how people feel when they believe that they did not get a fair hearing in the media.

In April 2020, another photo threw me and *The New York Times* back into hot waters, in the midst of another moment of crisis, provoked this time by the coronavirus. From my flat in Madrid, I spoke by phone to health specialists about how children were being affected by the lockdown, while my colleagues Elian Peltier and Aranda visited families in Barcelona. Our joint article received plaudits during 24 hours after its publication on a Saturday morning, but on the Sunday morning it turned instead into a major topic of controversy on Spanish social media, over whether the lead photo "misrepresented Spain" and "a traditional Spanish family." According to the data compiled by *The New York Times*, the photo controversy added about 500,000 viewers to the article, a vast majority of them based in Spain.

The main photo showed a couple who had moved to Barcelona from Bangladesh 17 years earlier, and shared a small apartment with their five-year old twins and a cousin. The family ran a bar and their children were born in Spain, yet my email inbox rapidly filled with criticism about how their family photo was an insult to Spain. Many of the messages I received were blatantly racists. Others were personal and violent, calling for my immediate deportation from Spain, or worse. Others seemed to be misplaced attempts to also revive the tensions over Catalonia. Like millions of others, the family supported the biggest football team in their city and had put a flag of F.C. Barcelona on their wall, yet several Spanish readers decided that their passion for football was also proof of their love of separatism.

The article landed at a difficult time for everybody, including myself. I had spent weeks interviewing doctors, nurses, patients as well as relatives of people who had died from the coronavirus. Right then, I just did not feel that I had the emotional strength needed to deal with such an unexpected and virulent criticism. Aranda kindly put out a disclaimer on Twitter to say that I was not involved in the photo selection, but I also found it depressing that nobody from that Sunday onward discussed with me the actual content of the article and its very important subject matter, the children of Spain. In fact, it was clear that many people had never read the article, nor even looked at the photo caption to see that the family was not "Arab."

But I did also have some more thoughtful exchanges with some upset friends and readers about why they considered the newspaper had not shown "the reality of Spain." I strongly argued that, in a multi-layered society, there are several realities rather than one. I said that I could understand they might not like the photo or object to having it chosen as the lead illustration, but I also reminded them that this story project was never about "representing the typical family," whatever that means. The five-year-old twins endured living conditions that were certainly one of the realities of Spain and its working class.

What in any case is a representative family in modern Spain? I asked them. Would they have preferred to have the article led by the photo of a single mother, or that of the mother of an autistic child, who also featured in the article? If so, why?

Of course, my response was probably tainted by my own background, as a Swiss of East European origin, without one percent of Swiss blood running through my veins. And while I have seen less evidence of xenophobia in Spain than in some other countries, I certainly believe many people in Spain should celebrate more diversity and be more willing to confront some of the country's economic disparities. The job of a journalist is not always to focus on what is average in a country, but also to show disparities.

The reaction to the photo also showed how some Spaniards continue to bear the weight of the past. A Spanish film producer, who had been living in Los Angeles for the past 35 years, wrote to me to complain that, since the late eighteenth century and the encyclopedists. Spain was excluded from Europe. "For them, we are more like Africans than Europeans. For them, we are backward, lazy, and atavistic people."

In a conversation on a morning show with Aranda, Susanna Griso, the television presenter, also argued that many people in Spain felt complexed that Americans looked down upon Spaniards. During her student days, she recalled staying in Colorado and getting asked if her family owned a fridge. There is ignorance everywhere, but I believe the many Americans who are among the more than 80 million people who choose to visit Spain each year know plenty about all the wonderful amenities that the country offers. And they certainly do not leave disappointed.

But to my amazement, several readers also wrote to insist that they did not object to the ethnicity of the family originating from

Bangladesh, but instead to the way that they lived, with child graffiti on the door, because "no Spanish family lives like this." I encourage these critics to visit one day the huge shanty town of Cañada Real outside Madrid, or even one of the several rundown apartment blocks that surround Barcelona. It is an eye-popping way of understanding how many families struggle on the periphery of Barcelona, earning on average about six times less than the residents of Pedralbes, the richest area of Barcelona.

El negocio de la tierra
El potencial de la mermelada, el vino y la trufa

My first visit to Seville felt like an attack on all the senses. I was struck by the visual beauty of its palaces and the size of its cathedral, by the heat that seemed to get trapped within its narrow streets, by the blend of loud debating, laughter and guitar music in its cafés and by the scent of its orange trees.

Seville's oranges stunned me. I had never been to a major city with such an abundance of fruit on its streets. I wanted to bite into one of these beautiful oranges hanging off the trees, but a friend warned me that it would be very bitter and unpleasant to eat. So what do you do with them? I asked. He told me that the oranges got either thrown away, or sold to the British so that they can make their marmalade.

I had finally discovered the origins of the pot of marmalade that was always placed at the center of the breakfast table, during my student days at Oxford University. But his answer also surprised me. If the only commercial value of these inedible oranges resided in turning them into marmalade, why did the entrepreneurs of Seville allow the owners of factories in English cities like Sheffield to produce the marmalade, rather than make it themselves? Did it not cost roughly the same to ship a crate of oranges as to send over jars of prepared marmalade?

I didn't get a clear answer that day, but I was left feeling that Spain was missing an opportunity. It sounded to me a bit like the story of how African cocoa had contributed to the chocolate wealth and fame of my own country, Switzerland. Somehow, the chocolate industry had been structured so that the Ivory Coast and other cocoa nations sold their cocoa beans to Switzerland and a handful of other countries, where food companies were then earning most of the money by transforming the cocoa into chocolate, wrapped in glittery boxes.

In 2015, I told this anecdote at a meeting in Madrid organized by luxury brand executives who belonged to an association called Circulo Fortuny. The gathering was presided by Carlos Falcó, an aristocrat who held the title of marques de Griñón and had a family estate that produces wine and olive oil. My orange story was met with what sounded like an embarrassed silence. One executive eventually told me that there was actually some marmalade production in Andalusia.

Spain has come a long way since this meeting, and gastronomy has been one of the areas in which it has made most progress. As part of a tourism boom that has made Spain among the most visited countries in the world, many Americans and other foreigners travel specifically to sample Spanish food and wine. Among them was one of my senior editors, who once arranged a holiday in the Basque Country that was scheduled around the table bookings that he had made at some of the region's award-winning restaurants. In 2019, the chefs working in the Basque Country held a combined 23 Michelin stars, which was the highest concentration per capita in the world.

New Yorkers no longer even have to travel to Spain to eat its food. In 2019, Mercado Little Spain opened as part of the city's new Hudson Yards. The project was the brainchild of the chef José Andrés, but also included Ferran and Albert Adrià among its collaborators. In its review of the mercado, *The New York Times* called Andrés the "unofficial one-man Spanish embassy," such is his fame in America. But despite such success stories, I think that it is still true that Spain continues to sell itself short — and not only with its oranges. The gap with countries like Italy is closing, but I still hear repeated complaints about how Spanish wine and olive oil do not get the recognition that they deserve and unfairly trail some of their rivals in terms of market value.

I am not a travel writer, but others have covered much ground in Spain for *The New York Times* to write about its beautiful hotels and restaurants. The newspaper's wine critic has also singled out amazing wines, sometimes made from lesser-known grapes, like the bobal variety.

Still, I have managed to write about the rich and diverse produce of Spain, mostly focusing on traditions and farming practices that seemed to me unusual enough to warrant the attention of American and other international readers. Even within Spain, I have often found that people are not fully aware of how diverse their land and its produce are, and I have sometimes tested my story ideas on Spanish friends to see whether they get as excited as me. Did you know that Spain produced caviar? I have asked them. Did you realize that almost all the Christmas biscuits known as polvorones are made in Estepa, a small Andalusian town?

As in many other places, I found in Estepa a story that opened a fascinating window onto Spain's rich cultural heritage, since the polvorones date back to Arab recipes from the Moorish occupation. Their history also reflects more recent economic hardship, as struggling farmers made polvorones in order to recycle pig's fat after the traditional slaughtering season. Almost nobody in the United States knowns the polvorones, whose consumption is surprisingly limited to Spain. In fact, Estepa's 23 factories export less than 10 percent of their production, mostly to Latin America.

But I still found in this Spanish food story plenty to interest my business editor, because the local economic monopoly of the polvorones was also tied to the peculiarities of Spain's labor market, heavily reliant on seasonal and temporary jobs. As the polvorones factories only operate for part of the year, Estepa's unemployment rate halves during the pre-Christmas months compared with the summer. "As a town, we win the lottery every Christmas," Miguel Fernández Baena, the mayor of Estepa, told me when I visited.

Encouraged by such reporting, I asked Falcó to meet again and explain to me why he was then lobbying politicians to alter the wine business in his region of Castilla-La Mancha. Over coffee in a Madrid five-star hotel, Falcó told me how he wanted to shift as soon as possible his region away from bulk wine, or granel, and improve the branding. "When I have a foreign customer visiting my cellar and I want to sell him a bottle for 20, 30 or 40 euros, the fact that he might know that there are bottles sold nearby for just a few cents doesn't really help," Falcó told me.

I traveled to Castilla-La Mancha to see for myself what upset Falcó, even though his region was promoting itself as Spain's wine heartland, producing half of all the country's wine. Soon enough, I understood that the land of wine could also be located within industrial polygons, far removed from the oak barrels housed in ancient wine cellars that are normally shown in the travel guides.

Isidro Rodríguez, the technical director of Virgen de las Viñas, took me around the facilities of his company, which was the region's biggest wine producer. There were massive steel deposits, hoses linked to tank trucks and workers on three shifts to make sure that production was maintained 24 hours a day in what he himself called "our factory." I was surprised to hear a wine merchant talk about his work in such industrial terms, but Rodríguez even corrected me when I then made a weak attempt to sound sophisticated and use the rich and colorful language of wine. "We don't elaborate wine here, we produce wine," he said.

Rodríguez and everybody else whom I met sounded very proud about how the dry and hot region of Castilla-La Mancha had been transformed by modern irrigation, harvest mechanization and storage systems, while its farming sector had used as much as possible European Union subsidies to finance this makeover. The outcome was an incredibly efficient industry, they insisted, in which people are willing to work hard and for relatively low wages. The producers told me about how the price of their granel wine was half that of France.

But there was a flip side to this pricing advantage, because of the reputation cost for Spanish wine, particularly when grown in the same region as much cheaper granel wine. However hard to measure, this problem turned into a personal battle for Falcó, which he fought until March 2020, when he sadly became one of the fatalities of coronavirus.

Of course, Falcó was not alone to fight for Spain's wine reputation. When I met Rafael del Rey, the director of the Spanish Observatory of the Wine Market, he backed his arguments by producing a folder filled with graphics and comparative charts showing the evolution of Spanish wine. As with the oranges of Seville, I was left feeling that Spain had been missing a trick. Wine producers had focused too much on short-term gains rather than developing their industry for the long run.

His data was revealing, particularly that which compared Spain with Italy. In 2000, both countries exported their wine at the same average price of 1.41 euros per liter. By 2014, however, Italy was selling its wine on average for 2.5 euros per liter, while the Spanish price was 1.17 euros. Spain had been outpacing Italy in terms of the volume of its exports, but their value had fallen to half that of Italian exports. "We have boosted our exports significantly, but probably too rapidly, so that we have now got the wrong price pyramid, with a lot of wine sold very cheaply," del Rey explained. Spain's relationship with France was just as unfavorable. Spain was selling about 500 million liters of wine to France, 90 percent as bulk. France was exporting half Spain's volume of bulk wine, but at a price that was three times higher than that of Spain.

Based on this mountain of statistics, del Rey reached an unfavorable conclusion, which was that massive Spanish wine exports helped make more profitable the wine business of other countries. It was similar to the complaints I had heard about Spanish olive oil that then got bottled in Italy. "I'm not saying that exactly the same liter that left Spain is then re-exported from France, but it is undeniable that some Spanish wine becomes part of French exports, with a lot of added value," he said.

Castilla-La Mancha's producers also switched to bulk wine after the European Union decided in 2009 to end subsidies for distilled alcohol. But the very thin profit margins of granel wine left its producers very vulnerable to any sudden shift in harvest volumes. When I visited Virgen de las Viñas, the company was hoping to break even for the year, after making a loss in the previous one. Enrique Cepeda, the chief executive, presented this precarious situation as inevitable. "Somebody who makes a Seat would be happy to sell instead a Porsche, but you can't make such a switch easily," he told me.

Still, Spain has several examples of producers who have followed a different approach, as well as a whole region whose international fame is based on its wine, La Rioja. The success of La Rioja was tied to a bold decision, taken in the 1990s, to force its producers to bottle their wine rather than sell any of it as granel. La Rioja then successfully defended this decision in court, going as far as a ruling by the European Court of Justice.

Could Castilla-La Mancha follow La Rioja's lead? That "sounds right but is simply not practical," because of the size of its vineyard and reliance on bulk, argued José Luis Lapuente, the director general of the Rioja wine regulatory council. When Rioja introduced its ban on bulk wine, such wine only accounted for 5 percent of its production, he told me, while in Castilla-La Mancha, "a lot of big producers absolutely rely on it and economies of scale." Still,

I could not avoid the feeling that bulk wine, however successful, would never allow Spain to reap the full benefits of being such a perfect country to plant grapes.

As I have mentioned elsewhere in this book, I get some criticism from people in Spain who believe that I have been focusing unnecessarily on the negative side of an otherwise positive story. Why do I write about granel rather than the fabulous and award-winning wines of Spain? I do not have the fine palate of a food or wine critic writing for *The New York Times*, so there are other journalists better placed to help cover the gastronomic potential of Spain. They have written about many of the lesser known treasures of Spain, including wines like the grenache that has been revived in the old vineyards of the Sierra de Gredos. Every year, *The New York Times* recommends 52 travel destinations. Inevitably, between one and three places in Spain are featured. While I have offered my own recommendations to the travel section editors who compile the list, I have nothing to do with the final selection, and a lucky travel journalist then gets to visit the place and write about it. What I do get sometimes, however, are undeserved thanks from local town officials who tell me about how making the newspaper's destination list has boosted their tourism, particularly from America.

But it is also true that, like in other countries, I have found that the poster tourism image of Spain sometimes hides a more contradictory reality, which also applies to its greatest produce. The most intriguing part of the story is sometimes hidden at the bottom of the barrel.

In 2015, I visited a truffles fair in the province of Teruel, after reading that Spain had become a major producer of a fine food mostly associated with neighboring France and Italy. The dry earth of Teruel offered fertile soil for truffles. As with wine, however, Spaniards consume relatively few truffles themselves. Instead, about 95 percent of Teruel's production is exported, much of it to France, where the black truffle has long been an essential component of French gastronomy, but production has been falling. "Spain is now producing what is missing in France," Eric Bienvenu, a French truffle broker, told me.

The Teruel fair was a fun and tasty occasion, with local producers proudly displaying their produce for visitors like Bienvenu, who buried his nose in the truffles to appreciate their pungent aroma and decide what kind should reach the kitchens of the French restaurants that he supplies. But despite his enthusiasm, Bienvenu also had a clear word of warning about the truffle business, which he described as "completely opaque" and clearly not confined to the nicely organized perimeter of Teruel's fair. He told me that three-quarters of his own transactions were made in cash, largely because farmers did not want any billing paperwork that could come under scrutiny from tax inspectors.

In fact, the regional authorities of Aragón only published their first official pricing list for truffles in December 2015, shedding light on an obscure trade in which truffles have been exchanging hands for at least 500 euros per kilo. Apart from the pricing issues, traders also told me that it was near-impossible to trace the exact origin of Spanish truffles, opening the door to registration fraud. Some probably got sold in France under the famous Périgord label.

So where did many of Teruel's farmers meet their clients? Long after the fair closed its doors, I drove to a semi-abandoned railway station, a few kilometers away. It was hard to imagine a more gloomy place to wait for some truffle action than the neon-lit and inhospitable cafeteria of this local train station. Eventually, I spotted the headlights of a few cars and pickup trucks driving slowly down the hill. They parked outside the station, but their occupants mostly stayed inside their vehicles, happy to keep their privacy in the darkness of the parking lot. When I approached one of them, he pointed his flashlight at my face and refused to talk to a journalist. From a distance, I then watched him walk around the parking lot, using his flashlight to inspect truffles that local farmers had piled into the trunks of their vehicles. There was a bit of haggling over the price, but eventually some precious truffles were stuffed into supermarket plastic bags.

Paradoxically, the authorities of Aragón had just granted millions in public subsidies to build a new irrigation system to help Teruel's farmers. But some of these same farmers then sold their produce on the black market.

Spain's truffle production is thriving, but partly in the darkness of a parking lot, in transactions that do little to contribute to the value of the produce of Spain.

Un mundo más o menos global
Vender sexo y colonialismo

In 2013, a sex story took me on a search for an American-owned factory that was located in an industrial park called Carretera de La Isla, outside the Andalusian town of Dos Hermanas. If the place had anything to do with an island, it was a deserted one. I knew that the area was then suffering from high unemployment, but it looked completely abandoned. On a weekday afternoon, many of the warehouses appeared to have been shuttered. Once I found the street on which the factory was meant to be located, I could not find the factory itself. I wondered whether I had been given the wrong address, or whether the factory had somehow suddenly joined the list of corporate casualties of Spain's economic crisis.

Eventually, I decided to make one final attempt to find the factory, before calling the boss of the factory to apologize for my delay and ask for help. I left the car and walked the street on foot, looking closely at each building. On one of the mail boxes, I finally found the name I was looking for, written only in fine print: Fleshlight. The factory itself had no logo on its outside walls and the delivery vans parked outside were all unmarked.

It was clear that this American company cared about discretion and wanted to remain a plain-brown-wrapper business. But once I walked inside, I found the place bustling with activity, with a dozen people working inside the factory, separated from the reception area by a glass wall. Juan Ziena, a Spanish software engineer who had become the manager of Fleshlight's factory, told to me that the lack of advertising outside the premises was very much part of Fleshlight's corporate policy, which was to advertise online but keep a low profile locally. "We don't really want to show" what is being made here, Ziena said.

Still, Ziena had plenty of reasons to feel proud, as the boss of a profitable factory, at a time when many other manufacturers in Spain were instead struggling to survive a devastating recession. The factory was on track to raise its profits that year by 300 percent and double its sales, he said. This staggering financial performance was attributable to growing demand for a male sex toy that was, as the company's name indicated, shaped like a flashlight. The sex toy came in different models, but the most popular one was then selling for 69.95 euros in Europe.

I had convinced my business editor to write about Fleshlight because it seemed an unusual counter-example to the slew of stories about Spain's corporate demise, but also because it was one of the rarely told and colorful success stories of global manufacturing. The story also had another selling point in that it was about American entrepreneurship in Europe. Last but not least, Fleshlight's founder and owner, Steve Shubin, did not exactly fit the typical profile of the business school graduate turned entrepreneur.

Before founding Fleshlight almost two decades earlier, Shubin had been on the SWAT team of the Los Angeles Police Department. But the career-changing event for Shubin came when his wife, Kathleen, became pregnant with twins and her doctor warned against having sex during what was ruled to be a complicated pregnancy. Shubin told me that he then asked for her permission to set up what he called a "home lab" in his garage, where he could develop something to help him masturbate. "It was clear that the products that were on the market for men were just garbage," he said.

Shubin presented himself as an altruist. He saw commercial potential in turning his personal invention into something that could help other men, so he worked on building a tool that could be "portable and concealable." As he explained to me, men had to be spared the hassle and embarrassment of traveling and getting seen with something as large and eye-popping as an inflatable sex doll. Shubin's sex toy, built within a plastic cylinder casing, could easily be mistaken for a large and rather heavy flashlight, weighing just over one kilogram. Within the casing, however, there is a soft, flesh-colored material, which Shubin patented as Superskin. He explained that he had developed it by trial and error in his garage lab, mixing polymers and heating them up with mineral oils, with the help of his son and then a chemical engineer. The result was a secret formula that Shubin felt had done for the sex industry what Coca-Cola did for the soft drinks sector.

I found some of Shubin's reasoning questionable. But I could not argue against his business acumen. By the time Shubin told me his story, he was a 61-year old millionaire, running a company alongside his wife that had sold 7 million sex toys and had big expansion plans. In terms of market potential, Shubin believed that Fleshlight had "hardly scratched the surface, when you think there are 3 billion men."

Fleshlight was based in Austin, Texas. Once he decided to manufacture also in Europe, Shubin looked at different countries. His final choice was made alongside his wife, Kathleen, driven by personal preferences rather than financial considerations, he said, even after visiting more tax-friendly locations for entrepreneurs. Discovering Andalusia "made us feel immediately comfortable, reminding us of Southern California 50 years ago," Shubin said. Kathleen, who was a former professional tennis player, was also fanatic about horses and found in Andalusia an incredible place to satisfy her equine passion. The couple acquired three horses that they kept on a property in Marbella.

"If this was a public company with shareholders making the decision, they would probably not have gone to Spain," he said, "not only because of its economic problems but because there are other countries, like Hungary or Romania, that offer much better tax advantages."

Fleshlight invested in Andalusia just as many foreign investors were instead trying to figure out whether to pull out of Spain, whose economy was cratering. Still, Andalusia offered a good corporate tax package that was almost half the amount that Fleshlight paid in Texas. Andalusia also then had an unemployment rate that had risen above 30 percent, which made it easy for Fleshlight to recruit a local workforce of 28 employees. "We had endless number of people to choose from, and they came with a higher level of education than what most of the jobs required," Shubin said. Although Fleshlight's American factory in Austin had to supply much of the machinery to its new and smaller Spanish counterpart, Shubin found it easier running a sex-related business in Andalusia than in United States, where "there is a much higher religious concentration and a lot more hang-ups about sex than in Europe."

In the United States, some banks rejected his corporate loan applications, he said, and some law firms refused to represent Fleshlight because of ethical concerns. "They don't want anything to blacken their résumé," he said. In contrast, Fleshlight had no problem finding companies to handle its banking and legal work in Spain (Fleshlight's banks were Banco Santander and Banco Pastor.)

During a tour of the factory, Ziena showed me how his company was developing premium products that were being made using a mould of a porn star's vagina. In return, the actress got a commission — usually 12 percent — on each toy that was sold. "We work

104

with the All-star team of porno," Ziena proudly told me. For clients with more freakish and fictional fantasies, there was even a line of sex toys decorated with vampire or Frankenstein designs. Although most clients were heterosexual men, the company also made some toys for gay men, as well as vibrators for women. "If a man buys one of our products, he may want his girlfriend or wife to have something as well," Ziena explained.

The employees, meanwhile, had just received a salary rise of 10 percent from the previous year. On average, the factory workers earned about 1,300 euros a month, which was almost twice the minimum salary in Spain. "I think the unemployment situation of Spain has made people value their work a lot more, because most know that to have a job around here now is like winning the lottery," Ziena said.

Among its permanent staff, the factory employed four women. One of them, Julia Vellloso, was a 29-year-old who had been the office accountant for almost three years. Working for a sex toy manufacturer "felt strange at first, but you get used to it," she told me. "My friends thought at first that I was joking, but I've been bringing them one of our products so that they can see it — and some have even bought it." On his office wall, Ziena had a set of screen monitors with minute-by-minute updates of the online orders for Fleshlight's products. The products were mostly being transported from the factory to Madrid's Barajas airport and then flown to Germany and other destinations across Europe.

It was an unusual production center, but what I found most interesting was talking to Ziena and other employees about how Spanish society related to their sex industry. When he met strangers, Ziena told me that he would normally say that he was working in "the plastics industry." Spain, he said, had "a problem of double morality," but nothing like the one he had encountered when he had visited the company headquarters in Texas. "We don't get the kind of "Burn in Hell" threats that get mailed to Fleshlight in the United States," he said.

As I returned to Madrid, I thought about what Shubin and Ziena had told me about Catholic Spain becoming a less conservative society than America. In fact, along the highways of Andalusia and other parts of Spain, neon-lit road signs invite drivers to stop in what are clearly brothels, evidence of a booming industry in a country where prostitution was decriminalized in 1995. This is part of the dark side of the story, one that has turned Spain into one of the brothel hubs of Europe, with also a worryingly high rate of human trafficking.

My editor edited the Fleshlight story carefully to avoid anything that could be interpreted as lewd. The final version said that Fleshlight made a product that was "meant for — how to put this — male auto eroticism." The story came with a set of photos taken by Laura León, the Seville-based photographer with whom I often worked. She had also been careful to avoid taking any picture that could be seen as offensive. In her set of photos, there was visually nothing that looked remotely like a vagina, nor any photo of the silicon replicas of a penis that were stacked on the factory shelves. Anybody looking at her photos would have struggled to guess what the workers were doing on the assembly line. Were they packing a cylindrical biscuit tin? Or perhaps assembling a flashlight?

Given the 24-hour news cycle, the story was published first in the newspaper's Asia edition, where it made the front page of the business section. But later that day, after concerns were raised in New York about how the story would be received by an American readership, the story was pulled.

A few months later, *El Mundo*, a newspaper considered to have a conservative readership, also visited Fleshlight's factory. It then published an article headlined "The 338.000 vaginas per year of Dos Hermanas." The article had a main, frontal photo of pink artificial vaginas. In the background, the photo also showed a poster of the porn stars who promote Fleshlight. Fleshlight's owner, Shubin, had told me that "in America, we don't even like talking about sex in schools." It turned out to be also a difficult topic to discuss in a liberal American newsroom.

Since 2018, the feminist Metoo movement has gathered significant strength, but not everywhere at the same pace or in the same way. The indictment of the film producer Harvey Weinstein in 2018, on rape charges, was followed by a plethora of similar accusations in the United States. In Spain, however, hardly a male celebrity had come under the spotlight for sexual misbehavior at the time of writing this book. The response to accusations has also differed.

In August 2019, the tenor Plácido Domingo found himself accused of sexual misconduct by several women and was quickly pushed out of the American music scene. Major opera houses canceled his assignments and Domingo resigned two months later as director general of the Los Angeles opera. But throughout the summer, he continued to perform to wild applause at the Salzburg Festival and other major European events. Upon returning to Valencia's opera house, he received a hero's welcome.

Still, Spanish women have recently taken part in some of the world's largest demonstrations to mark International Women's Day, on March 8. They also took to the streets in large numbers to protest specific court rulings and voice their frustration against what they viewed to be a bias legal system, which offered women insufficient protection against sex assault. Such protests probably helped win an appeal before the Supreme Court in June 2019, which overruled the more lenient sentencing for sex abuse, handed down by a lower court in Pamplona, against a group of men known as the "manada," or wolf pack, who had attacked a woman. Instead, the Supreme Court found the men guilty of raping the woman during Pamplona's world famous festival of the running of the bulls.

The crusade by women against Spain's patriarchal judiciary has been closely watched in America. Some of my stories about the Pamplona attack were among my most read. My article in October 2019 about a similar gang sex assault — on an unconscious teenager at a party in Manresa — was also read by over 150,000 people, 80 percent of whom were subscribers in the United States, according to the data that the newspaper collects.

Sex, of course, is only one of the issues over which attitudes vary across the world. What might be considered a political or racial affront in Canada is perhaps tolerable in the Middle East. The fight against climate change has been not gaining the same traction in every country and government, as was shown by the standoff over forest fires in the Amazon in 2019 between Jair Bolsonaro of Brazil and Emmanuel Macron of France. Issues like the environment are also often impacted by election switches in administration, like that from the presidency of Barack Obama to Donald Trump or, more locally, like that in 2019 in the Madrid city hall, once a right-wing mayor took over from Manuela Carmena, after campaigning against her no-driving "Madrid Central" zone.

The treatment of history has also become more complex, in a world in which more and more people resent their past being viewed through an American or European lens. I once got a complaint from a reader in Brazil about an article that talked about the relationship between Portugal and Brazil and in which I mentioned that Brazil was a former Portuguese colony. The reader noted that Brazil was declared independent in 1822, only a few decades after American independence. But when did an American newspaper write an article that described the United States as a former colony of England?

One people's hero can be another's villain. In my book on Catalonia, I wrote about how some people in Barcelona wanted to stop celebrating Christopher Columbus and even perhaps remove his statue, which dominates Barcelona's seafront. I listened to complaints about honoring Columbus from some Catalan separatists, but also from a Peruvian artist and other Latin Americans who were upset about the celebration of Spanish imperialism.

In March 2019, I followed the debate sparked by Mexico's president, Andrés Manuel López Obrador, who wrote to King Felipe VI and Pope Francis asking them to acknowledge the brutality of the Spanish conquest. Pablo Casado, the leader of the conservative Popular Party, described the Mexican demand as an affront to the Spanish people. Spain, he said, should instead celebrate "with pride" its historical role in Mexico, "the way great nations do it, those that have contributed to the discovery of other people."

Later that year, to mark the 500th anniversary of the launch of the world's first circumnavigation, Spain celebrated Juan Sebastián Elcano, the sailor who completed the journey and managed to bring his ship back to Spain.

I visited Getaria, Elcano's birthplace, and wrote an article about how Spain also wanted to use the celebration to put Elcano on an equal footing to Ferdinand Magellan, the Portuguese leader of the expedition, who was killed half-way through the trip. But there was also a more local dimension that added another layer of complexity to this story, because Getaria's town hall was at the time run by a mayor from EH Bildu, who had boycotted a sailing commemoration centered on the four-masted Juan Sebastián de Elcano, a famous training ship of the Spanish Navy. In the Basque Country, there were plenty of nationalist politicians and historians who were unhappy that Elcano was being showcased as Spanish rather than Basque.

After I filed my story, an editor in New York called me to ask whether there was no discussion in Spain about how the circumnavigation was seen from the perspective of indigenous people, who suffered the imperial ambitions of Spain and Portugal. I told her that, although Spain and Portugal were preparing dozens of events to commemorate this landmark journey, none of the officials I spoke to had mentioned to me the destructive colonial dimension of this extraordinary journey.

I was grateful for the editor's view and added some paragraphs that made specific reference to this wider perspective of history, which I feel is little acknowledged in Spain. For instance, Lapu-Lapu, the ruler whose troops killed Magellan, now has a city named after him and is celebrated in the Philippines as a hero of resistance to European imperialism. *The New York Times* is a global newspaper operating in a world where sensitivities differ.

SOCIETY

Drogas sin violencia
La vía de escape de Barbate en plena crisis

In 2011, I visited Barbate, a coastal town of Andalusia, to report about drugs trafficking. But the first problem I encountered there had to do with law enforcement, rather than criminality. Barbate's main police station was filled with officers complaining that, if anyone wanted them to stop drugs, they should first get paid.

I didn't even have to speak to these policemen to know that they were disgruntled. Their frustration was posted on the walls of their police station, for any visitor to see. In the reception area, the officers had pinned a hand-written poster that read "they owe us April," to complain about the late payment of their salaries.

"It's a disastrous and chaotic situation here," Rafael Romero, one of the officers, told me, as soon as I asked him how things were going in Barbate. Romero was indignant that police officers were expected to do a good job when they were getting paid late, or possibly not at all. He also had a long list of other demands. "We need more boats, vehicles and everything, but there's not even money to repair our two broken surveillance cameras," he said. At the time, Barbate seemed to be caught in a perfect storm. The financial crisis had crippled the town hall's finances, a faltering fishing industry was exacerbating one of Spain's worst unemployment situations and the only profitable business in town seemed to be drugs trafficking, thanks to Barbate's proximity to North Africa.

Only a 40-minute boat ride separates Barbate and the beaches of Morocco, from where significant quantities of drugs are sent to supply European consumers. Most of this drug is Moroccan-grown hashish, which is generally carried in light but powerful rubber boats that can ride big waves. In the nearby town of Conil, I visited a pound operated by the Guardia Civil, where the police stored vehicles under judicial investigation. In a shed, rubber boats with large outboard motors had been stacked up four-high. Since the start of the financial crisis, a Guardia Civil officer told me that the drug business was thriving. "Those who control the drugs used to have other legal businesses, but the crisis has wiped out those businesses, so they're back focusing on the drugs," he said.

In Barbate, some of the frustrated police officers had harsh words for the local politicians. They blamed them for failing to acknowledge the size of the drugs problem and instead almost halve police staffing in Barbate compared to a decade earlier, as part of budgetary cuts. "I invite any politician who is claiming that the drugs problem is under control to come and tell me that to my face," said José Manuel Jiménez, a 44-year old who had joined the local police force 15 years earlier.

Some policemen also questioned why Spain could not stop the drugs trafficking, even though an upgraded system of infrared camera surveillance had been installed along its southern coast, to monitor boats traveling from North Africa to Andalusia. "Why so much chocolate is still getting through is something that I just can't understand," said Jiménez, the policeman, using "chocolate" as the common slang term for hashish. "There must be stronger interests behind the drugs trafficking and more money to be made" than from illegal migration, he suggested. Occasionally, the drugs smuggling around Barbate had also been of a more serious kind than hashish. A few months before my visit, the Guardia Civil had arrested five people in Barbate as part of a nationwide investigation into a cocaine and heroine network.

I had not expected police officers to speak so openly with me about their problems. I next wanted to hear from the politicians. Barbate's mayor, Rafael Quirós, told me that as many as 300 of his town's 22,000 citizens were sitting in jail after getting sentenced for drugs trafficking. Meanwhile, he had a debt pile of 50 million euros, as a result of unchecked spending during Spain's economic boom. The central government in Madrid, he said, "wants us to pay back 30 million euros in the next 10 years, but that's just an impossible schedule if basic services are to be maintained."

Quirós acknowledged that the drugs activity had revived since the start of the financial crisis, although it remained below what it was around the start of this century, when "there was just complete impunity here." He added: "You can nowadays get sentenced to five years in jail, so it does make some people think twice, however desperate their economic situation."

We talked at length about how Spanish society suffered from a strong sense of impunity, which made some people move for themselves the boundaries between what they considered criminal and acceptable.

But I also told him about I had seen that an effective legal crack-down could help change attitudes within a society quickly. When I first visited Spain as a holidaying teenager, I saw some people drive home from a nightclub so drunk that they could hardly fit their key into the car door. I was now back in a Spain where drink-driving was limited to the very foolhardy, willing to risk the loss of their license and a huge fine.

Similarly, a few months before visiting Barbate, I had reported on the public debate that had been generated by Parliament's approval of a ban on smoking in bars and restaurants. Before the *ley antitabaco* was introduced, in January 2011, some prominent intellectuals criticized it vehemently, in the name of the "principle of liberty" and the individual right to smoke. Soon enough, a few establishments proudly declared themselves *"bar piratas,"* raising their flag in defiance of the smoking ban. They then either got heavy fines or had their licenses suspended, and I soon stopped hearing about whether the law was an attack on "the fundamental rights of Spanish society." My Spanish smoking friends now quietly step outside for a few puffs, just like they do in most other Western countries.

But from Barbate, Quirós had fueled a slightly different national debate about the limits of criminality, after newspapers picked up his controversial comments about drugs. During an election campaign, the mayor had suggested that a young drug-dealer who could not find legal employment should not automatically be called a delinquent. When we met in his town hall office, Quirós told me that Spain's real problem was clearly not drugs trafficking, but the fact that a young person could not find work. "A youngster has absolutely zero chance right now of finding a fixed job here," he told me.

Quirós also questioned how Spain was defining its black economy, and why the authorities were doing so little about enforcing some basic laws if this underground economy was really considered a big problem. Earlier that year, Valeriano Gómez, Spain's labor and immigration minister, had estimated that Spain's underground economy was equivalent to about 20 percent of its gross domestic product. But in Barbate, Quirós calculated that the underground economy represented about 40 percent of the local GDP, and for the most part had nothing to do with drugs. Some residents, Quirós explained, had become "professionals at living off

115

social security" and other benefits, even though they were holding a temporary job on the side. Others were enlisting in work training programs for the sake of getting subsidies, acquiring skills that they knew would never give them a fixed job.

The job landscape certainly looked bleak. Andalusia suffered at the time from the highest unemployment among Spain's 17 regions, with a jobless rate of 32 percent. That was almost three times higher than the average in the European Union. Barbate itself was the town with the second-highest joblessness in mainland Spain, according to national statistics, only behind Ubrique, another Andalusian town whose traditional leather manufacturing activities had been shrinking. Quirós felt that it was not for him to tackle the black economy. But he assured me that he was working hard to create jobs and also reduce Barbate's reliance on fishing, a steadily declining industry that still represented 60 percent of the town's economy. The financial crisis accelerated the decline, he said, because Spanish consumers switched to cheaper food than fish.

Over the next two days, I met plenty of people in the kind of "idle but livable" situation that the mayor had described. I had a coffee with Joaquín Gil Narváez, a 23-year old who wanted to work in the fishing industry but had instead been jobless for two years. "The problem of Barbate is that there are plenty of guys like me who have work experience, but none of which ever came with a proper work contract," he told me. He had recently enrolled in a course to get a boat captain's license, while relying on his unemployment subsidies and living in his mother's home. His course was due to last 605 hours. "There's no future in fishing around here, but the course is free and it's at least something to keep myself busy," he said, shrugging his shoulders.

Was there no other kind of business that Barbate could develop? Quirós listed a few projects, among them a light bulb factory that could employ about 200 people. But overall, the mayor concluded, "this isn't exactly the easiest time to find investors." As long as the job situation stayed so gloomy, Quirós expected young residents to continue to turn to drugs trafficking as their only viable alternative, in a town where the official rate of youth unemployment stood then at a staggering 60 percent. "The politicians in Madrid who consider my views on youngsters occasionally dealing drugs to be those of a caveman either don't understand or don't care about how much people are struggling here," Quirós said.

Quirós' empathy must have struck a chord with voters. Shortly before my visit, he was one of the few Socialist mayors of Andalusia to win re-election. But not everybody in Barbate agreed about the scale of the drugs problem. Miguel Molina, the local leader of a regional political force known as the Andalusian Party, suggested that the mayor was using the drugs problem to avoid discussing his other failures. "Some people seem determined to give Barbate a bad reputation, but in all my life here, I have never once been offered drugs," he told me.

Five minutes from Molina's party headquarters, however, I walked into a neighborhood that seemed to be a hub for drug dealers. At one of its street intersections, I spotted above my head a pair of shoes hanging off an electricity cable. A police officer had told me that shoes were used by drug dealers to indicate points of sale.

On Calle Vejer, two young men parked right in front of me their shiny black BMW, equipped with powerful loudspeakers that blared music from the boot. After hesitating for a short while, I engaged the driver in conversation and congratulated him on having a beautiful car. He sniggered and said that he had bought his BMW by doing good business. After a pause, he added: "By selling drugs, of course." There were a few other impressive cars parked along the street, surrounded by young people chatting and smoking. Like the BMW driver, several openly admitted to drugs dealing. One even offered me a sample of his hashish.

Although it took some effort to get them to talk, a few of the dealers eventually opened up. Paco, a 30-year old with a bright pink tee-shirt and a frog tattooed on his neck, told me about how he had moved from helping dealer friends to selling drugs himself. In early 2006, along with ten other men, Paco was arrested while trying to smuggle into Barbate a boatload of 600 kilos of hashish. He was sentenced to three years and nine months in prison. Since his release, he had not found a job and instead relied on "all sorts of things" to keep going, as well as maintain his two young daughters. Even though he had spent time in prison for trafficking drugs, he was unrepentant. If anything, he said, he had come out of jail knowing how to "handle this better."

He also walked me through the strong economics of drugs. The retail price of hashish had climbed to about 2000 euros per kilo, up from 800 euros when he entered jail in 2006. "Just name me one

117

other thing that I could now sell so easily and for that kind of money," he asked me defiantly.

As I finally left Barbate, I couldn't help thinking that perhaps the weirdest aspect of its drugs trafficking was how peaceful and relaxed it felt. Local business owners and the police had also told me that there was no evidence of a surge in criminality. Except for the few flashy cars and their tattooed occupants, Calle Vejer felt like any other street in the province of Cádiz. "Drugs is seen as a way to make money and survive in this disastrous economy, but it doesn't mean that people have become nasty or violent here," Narciso Corrales, the owner of a local café, told me.

I had approached the owner of the BMW with some apprehension. But he seemed nonplussed by my arrival, as did most of the other drug dealers I met that afternoon, even once I had identified myself as a journalist rather than a potential client. I was working alongside a photographer, Laura León, and her presence also didn't ruffle feathers. Some of the dealers asked not be photographed, but she was skillful enough to convince a few others to show off in front of her camera their tattoos and designer sneakers. This really didn't feel like an encounter with hardened criminals, even though some of the people whom I interviewed had already spent years in prison.

I have found myself reporting in other troubled cities or neighborhoods of Spain with surprisingly little difficulty. In April 2015, I visited Algeciras with León to find people who knew Ayoub El Khazzani, a man who had boarded a week earlier the high-speed train that runs between Amsterdam and Paris, armed with an assault rifle. Only the fortuitous presence of some off-duty American army men and other brave passengers prevented him from going ahead with a mass shooting.

I was walking into an Algeciras neighborhood where everybody knew about the train attack and the unwanted media spotlight that it had brought onto their community. But I still managed to meet the gunman's distressed father, who spoke to me on the doorstep of his run-down apartment and came close to tears as he explained how he could not believe his son had planned a bloodbath. I also talked to several other people who had worshiped alongside him at a local mosque, or instead played football with him in the evenings. Some of my questions about how radical Islamic thinking had reached Algeciras made the conversations very tense. León, the photographer, also got an angry response from some men who didn't want her to take any pictures in their neighborhood. But we somehow managed to put together a story, with great photos, even at a time when the local Muslim community was very wary about media coverage.

Of course, places can change quickly. A few years after my story on the drugs trade in Barbate, the situation there and in other towns of the Cádiz province became more tense after police officers were injured while confronting drug gangs. León told me that the drug gangs had made it near-impossible to take the kind of portrait photos that she took of Barbate's drug dealers in 2011.

At the time of writing this book, stories about traffickers fighting to control the arrival of drugs in the Campo de Gibraltar continue to fill the pages of Spanish newspapers, despite a *"Plan Especial de Seguridad"* for the area that was put into place by the Socialist government in August 2018, shortly after it took office. In the following 18 months, police intercepted over 200 tonnes of drugs and detained over 7,000 people, which is worrying evidence that the Campo is a crime hotspot.

But still, my visit to Barbate confirmed one of the more surprising observations that I made while Spain sunk into financial crisis. Many people were involved in criminal activities, from the trafficking of drugs to that of prostitutes, but overall, the country's violent crime statistics had not worsened, even as Spain's unemployment rate climbed to a record 27 percent.

Some foreigners visiting Madrid had asked me whether they should worry about street violence, given the surge in joblessness. How safe was Spain at a time of economic distress? I always did my best to reassure them. The stories about Spain's economic downturn were real, but this did not mean that Madrid or any other city had become a place where people had to fear constantly for their belongings, let alone their physical safety. I remember being struck by how many people walked home alone very late at night in Madrid, after an evening of drinking and partying. Sometimes, I have seen women walk barefoot, holding their high-heeled shoes in their hand, after a long night out. I remember thinking that I would be fearing for their safety if this scene took place in many other big cities of Europe and the United States.

Comparative crime studies always tend to favor Spain. During the financial crisis, some even suggested that violent crime was falling. Even without looking at the numbers, I use a simple litmus test as a journalist, which is to look at what gets reported in the local media. In many cities around the world, sadly, incidents like supermarket robberies or carjackings no longer make the local news. In Madrid and other parts of Spain, thankfully, they still do.

La limosna del rico
La endeble cultura de la filantropía española

In May 2019, the foundation of Amancio Ortega, Spain's richest man, offered to donate about 310 million euros to hospitals to buy medical equipment and help Spain's fight against cancer. The donation was not welcomed by everybody. Pablo Iglesias, the leader of Unidas Podemos, wrote on Twitter that "a dignified democracy should not accept alms from multimillionaires to boost its health system."

I was struck by the debate that followed. After all, several countries do not have as strong a health system as Spain's, but nevertheless consider themselves to be solid democracies. And in many places, philanthropy is not only welcomed but also clearly encouraged.

Anybody who has visited the United States knows that it has become hard to find a sports stadium, a museum gallery, a university building or a theater that does not bear the name of one or several generous donors. In 2010, two of America's richest men, Warren Buffett and Bill Gates, launched their Giving Pledge campaign, to encourage wealthy people to give at least half of their net worth to philanthropy, either during their lifetime or upon their death. By 2019, they had convinced about 200 other wealthy individuals or couples to join them, which amounted to a combined pledge to donate more than $500 billion.

Such American philanthropy is an appeal to the heart and the generosity of the wealthy. But it also taps into their ego and vanity. The list of those on the Giving Pledge campaign is public information and the names of donors are often engraved in golden letters on the buildings that they sponsor. Just as importantly, American philanthropy draws on financial common sense. The wealthy know that a gifted dollar is one that can be deducted from their tax bill.

This is a model that other countries can replicate, and some have been doing just that. But in Spain, philanthropy remains in its infancy. Over the past decade, I have followed a political debate that has taken place on and off, over the law of patronage (*Ley de Mecenazgo*), which should set a new fiscal arrangement to encourage people to make cultural donations in return for a tax rebate.

At the time of writing this book, the law remained on the shelf, despite the efforts of some politicians and pressure from museum and theater directors who have been demanding tax rebates to help their institutions stay afloat, also as a substitute for reduced state subsidies. But even during the years of the conservative government of Mariano Rajoy, this idea ran into firm opposition from Cristóbal Montoro, his treasury minister. As a result, institutions like the Prado museum and the Teatro Real opera house have used financial vehicles to allow them to tap into overseas donations, notably from the United States. The Teatro Real, for instance, uses an American foundation, set up in the state of Delaware by a Miami-based lawyer, to allow American citizens to get tax breaks on donations made to the foundation. The foundation then transfers the money to Madrid's opera house. In the Prado and its other painting museums, Madrid displays some of the best artwork in the world, admired by millions of visitors every year. On the other hand, it also has some amazing works that are privately owned and almost impossible for the public to view, even when housed in structures that resemble a museum.

I once got to accompany a group of British art lovers on a visit of the collection of Juan Miguel Villar Mir, which is assembled in a beautiful space at the top of the Madrid skyscraper that is also the home of his family's construction company, OHL (*Obrascón Huarte Lain*). I could not believe that this art was only shown on special occasions to outsiders, including of course the business partners of OHL.

In November 2012, I visited the Liria Palace in Madrid, which belongs to the Alba family, arguably the most famous name in Spanish aristocracy. My guide was Carlos Fitz-James Stuart y Martínez de Irujo, who was then the family heir and Duke of Huéscar. I was invited to see the family's art collection shortly before 150 of its works would get showcased in a temporary exhibition held in the gallery space within Madrid's city hall, the

Cibeles Palace. The Duke was clearly proud that some of the family's collection would for the first time go on public display. When I asked him why such an initiative was not taken before, he said that "My mother was very afraid of letting things go out." But, he added, "People evolve, circumstances change, and we have convinced her."

Looking around the sumptuous palace, it seemed clear to me that the Cibeles exhibition would be successful. The Alba family owns several of the most precious items in Spain's cultural and historical heritage, some intimately connected to the family itself, like Francisco Goya's portrait of the *Duchess of Alba, The White Duchess*. Beside all their paintings and sculptures, the Alba family also has the largest number of handwritten manuscripts from Christopher Columbus, including his drawing of the coastline of Hispaniola, the first island that he reached in the Americas. The Albas inherited them after a descendant of the explorer married into the family.

The Alba exhibition took place during the worst year of Spain's banking crisis, at a time when public museums were facing budgetary squeezing. After his mother's death, the Duke was true to his words, opening gradually the family's properties to the public, including the Liria palace, which started organizing daily guided tours in September 2019. But the change of attitude in the Alba household has remained an exception rather than the norm, even if a few other families have followed the same path. Two years after the Alba show, I returned to the Cibeles Palace to admire 160 great works on loan from the collection of Juan Abelló and his wife. It was also their first major public show.

Such family gestures are noteworthy in Spain, in contrast to the United States where museums inherit or get loaned works regularly by private collectors. I have also been struck by the comparison between the aristocracy of Spain and Britain. In Britain, cash-strapped aristocratic families have long made a business out of renting their estates for private events, converting them into hotels or opening them to visitors at weekends. In Spain, again, being able to visit a private palace or estate is an anomaly.

I started asking some culture experts about why philanthropy was so weak in Spain. One of them was José Guirao Cabrera, whom I got to know as the director of *La Casa Encendida* in Madrid, but then became Spain's culture minister in 2018.

Guirao talked to me about the mismatch between the concepts of giving and receiving in Spain. While philanthropists were hard to find, society continued to expect the government and other public authorities to showcase the country's culture for free, since it is maintained with taxpayers' money. Part of Spain's problem, he explained, was that when public money started to run out during the financial crisis, every institution was left scrambling to find substitute private funding. "Moving Spanish culture away from its reliance on the state is proving a very difficult transition," he said.

Because of the changes brought about by Spain's banking crisis, his own cultural center, *La Casa Encendida*, started charging two euros for a concert ticket, instead of offering such events for free. There was a silver lining to this change, however, as it allowed *La Casa Encendida* to forecast accurately how big its audience would be. When entrance had been free, many people would book their concert tickets, but then make alternative plans and never come. *La Casa Encendida* would end up with empty seats.

"Spain has been living in the *cultura del gratis*, in which people also behave without thinking about the impact on others," Guirao said. "Two euros is only the price of a beer, but almost nobody who has paid money will then not show up."

As for the willingness of the rich to share their artwork with a wider audience, "I know some Spanish families with great collections who have never lent anything at all," Guirao told me at the time of the Alba exhibition. Elena Ochoa Foster, who runs IvoryPress, a Madrid art gallery and publishing house, talked to me about how Spain was losing some of its artwork because more families were auctioning paintings abroad, to get higher valuations. On the other hand, Spanish collectors prefer to buy their works in countries like Britain that apply no value added taxation on art purchases, rather than acquire them in Spain at an added rate of 21 percent. Some important artwork is then not shown because its owners never declare it fiscally. A curator once ran me through a list of very wealthy Spaniards whom she knew had masterpieces undeclared.

Unexpected events have sometimes shed light on the unexpected ways in which some of the wealthy keep their collection. In 2001, Esther Koplowitz was the victim of a house robbery in which several paintings worth millions were stolen. Investigators were surprised to find out that most of her stolen paintings had not even been insured. When Spain's tax agency intervenes, its inspectors can strike forcefully. In 2015, police raided a boat in Italian waters and seized a Picasso portrait owned by the banker Jaime Botín. He was then charged and found guilty of illegally smuggling the masterpiece out of Spain. At the time of writing, Botín was appealing against a prison sentence of 18 months and a fine of 52 million euros, while his confiscated Picasso was languishing in the warehouse of a Madrid museum. Again, the comments I have heard about Botín's painting have suggested to me that Spain is a country that has a very advanced concept of social solidarity and egalitarianism, while keeping a complicated relationship with wealth. There is plenty of inherited family money in Spain, but it does not generate the perception that its owners are trying to help society, even though many have set up charitable foundations.

The connection between the state and culture was reinforced during the construction boom, in part because money was plentiful, but also because of the so-called "Guggenheim factor." After Bilbao successfully inaugurated its Guggenheim museum in 1997, almost every city in Spain decided that a flagship cultural project would guarantee its tourism status and urban revival. Some projects were successful, but just as many proved disastrous, leaving Spain littered with uncompleted or unvisited buildings. In a country that does not punish severely cost overruns, it all ended up costing far more than budgeted, whether for fraudulent reasons or not. The politicians certainly never picked up the bill.

Yet, however costly the outcome, I have rarely heard local residents voice shame or sadness at the fact that public money was used to add an expensive and underused museum to their city. The view seems to be that, once something is built, it might as well be appreciated. There is no point crying over spilt milk.

I have heard such expressions of tolerance across Spain, from Santiago de Compostela and its Cultural City — inaugurated in 2011 with only two of its planned six buildings – to Valencia, where high winds ripped off part of the roof of the opera house and forced its temporary closure in 2013, only eight years after it was inaugurated, as part of the Pharaonic works of the City of Arts and Sciences complex designed by architect Santiago Calatrava.

Why are Spaniards more forgiving toward collective waste or failure rather than individual setbacks? In general, like in many other Europeans, I have found that Spaniards do not really value individual success (outside a few areas like sports.) And they certainly do not worship failure, unlike Americans who often see it as a badge of honor on the path toward professional glory. When successful American businessmen give speeches about their track record, they love to mention all that went wrong before they got it right. Or they like to talk about famous examples, like that of Sam Walton, whose first store was declared bankrupt and left him penniless. Walton, of course, recovered to develop instead America's largest retailer, WalMart.

Philanthropic money can draw controversy in America too, and the backlash against disgraced donors can be stunning. America's opioid crisis ensured that the Sackler family became persona non grata in the museum world, even though they had financed major institutions for decades. The divorce was prompted by public fury over the fact that the family's pharmaceutical company made OxyContin, an opioid drug. In 2019, New York's Metropolitan Museum of Art announced that it would no longer accept gifts from the Sackler family, thereby ending its relationship with one of its most important philanthropic families. One of the wings of the Metropolitan museum was named after the Sackler family and is home to one of its main treasures, the ancient Temple of Dendur.

But producing drugs that kill Americans is not the same as Inditex using tax loopholes, or for that matter using cheap Asian labor to make some of its clothing (while also paying thousands of factory employees in Spain, Portugal and Morocco).

When I arrived in Spain, Ortega was the only first-generation owner of a company that was listed in the Ibex35 index, which reflected well on him but poorly on the country's culture of entrepreneurship. Instead, much of the rest of the Ibex35 membership had once been directly owned by the state. But his cancer donation sparked a debate, particularly heated on social media, in which Ortega was sometimes presented as a corporate criminal, accused of stealing from the state by not paying fully his taxes. How could this backlash encourage any other rich person to follow his example?

A friend once lent me a book to help understand what she called "the Cainism of Spain." Written by Miguel de Unamuno in 1917, *Abel Sánchez: The History of a Passion* is more than a reinterpretation of the Biblical story of Cain and Abel. Unamuno also felt compelled to add a striking prologue to the second edition, in which he wrote about his return to Spain, after five years abroad, to find that envy had become "the national leprosy." Two decades after writing *Abel Sánchez*, Unamuno died, isolated and discredited by Franco in his beloved Salamanca, amidst a civil war that showcased the worst of Spain, including much of the envy that Unamuno had identified.

Spain also has a deeply egalitarian streak that notably brought about the 1932 agrarian reform that the short-lived Second Republic sought to implement. In the summer of 2012, I found myself reporting a story that felt like a journey back in time, as I joined a group of protestors in the sun-baked farming heartland of Andalusia. In Madrid, officials had just agreed the terms of a European banking bailout. In Andalusia, hundreds of jobless farmworkers wanted the government to save them and their jobs, rather than the bankers. They believed Spain needed to change urgently its economic model and focus on those who really fed the country.

For weeks, I had been in touch with representatives of the Andalusian Union of Workers, while following in the national media the outbursts of Juan Manuel Sánchez Gordillo, the left-wing mayor of the farming town of Marinaleda. Sánchez Gordillo had somehow managed to convert himself into the Robin Hood of Spain, even though he was an elected politician who made controversial usage of public subsidies for housing and was in fact openly breaking the law. He had even helped coordinate food raids on supermarkets, after which the police detained some other participants and charged them for robbery with violence.

I wanted to meet him and the other leaders of this struggle that sounded like a return to the class conflict from a century earlier. I spoke to my editor about this, who sounded both fascinated and incredulous. How come this mayor isn't also in jail? he asked me.

My editor asked for a story as soon as possible. The Andalusian Union of Workers told me that I should wait to visit once they were ready to stage another of their special protest actions. The following week, somebody from the Union called to tell me to travel immediately to Andalusia. I took the Ave high-speed train to Seville, where the photographer Laura León was waiting for me in the car park of the station. It was early evening by the time we reached a farmhouse in the middle of nowhere, which was occupied by protestors. They were busy picking fruit and other produce from its orchard and vegetable garden and they then started to prepare dinner. We ate some deliciously fresh food, but spent a very uncomfortable and short night.

The switch in scenery felt extraordinary. I had left Spain's modern capital and traveled on one of the most efficient train networks in the world to find myself only a few hours later plunged into revolution-related conversations that sounded like those I had read in books about life in rural Spain ahead of the civil war.

At about 5 a.m., we drove to a near-by town, where hundreds of other people had already gathered. Some were busy preparing their protest banners, as well as consolidating the edges of an imposing and worn-down Republican flag. We then started out on the road, forming a long column. I moved up-and-down, doing my best to interview protestors while keeping up with the walking pace. Along the way, I had long conversations with Diego Cañamero, the leader of the Andalusian Union of Workers, and later on with Sánchez Gordillo, whose beard and necktie had already given him one of Spain's most recognized faces.

We walked for hours, the heat was getting worse and it was lunchtime. Nobody would tell me where we were going. Eventually, the column came to a stop and the organizers ordered everybody to fold their flags and protest banners. I could see nothing special around us, except for a long fence that was running alongside the road. A few minutes later, some people started running toward a hole in this fence, and everybody else followed and broke into the enclosure. We had trespassed into an enormous private property called the Palacio de Moratalla. But its owner, the Duke of Segorbe, was not there to welcome us and instead was living about one hour away, in Seville.

The next few hours delivered a surreal spectacle, to the delight of León, who took photos that could have been shot on the set of a movie. To me, it felt like a modern version of the French Revolution, perhaps blended in with scenes from the hacienda in Viridiana, one of the masterpieces of Luis Buñuel. The protesting farmers dive-bombed into the duke's swimming pool and splashed around in the water to cool down. They prepared a paella and played cards in the shade of the pink palace's terrace. They drank beer while listening to Cañamero deliver a speech in which he lambasted the Spanish aristocracy "who leaves such places to waste," while farm workers across Andalusia can no longer find a job that earns them a decent living.

I expected to see at anytime the Swiss guards come out to fight them, as they tried in the Tuileries palace of Louis XVI in 1792. Instead, a small contingent from the Civil Guard arrived at the palace, but waited patiently outside its gates. When León and I finally left the estate, the officers took down the details on our identity cards, warning us that we could get charged for violating private property. We were thankfully never charged. The Civil Guard waited for the last group of farmers to step out the following day, after spending the night in its beautiful gardens. Our article, with a set of fabulous photos by León, was published on the front page of the newspaper's international edition. The farmers' protest movement eventually died down, without ever facing a strong clampdown from the authorities, who also hesitated about taking action against the illegal occupiers of abandoned farmhouses.

Spain witnessed massive protests during the financial crisis, but never came close to the kind of downward spiral that brought about the civil war. In 2011, I spent weeks covering the rise of the 15-M movement and its unexpected occupation of Puerta del Sol, which helped inspire other similar protests elsewhere, including the Occupy Wall Street movement that began later that year. Watching people join the tent city on Puerta del Sol, the place was at times marked by organized chaos. It was a cacophony in which people vented their anger against the corrupt elites and rising inequality without always listening to the opinions of others. During those days Puerta del Sol certainly emanated incredible energy, while never looking likely to turn aggressive or violent. Three years later, Podemos was founded and initially grew very rapidly because its leaders were able to reactivate the protest feelings of the 15-M.

In Andalusia, the protesting farmers seemed to have a slightly different approach. They were worrying about their future, but also kept looking back at their history, drawing very clear parallels with the situation of their grandfathers, almost a century earlier. "We are not anarchists looking for conflict, but our claims are similar to those of the 1930s," Cañamero told me, "because the land is, unfortunately, under the control now of even fewer people than at that time."

I feel that the relationship between people and wealth varies from country to country, but also even slightly within Spain, reflecting its huge economic diversity. Anarchism grew in Barcelona once the city started to spearhead Spain's industrial revolution. The creation of the first labor unions came hand-in-hand with violence on the streets, which culminated in terrifying episodes like the Semana Trágica of 1909. In contrast, anarchism in Andalusia has historically revolved around the ownership of land because it is Spain's largest region and has long been the bread basket of the country.

I have also observed some differences in the way people display their wealth. The level of ostentation varies. For instance, in my encounters with rich Catalans, I have found that many almost share the Calvinist culture of the wealthy in my home city of Geneva. They tend to avoid gold watches, often drive themselves in a normal car, restore traditional fishing boats rather than acquire flamboyant yachts. When they display their wealth, it is mostly within the secure and private confines of their own house.

In Andalusia, in contrast, some newly-rich sought to live the lifestyle of the oil tycoons in the Dallas television series during Spain's boom years. I found a tragic example of this while reporting on a story about the illegal killing of horses. Many horses had been acquired by hacienda owners who wanted to gain rapidly and visibly the social status of landed gentry, but who could then no longer afford the upkeep of their beautiful animals once the property bubble burst. I worked on this story in 2013, shortly after police unearthed an illegal horse cemetery in the hills near Algeciras that contained the unidentifiable remains of around 20 horses.

There seems to be a tacit agreement, particularly among the Spanish left-wing electorate, that people can make money, but never on the back of others. The huge pile of political corruption cases that came to light after the bursting of the construction bubble particularly angered people, I feel, because it involved so much taxpayers' money.

I remember a long discussion with a freelance photographer who told me about the difficult financial balancing act that he kept facing. Some publications were not paying him on time for his photos, while his social security contribution had to be made on the same day of every month, as an autonomous worker. It was a tough situation, he said, but he had been willing to tighten his belt until he started reading almost daily about the massive bribes paid to politicians for the award of public work contracts. "Why should I continue to pay my taxes when I am not getting paid properly and others are then stealing my tax money?" he asked.

The alms of the wealthy

I have been fascinated by the yearly publication by the national tax agency of the list of the bad tax payers, who owe money to Spain, as part of a naming and shaming exercise that hopefully helps fill the coffers of the state, but also fuels the public debate over the flaws in the tax system. After the agency releases the list, every newspaper then publishes photos of famous people who owe tax money, along with a text that clearly delights in ridiculing them. In 2019, the newspaper *ABC* started its annual review of the famous bad tax payers, or *"morosos,"* by saying that "some have got to enjoy it and are doing it again, others are starting out while others are bidding farewell to the list." *ABC* made it sound as if tax evasion was a national competition, but I have also often wondered whether these celebrities then decide to cancel all their lunch appointments and stay home for a month.

After the Ortega donation was announced in 2019, I asked a friend who was a Podemos voter how she felt about it. I was hoping for a short answer, but instead heard the same kind of diatribe that I had got from the freelance photographer. In fact, my friend seemed to know details about Ortega's tax situation that I had never heard before. I found it weird that she sounded more upset about Ortega than her own problems at work, which led her to change jobs a few months later.

Ortega displayed generosity again during the coronavirus crisis, particularly by making available some of Inditex's cargo planes, normally reserved for the company's clothing orders from China. One of Spain's first shipments of emergency medical equipment landed in Zaragoza exactly one week after Spain was put under a state of emergency, in March 20. The Inditex plane carried much-needed face masks as well as medical suits, delivered on wooden pallets that had a message written on them, both in Mandarin and Castilian: "Although oceans separate us, the same moon unites us." In return for his contribution, Ortega got some of the daily applauses normally reserved by citizens to thank their medical workers. Perhaps the most poignant one was delivered by a cohort of ambulance drivers, who drove their vehicles one evening past Ortega's house in La Coruña and serenaded him with their sirens.

In many ways, the Covid-19 crisis brought to the forefront the grassroots solidarity and generosity that I have found in Spain, often on a far greater scale than in most other countries that I know. This is the topic of my next chapter.

Salto de vallas
Las puertas de la inmigración quedan al sur

In January 2018, I drove about one hour inland from Málaga, to a new prison built outside the town of Archidona. The prison was not yet officially opened, but it was already being misused.

Two months earlier, Spanish police had intercepted about 500 Algerian migrants who had crossed the Mediterranean by boat to the southeastern coast. Their arrival created a logistics problem for the authorities, at a time when more migrants were crossing to Spain rather than Italy, after Matteo Salvini and his Italian government closed off access to Italy's territorial waters. Spain's migrant detention centers, known as CIE (Centros de Internamiento de Extranjeros), were full, so the authorities turned Archidona's prison into a temporary home for the Algerians.

It was a cold day, but I had not expected to run into a snow storm by the time I crossed the hills surrounding Málaga. Still, braving the wind and thick fog, I found a small group of activists standing outside the prison entrance, holding protest banners. They had also painted slogans along the road to denounce the mistreatment of migrants. They told me that they kept vigil day and night, to stop the police from deporting the migrants. Every time a police bus left the prison, the activists tried to block it and check whether Algerians sat inside and were being driven to board a ship bound for Algeria.

There are brave and determined activists all over the world, fighting over issues ranging from climate change to sexual abuse. But what really struck me in Archidona was how much solidarity the town's inhabitants were displaying toward the imprisoned Algerians. After all, they had reached Spain illegally.

The prison was due to open soon and was designed to hold about 2,000 prisoners, with a staff of almost 600. For the nearby town, it represented an economic opportunity. Some residents in fact worried that the migrants could damage the prison's infrastructure even before its official opening.

To protest their detention, the migrants had recently been smashing windows and furniture. Riot police officers were dispatched to Archidona, but tensions rose after one migrant was found dead in his cell, strangled with a bedsheet, a few days after

Christmas. The police said an autopsy had confirmed a suicide, but activists and some local politicians were demanding a full investigation.

Mostly, the town's 8,400 residents seemed to care deeply about the wellbeing of the migrants rather than to worry about the prison turmoil. People helped collect food and clothing for the Algerians. The mayor, Mercedes Montero, told me that her people needed the prison jobs, but this did not mean that they wanted Spain to flout its human rights obligations by keeping migrants in a prison that had not yet even been equipped with a medical center and access to drinking water. "Nobody here wants Archidona to be a place where migrants get mistreated," she said. I added her comments to the long list of interviews in which I have been struck by the willingness of Spanish people to feel for the plight of others, even people from a different culture and a distant African land.

My visit to Archidona coincided with a worrying rise in anti-migration and xenophobic feelings across Europe. Eventually, such feelings would also come to the forefront in Spain. In fact, Vox made its electoral breakthrough eleven months later, in the December 2018 in the regional elections of Andalusia. Another eleven months later it had become the third-largest party in Spain, after winning 52 seats in Congress in a general election.

But neither the sudden rise of Vox nor some isolated incidents of racism have changed my perception that Spain is remarkably open and tolerant. When I was studying in England, I often went on holiday to Spain. During the 1980s, my parents owned an apartment-share in Ibiza. Of course, I was among thousands of other foreign tourists, but I was struck by the homogeneity of Spain, as a white and Catholic society. When I returned in 2010, Spain had been transformed by the arrival of about five million migrants during a decade-long property boom. Once the housing bubble burst and the jobs dried up, many left Spain. But no Spanish politician was telling them to get out, nor were their neighbors, even in the cities that had the highest unemployment.

In contrast, the financial crisis triggered many social tensions and changes, including unfortunately a rise in xenophobia in several other European countries, some of which already had large and established migrant communities. In 2015, the Greek island of Lesbos became the epicenter of the Syrian refugee crisis, moving migration further up on the EU agenda. This migration crisis sadly strained the EU's political cohesion, even when debating human rights that all EU member states were meant to defend.

Over this past decade, I have read stories filed by correspondents about racism and anti-Semitism across most of Europe, whether in the form of violent attacks or vile acts like the desecration of Jewish graves. Such events have been common place from the France of Marine Le Pen and the Italy of Matteo Salvini to Hungary, Poland and the other former Communist countries. But in Spain and Portugal, people took to the streets after the financial crisis to protest against almost everything except the presence of foreigners. During this decade, Spanish opinion surveys have repeatedly showed that only a small proportion of Spaniards felt hostility toward migrants. In February 2017, Barcelona staged the largest demonstration in Europe in favor of Syrian refugees, with protesters demanding that the Spanish government welcome more of them.

Of course, Spain has at times struggled in its response to illegal migration, like in Archidona. Over recent years, I also witnessed several disturbing scenes related to migration, including in the port town of Tarifa. During one reporting trip, the photographer Laura León and I watched the cat-and-mouse encounter between Spanish police officers and two Moroccans who were stowaways and jumped off a ferry as it entered the port. They then swam toward the pontoon, but were spotted by port officials who alerted the police. When the police officers ordered them to come out, the Moroccans hid instead for two hours in the waters below the pontoon's platform, until the rising tide came close to drowning them.

During another trip to Tarifa, we visited an overcrowded sports complex that had been transformed into a makeshift refugee center. On its basketball court, exhausted migrants were slowly recovering from their frightening boat journey, wrapped in blankets provided by the Red Cross. As we finished our harrowing visit, we found a group of tourists just outside the sports center, who were watching the sunset while laughing and sipping caipirinhas, completely unaware of the human distress housed in the sports center next to them. It seemed to me a telling example of a digital world in which we sometimes learn quicker about a tragedy unfolding on the other side of the world than the one on our doorstep.

It can be hard to write about a subject like migration without falling into cliches, making sweeping generalizations or reheating oversold stories. When looking at the world, the media also often tries to draw broad brushed conclusions that can be presented to readers in a clear and impactful way.

While working in Europe in the 1990s, I remember following many stories about the development of Asia that talked about the continent as if it was a monolith. Western newspapers warned about the rise of Asian exports, weak Asian labor laws or counterfeiting in Asia. When I later moved to Hong Kong to become the regional correspondent for Asia at the *Financial Times*, I soon understood that it was very hard to write any story that even fitted my job description. Asia had limited regional integration. Exports were rising, but not at the same pace and in the same sectors everywhere, which made it hard to write anything that did not sound simplistic or confusing. The labor laws varied, as did the production costs. Counterfeiting was also not a major trend everywhere, and it was a lot more sophisticated in places like China than Indonesia. Much of my reporting ended up focusing on differences within Asia, rather than highlighting the homogeneity of Asia.

Within the European Union, politicians love to talk about their common goals and principles, which naturally helps fuel the idea that American readers should receive stories "about Europe." This approach works sometimes, but not always.

A famous joke about journalism is that nobody should ever let facts get in the way of a good story. When it came to migration, Spain did not fit perfectly into some of the broader stories that *The New York Times* was chronicling, and sometimes I could not even explain to my editors just why this was the case. Of course, Spain's proximity to Africa made it a major port of call for migrants. But apart from some sporadic incidents, like clashes between Spanish police officers and African street vendors, Spain was not turning into a hub of race-related tensions. Thankfully, no editor ever encouraged me to exaggerate events in order to fit the script. On the contrary.

As a correspondent, there is also always the risk to repeat the same explanations, without being really sure whether they still hold. In Spain, there is some truth to the notion that politicians did not attack migrants because far-right rhetoric was stigmatized by the decades of Franco's dictatorship.

But then came Vox, whose rise is probably too new to undergo a reliable and complete analysis. In February 2019, I visited

El Ejido, to write an analysis of why Vox had just come top and won almost 30 percent of the votes in the municipality in the Andalusian elections. I heard from El Ejido's residents about economic hardship, the need to defend Spanish sovereignty against Catalan secessionism and how it was time for a strong leader like Donald Trump in America or Jair Bolsonaro in Brazil to end Spain's political fragility. Some local businessmen seemed to have developed a love-hate relationship with their migrant workers, happy to have them pick tomatoes in their greenhouses but at the same time resentful of some of their demands and the way that Muslim cafés serving mint tea were increasingly filling their neighborhoods, rather than Spanish bars serving whiskey or rum in tall glasses, filled with ice cubes and a splash of Coca-Cola.

In a local mosque that was built on the premises of a disused car workshop, I shared a couscous dinner with photographer Samuel Aranda and a group of worshippers. Sitting on a carpet, I listened to their own financial problems, but also heard them sound confident that their contribution was now part of the economic fabric of El Ejido. "Whatever Vox or any other party says, people need us to come and work here," said Issam Mehdaj, who distributed water to local households.

But perhaps my most insightful encounter in El Ejido came during a morning spent in the Fuente Nueva secondary school alongside Javier Adolfo Iglesias, a teacher and journalist with a passion for John Lennon and other foreign celebrities who spent time in Almería. He proudly introduced me to his students and opened his class by arguing that "Xenophobia cannot be the reason for Vox, because I've never seen it in my classroom, nor in my local bar."

Still, when I was later allowed to ask myself the 15 students about politics and whether they would vote for Vox, five raised their hands. The result was slightly higher than that obtained by Vox in the Andalusian elections, and it immediately prompted a classroom debate about the lack of integration among adolescents of different backgrounds. One of the Vox teenagers related the work problems of his father to migration, while others gave examples of unwanted behavior by some Arabs. It was clear to me that the school needed to spend more time discussing xenophobia with its students.

As I am writing these lines, I cannot forecast whether the next generation of Spanish voters will support Vox more, or instead the party will lose ground as its novelty factor evaporates and its lawmakers come under closer scrutiny, as elected members of Congress.

I think that much will also depend on whether other conservative politicians adopt the anti-migration rhetoric of Vox rather than oppose it. Two weeks after Vox won 52 seats in Congress, José María Aznar, Spain's former leader, shared a podium with Nicolas Sarkozy, his former French counterpart, at the Francisco de Vitoria University in Madrid, within which Aznar had founded his own education center. That day, Aznar's warning about migration and allowing more "multiculturalism" into Western societies sounded to me like a copy paste of a campaign speech by Santiago Abascal, the leader of Vox. "Multicultural societies break up the values that we have in Western countries because they generate more radicalism and more confrontation — and we should be aware of this," Aznar told his audience.

There is often a thin line between extremism and mainstream, which is breached once the words of extremism get spoken loud and clear by enough people for them to become part of the mainstream. The risk is not what Abascal has been saying, but that some of his words have been endorsed by some rivals, or at least unopposed. My heart sunk during the televised debate before the election in November 2019, when Pedro Sánchez, the Socialist candidate, allowed Abascal to expand on the dangers of Islamic migration. Sánchez produced data to defend his government's track record against illegal migration, rather than reminding Abascal that Spain protects religious freedom.

It is hard to forecast just how tolerant Spanish society will remain, just as I find it hard to explain how it has evolved in recent years. Some of the common explanations also never leave me fully convinced, for example when it comes to understanding why social and racial tensions have rarely spilled over into street violence in Spain.

Yes, it is true that Spanish people spend their life outside rather than inside their home, which means a lot more greeting and meeting helps create a more open neighborhood community. But does this explain the whole story, or does it tell us that Spain is immune to more open expressions of racism? Italy also has a hot climate, where people gather for morning coffee and enjoy their piazza just as Spaniards worship their plaza, but Italy's record on racism has recently been deplorable compared to that of Spain. Its football stadiums have become a cesspit of hatred toward black players, even against those who have played at the highest level for Italy, like Mario Balotelli. In 2019, for the first time in a decade, a majority of Italians surveyed did not question racism outright, according to an annual survey by SWG, a European polling firm.

I have felt the same sense of "incomplete understanding" when looking at why crime has remained comparatively low in Spain, even at the height of the unemployment crisis, which I discuss in another chapter. Perhaps, later on in life, I will return to university to study sociology.

Writing about such issues, the difficulty has sometimes simply been to find a fresh angle to a well-known situation. In November 2014, I went to Melilla to meet sub-Saharan Africans who were trying to climb its border fences. As the year was coming to a close, about 14,000 migrants had already tried to jump over Melilla's border fences and 2,000 had succeeded. These numbers were in themselves an important leap from previous years. The situation in Melilla had also caught the world's attention because of the work of local activists. An NGO called Prodein had filmed Spanish police officers beating an African migrant after he jumped the last fence to Melilla. Possibly unconscious, he was then carried by the Spanish police officers to the Moroccan side of the border.

José Palazón, the director of Prodein, had also taken a picture of African migrants sitting on a border fence, just next to golfers dressed in white who were enjoying their sports morning on the greens, oblivious to the stranded Africans. This shocking contrast meant that his photo caught the attention of people both in Spain and overseas, and among them was one of my editors.

But I was facing a very common challenge for a correspondent. An editor gets excited about a story in a remote location. Unless the story is major breaking news, like a terrorist attack, it can take a while to get the final green light from the newsroom, and it then takes even longer to arrange the trip and get there. Yet the correspondent is sent in order to narrate the story as if it was unfolding right in that moment. Over the years, I have read some accounts by correspondents who clearly reached a place way too late, like somebody who arrives at a big party just in time to clean the dance floor and wash the last champagne glasses. Sometimes their reporting and writing skills save the day, but also their power of imagination.

I also arrived in Melilla late, but many migrants were still camping in a Moroccan forest on the other side of Melilla's border, preparing for their next attempt to climb the fences. I could see that this assignment would work well as a visual story, for the Barcelona-based photographer Arnau Bach who had joined me in Melilla. But as a writer, I was not sure what I could add to the dozens of other great stories that I had already read about the border crossings.

From the start, almost everything went wrong for us. We crossed the border into Morocco with the help of a local fixer, who was hired by *The New York Times* to help us on the ground. He took us into the forest, but looked very nervous and explained to us that some Sub-Saharan Africans had stolen things from him on a previous visit. As we reached a group of Africans who sat around a fireplace next to their makeshift plastic tent, one of them started screaming at our fixer. He was from Western Africa, spoke French and I asked him what the problem was. He told me that our fixer, who had been recommended to me by a Spanish journalist, was in fact an informant for the Spanish secret service. We left their fireplace and I started talking instead with other Africans scattered across the forest. It all felt very uncomfortable. On the way back, the fixer admitted to me that he had traveled once to Madrid, on a trip paid by the Spanish authorities, to help corroborate police evidence that they were gathering about migrants. I told him this presented a very serious conflict of interest, which would likely mean that we would not be able to continue working much longer together.

The fixer said that he still wanted to help us and that he would ring us during the night if he heard about Africans planning another border crossing. I was exhausted and went to bed early. Bach, however, decided not to rely on our fixer and set his alarm clock for 4 a.m. to go to the border fence. When Bach returned to our hotel, after spending five hours along the border, he had taken great photos of migrants trying to climb the fences. But he had also accidentally bumped into our fixer, who had been assisting instead a French television crew. Journalism has allowed me to work alongside exceptional people, sometimes while working on the same story, but for rival publications. Unfortunately, there are also some more unpleasant encounters, with people who seems to lack ethics and professionalism.

Before traveling to Melilla, I had asked the Guardia Civil, Spain's military police, for a tour of the border area and an interview with a commander. When we arrived at the headquarters of the Guardia Civil, a spokesman said the tour was scheduled, but there would be no interview. A judge in Melilla had indicted the local head of the Guardia Civil, Colonel Ambrosio Martín Villaseñor, after a complaint filed by Prodein and other NGOs, who accused him of allowing illegal expulsions. Although I did my best to sweet talk the spokesman, he insisted that he was the only officer whom I could speak to.

Just as we were preparing to leave the compound, we ran into an officer whose uniform indicated he held a high rank. I stopped him, introduced myself and told him that it was a big shame that no commander of the Guardia Civil wanted to explain their work properly. "Why not? I can certainly tell you why we are needed here," he replied, with a blend of indignation and surprise. The officer was in fact Colonel Martín Villaseñor. He ushered us into his office, to the dismay of the press spokesman who had wanted to show us the exit door instead.

Bach later shared with me a photo of the colonel, which captured perfectly his mood during a tense part of our interview. The colonel is seen raising his finger menacingly as he spoke to me. Behind him, there is an aerial photo of Melilla, a crucifix and a portrait of King Juan Carlos. We had started by talking about the great job that his police officers were doing in difficult circumstances, but our conversation got more tense as I then shifted onto the topic of his legal problems. He argued that the court case would go nowhere, as nobody had been expelled from Spanish soil.

"Do you even know what a border is?" the colonel asked me, clearly irritated. He then drew an analogy for me, assuming that I was an annoying American, and asked whether, if I got off the plane at John F. Kennedy airport in New York, I could say that I was in America. Yes, I told him. "Completely wrong!" he shouted, while banging his fist on his desk. "Nobody is legally in the United States until the immigration police control has been crossed."

The colonel had done much more than just make a valid point and also make me feel ignorant. He had given me a new focus for my story. I decided that my article would not tell another story of African tragedy, which others had already written better than I could, but instead mostly look at the issue of what defined a border, and why that mattered in Melilla. My report from Melilla was head-lined: "At Spanish enclave, a debate over what makes a border." It talked about the fact that Morocco was preparing to build a third fence, which would require rethinking about how many fences an African needed to cross before entering Spain. I also talked to experts about the history of Melilla, which was conquered by the Spanish monarchy in 1497, controlled from a fort and then consolidated as Spanish in the Treaty of Wad-Ras in 1860, which Morocco signed after suffering several military defeats. But even though Morocco signed border treaties relating to Melilla, it never recognized Spanish sovereignty over the territory. In another twist in 1998, Spain built its first fence without allowing any Spanish bulldozer to operate on Moroccan soil. The fence, therefore, could not be erected exactly along the line that had been drawn by cartographers on the map. In short, I wrote, "the case raises the question of what, exactly, is a border: a physical barrier or something more notional?"

I felt that readers could relate to this question wherever they were, and whether or not they cared about Melilla. More recently, the United States has been gripped by a similar border debate, triggered by President Donald Trump's promise to erect a wall along the border with Mexico.

In Melilla, I also heard tales about economic hardship and how the arrival of sub-Saharan Africans was straining Melilla, but without triggering street protests. In fact, many residents were trying to help the migrants, in line with the gestures of solidarity that I have seen in other places like Archidona. Activists were also working hard. Palazón, the director of Prodein, seemed happy to spend a late night with me talking about police officers mistreating Africans who had already risked their lives to reach Melilla.

A few residents sounded upset by the influx of migrants, but not furious. In fact, they mostly complained about how the media coverage was hurting the reputation of Melilla. They told me that journalists should forget this fence story and move on. Like the people who just enjoyed playing their morning golf.

Salir del coma
La lucha por la justicia tras una negligencia médica

On an autumn Saturday of 2010, I was crossing the historic center of Madrid, on my way to meeting friends, when I noticed a blue tent pitched on the square of Jacinto Benavente, in front of a large building occupied by the ministry of justice. I stopped to look at this unexpected tent, erected in a deserted square, and started to read some of the signs hung outside it, which were mostly complaints about the justice system. There was one reading: "Where is justice? In a coma?"

While I was trying to decipher some of the other handwritten messages, using the flashlight from my mobile phone, a woman stepped out of the tent. She told me that she and her husband had been living there for almost 500 days, while looking after their son who was lying on a bed inside. He had been in a coma for 21 years, after he got deprived of oxygen while undergoing cosmetic surgery on his nose. As she continued talking about her tragic family situation, I realized that I was running very late to meet my friends, so I mumbled an apology about having to leave. I told her that I was a journalist and that I hoped to come back another day. She smiled benevolently, as if she had heard plenty of other lame excuses before. But before I left, she still offered to introduce me to her son, Antonio. The tent was lit with a weak lightbulb, making it too dark to see anything properly, but I could see the emaciated face of a young man, wearing an oxygen mask and sweating profusely.

I finally left the tent, feeling ashamed about my rush to join friends for a fun Saturday evening. I joined them in one of the bars of the La Latina district, but I found that I had lost any appetite for eating and drinking. While we talked, my mind kept switching back to the son in a coma, called Antonio Meño Ortega. I was unsure whether he had actually been aware of my presence as I stood next to his bed. I also had in mind the image of the far younger face that I had seen in a photocopied picture that was displayed on a table at the entrance to the tent. The photo had been taken when Antonio was a student, shortly before he underwent his nose surgery. It highlighted his piercing black eyes, as well as a nose that made him look tough, but not in any way ugly.

During our brief conservation, I had told Antonio's mother, Juana Ortega, that I was Swiss, so she told me about how Antonio loved climbing mountains. Antonio was also almost the same age as me. Why had our lives followed such dramatically different paths? After bidding an early farewell to my friends, I rushed home to read more about Antonio's case. It had been widely reported in the Spanish media because the Supreme Court had just re-opened his legal case against the Nuestra Señora de América hospital, where he had undergone his botched nose operation in 1989.

On the Monday, I wrote to my editor to tell him that I really wanted to write an article about Antonio and his family, almost as a personal project. We then spoke and I convinced him that it was not only a story of human tragedy, but also one that tapped into the broader theme of the struggle of the individual against the system. The following day, I visited Antonio again and talked to his parents about their downward spiral into poverty and indignation. I watched him closely as his mother spoke softly to him while adjusting his bed sheet and realigning his crooked arms. He would twitch, grimace and sometimes even blink furiously when she spoke. But she told me that it was unclear whether her son understood her words or simply felt her move around his bed.

What was certain, however, is that his family had taken every conceivable step to be granted justice, making huge sacrifices along the way. They had fought a long legal battle to demonstrate that medical negligence led to their son's coma, losing in the process their family fruit store, as well as their house. By the time we met, they still owed 400,000 euros in unpaid legal costs from their previously lost court cases. Juana told me the story of Antonio's nose surgery as if it had happened the day before, rather than on 3 July 1989. "I accompanied him and last saw him normal at 10:45 a.m., when I was told to leave," she said, her eyes welling up with tears.

She said the hospital refused to acknowledge an error by one of its doctors and instead attributed the accident to Antonio unexpectedly choking on his own vomit. I repeatedly tried to get the hospital's own version of the story, but never got a response.

After the botched surgery, Antonio was transferred to a public hospital, spending several months on a floor assigned to patients with AIDS and serious infectious diseases. With the hospital not carrying out any specific treatment on him and refusing to move him out of what his mother called "an unsuitable and very risky area," she eventually decided to bring him home.

For the next two decades, Antonio's mother almost never left his bedside, except for court proceedings, whose paperwork she kept carefully archived in a corner of the tent. "I'm looking after a four-month old who's in fact 42, and that's a lot of work," she said. Her three other children also visited their brother regularly and helped finance his upkeep. Next to Antonio's bed, her mother kept a pack of diapers and three water cans that she used to wash him twice a day. She stacked his baby purees beside a portable gas cooker. The nearby newsstand had agreed to run an electricity cable to their shelter, with one light bulb shining directly above Antonio's bed, thereby also illuminating a few pictures of saints and other religious icons that were placed around the tent. These, however, were gifts from friends and visitors, Juana insisted. "This tragedy hasn't helped my own faith," she said, with a stern face.

Feisty and stocky, Juana was clearly in charge of Antonio. Her husband, Antonio Meño, split his time between sitting on one of the shelter's foldable chairs, watching a small television, and running errands. He told me that he preferred to let his wife deal with visitors and seemed reluctant to discuss his own feelings with me. But he reacted forcefully when I asked whether he had ever wanted his wife to abandon their legal fight. "I'll do whatever can be done for our son," he said. "If being a father means anything, it must mean remaining strong and present in the hardest of times."

The family moved Antonio to the square after receiving a city permit to hold a protest outside the justice ministry. Juana first showed up with her son in a wheelchair and an umbrella to protect him from the sun. When her husband then started constructing the shelter, the city authorities turned a blind eye. "Nobody does something like this in Madrid, so they probably didn't know how to react," Juana Ortega told me. "But I also believe that everybody knows, deep down, that we deserve justice."

Every morning, Ortega rewrote the sign outside their shelter to show exactly how many days they had spent there. Adjusting to such a cramped and makeshift space was "a real challenge," she said. There was street noise at night, as well as drunkards occasionally relieving themselves behind the shelter, "as if they're trying to piss all over my son," she said. Still, Ortega harbored no regrets about moving into the tent. Living on a Madrid square, she said, had allowed her to make "amazing people" aware of Antonio's plight."We've received here the respect and attention sadly denied to us by the judicial system," she said. "Ordinary folks can relate to us, unlike these big and powerful judges who see us just as case numbers."

I increasingly felt an emotional attachment to Antonio. But as I had told my editor, I also wanted this story to be read from a different perspective. In a way, it talked about the struggle of a working-class family to get a fair hearing in court and how slow and costly the judiciary can be. At the same time, I did not want my article to read as criticism of Spain's otherwise exemplary health system. Antonio had been mishandled, but he was particularly unfortunate. I knew many other people who have been treated fast and successfully, whether in a public or private hospital. They often underwent surgery far more complicated than a nose job, at the hands of some of the world's best-trained doctors.

My personal experience of the Spanish public health system has thankfully been limited, but almost invariably positive. Most doctors and nurses also take the time to explain clearly what they are doing.

For a story, I once toured medical centers in the Basque Country and discussed with local officials how residents were getting tested early for diseases, as part of a shift toward preventative healthcare. In 2018, the Basque authorities launched a free screening program for cervical cancer, on top of their programs to detect cancer of the breast and colon. Statistics show that Spain spends less than France, Germany and the other larger European nations on health, but is producing some of the best results, as measured by mortality and other indices.

Five centuries ago, the Spanish explorer Juan Ponce de León landed in Florida while searching for the fountain of youth. Nowadays, Spain is instead exploring the boundaries of old age. By 2040, Spain should overtake Japan as the country with the longest life expectancy, according to an American study published in 2018 by the Institute for Health Metrics and Evaluation, based in Seattle. Lifestyle, diet and other factors contribute, but this advance would not have been possible without a solid and accessible health care system.

After the financial crisis hit Spain, members of the medical staff held many protests about budgetary cuts, their salaries and working conditions. But they have never threatened to collapse a Spanish health system that generates a mix of admiration and envy among most foreign tourists and other visitors. Spain's health treatment problems pale in comparison with those of some other major European countries, like Britain and its overstretched National Health System. For many Americans who have been distraught by the heated and lengthy debate over Obamacare, the priority is not to guarantee good healthcare, but at the very least basic access and treatment, in a country where people struggle to enter hospital without first being able to demonstrate that their credit card works.

Doctors can make mistakes. In fact, I believe there should be more praise for them saving lives, rather than only blame when somebody falters. Public recognition is not everything, but it can go a long way toward alleviating discontent.

In the spring of 2020, this recognition turned into a huge show of solidarity across Spain, when the country found itself among the worst hit by the coronavirus. The pandemic revealed serious problems and shortfalls within Spain's national healthcare system, in particular in Madrid where hospitals soon overflowed with Covid-19 patients. It sadly forced doctors and nurses to go beyond the call of duty, working sometimes in unsafe conditions that left many of them infected with the disease.

To show their appreciation for their health care workers, Spaniards started to gather every evening at 8 p.m. for a round of applause, delivered from their windows or balconies since everybody was kept under lockdown. While the pandemic continued to rage for more than a year, the applause stopped after a few months. I can only hope that once life returns to normal, the doctors and nurses will receive the salary rises and other improvements that they have been calling for, so that the country can also be better prepared to tackle the next health emergency.

Of course, every nation has been engaged in a roller coaster fight against the pandemic, with moments of relief often followed by episodes of despair. But Spain's struggle in the spring of 2020 was a shock to many who had assumed that the country was better prepared, at least in terms of supplying gloves, face masks and other basic protection gear to its frontline health workers. At the time of writing, nobody had yet assumed responsibility for some of the most glaring shortcomings in Spain's emergency response system.

The real problem with Antonio's case was not that nobody claimed responsibility, but that the mistake was actually denied. In November 2010, Antonio's family finally managed to get their claim heard before the Supreme Court, thanks to a new witness who also came across their tent, and later provided damming testimony against the hospital. The witness had been an apprentice doctor at the Nuestra Señora de América hospital when Antonio was operated there. He told the court that Antonio's anesthetist had been summoned to another operating theatre during Antonio's surgery. When he returned, the anesthetist discovered that Antonio's oxygen supply tube had come unstuck, leaving him in a disastrous situation.

After hearing the doctor's account, the court overruled the previous decisions against the family and cleared them of any obligation to pay their legal costs of 400,000 euros. The court also canceled the seizure of their house, allowing Antonio and his family to return home in time for Christmas. In a final ruling in July 2011, the Supreme Court awarded the family just over one million euros in compensation for the gross negligence suffered by their son.

Antonio died on 28 October 2012, after spending 23 years in a coma. The long battle waged by his parents had not helped him recover his health, but it had at least given back to the family their dignity and home.

I did not get to write about his death, nor did my initial reporting contain any groundbreaking revelation. But my article about the struggle of Antonio's family triggered many comments from readers of *The New York Times*, precisely because it touched their emotions, rather than any particular interest in Spain. This was not about the uniqueness or importance of the country that I was covering as a correspondent, but rather about how people are driven by their desires and fears and how they sometimes miscalculate or are desperately unlucky. Any reader who ever worried about their looks could probably imagine getting caught in a medical tragedy like that of Antonio.

Un olvido a la americana
Décadas de residuos nucleares en Palomares

One of the darkest moments in the relationship between the United States and Spain occurred on a clear winter day, high above the Andalusian seaside village of Palomares. On 17 January 1966, the U.S. Air Force almost provoked a world nuclear tragedy when one of its bombers dropped four hydrogen bombs after hitting a refueling tanker while flying above Palomares. Two of the bombs released plutonium into the atmosphere, but miraculously no warheads detonated. Following the crash, there was a botched attempt to clean the site, as well as a political cover-up operation. The cleaning exercise was incomplete, while the diplomatic white-washing proved much more thorough.

Of course, the accident took place in the midst of a Cold War in which the United States was tussling with the Soviet Union, while Spain was under a dictatorship that censored information. Franco's regime did not want to upset an important American alliance that had been cemented by the visit to Madrid of President Dwight Eisenhower in 1959. The Cold War eventually ended, but not the diplomatic tensions over Palomares. This is why I have occasionally reported from the village.

The New York Times covered Palomares from the moment that news filtered out about this strange and worrying accident. One of the newspaper's foreign correspondents, Tad Szulc, visited Palomares two weeks after the plane collision and eventually turned his reporting into a book, titled *The Bombs of Palomares*, which the director Luis Buñuel even considered making into a movie. At the time of his visit, Szulc wrote for the newspaper about how "a stark awareness of the nuclear age weighs heavily over this tiny Spanish farm community." He described the search and rescue mission that was underway, which included the decision to abandon tomatoes grown in the surrounding fields because of the fear of radioactivity. But his article did not criticize forcefully the handling of the cleanup.

During my first visit to Palomares, in March 2011, I discovered that tomatoes remained an issue in Palomares, because those in charge of the cleanup decided to burn the tomato crop, which helped spread contimation, rather than remove the tomatoes or at least bury them. Farmers in Palomares told me how their production of tomato, lettuce and watermelon was long stigmatized and did not carry a Palomares label until the 1980s, because of fears about the contamination.

Apart from a few farmers working the fields, Palomares is a sleepy village, particularly in the winter. The wind gusts can get so strong that it becomes hard to walk on the beach. I remember thinking that this was not the kind of windy weather in which radioactive particles should be allowed to float in the air.

My visit in 2011 was prompted by the fact that the governments in Washington and Madrid seemed close to finally signing an agreement to clean Palomares of any remaining land contamination. A month before my trip, Trinidad Jiménez, the then foreign minister, had told the Spanish Senate that clearing Palomares was "a priority." Days later, Washington had sent a team of experts to Palomares to help evaluate how to clean what had become Western Europe's most radioactive site.

Everybody agreed that Palomares remained contaminated because the initial clearance had been insufficient and badly managed. About 5,000 barrels of toxic earth were shipped from Palomares to South Carolina after the crash, but that still left some plutonium in Palomares, which Spain also wanted the Americans to transport home because Spain did not have a facility to store such poisoned soil. In fact, Spain's own research had raised major concerns about the radioactivity levels around Palomares. The main scientific concern was that plutonium was being allowed to degenerate into other radioactive components like americium, which emits gamma rays that travel further and are harder to block.

The sophistication of this analytical work contrasted with the makeshift safety steps that I discovered on the ground. After a survey was completed in 2008, the Spanish authorities divided the contaminated land into three main sections, covering a total of about 40 hectares, some of which almost touched private homes, as well as fields and greenhouses. The steepest section of scrubland was cordoned off rather than fenced off, which meant that a shepherd and his goats, blissfully unaware of the health risks, had crossed the area a month before my visit. Spain's nuclear agency then filed a police complaint against the shepherd. I remember thinking that, if there had to be a court case, it should probably involve the shepherd filing a lawsuit against Ciemat, Spain's nuclear agency, for not putting a solid fence to stop his animals from crossing the land. In a modern country like Spain, I found it weird that anybody would think a tape cordon would be considered sufficient protection.

A few months after my trip to Palomares, Hillary Clinton visited Spain for the first time as U.S. State Secretary. In February 2012, she met again with José Manuel García Margallo, Spain's then foreign minister, who later told Spanish media that Clinton had promised him some "good news" soon about America's commitment to the cleanup Palomares. She never delivered this good news.

Instead, in 2016, I found myself involved in an extensive *New York Times* investigation into the consequences of Palomares, 50 years after the US aircraft had nearly provoked a nuclear Armageddon. The investigation was led by my colleague in Washington, Dave Philipps, who interviewed dozens of former airmen and got the first access to freshly declassified documents relating to the Palomares crash. His investigation clearly countered the longstanding claim by the U.S. Air Force that there had been no harmful radiation at the crash site and that adequate safety measures had been taken to protect all of the 1,600 troops who worked around Palomares after the crash.

Philipps produced some groundbreaking reporting into how the U.S. Air Force had purposefully kept radiation test results out of the medical files of some of the military staff who cleaned Palomares in 1966, and about how many of these people then suffered from plutonium poisoning. Of the 40 veterans whom Philipps identified as having worked in Palomares, 21 had cancer.

My reporting assignment was far more straightforward. I was sent back to Palomares to talk once more to residents who had witnessed the crash or its aftermath. I heard from villagers who had understood that a major accident had occurred, but were never told about the contamination risks. Some even treated the crash as an opportunity to retrieve desirable material from the aircraft, like José Manuel González Navarro, a mechanic, who told me about how it had driven on his motorbike to the crash site, after checking that his house had not been damaged, to search the debris. He found an undetonated bomb attached to a parachute. He cut off the straps of the parachute and took them home, alongside some work tools and bolts that he found scattered on the ground.

"I was just thinking about what objects might prove useful," he told me. "I liked fishing and those parachute straps, thin but very solid, were clearly perfect to be turned into a weight belt for diving." I spent the day talking to people who had risked their health, if not life, without realizing it. Among them was Martin Moreno, who was 81 years old when we spoke, but recalled vividly how he had rushed with a friend toward the local cemetery after seeing the crash overhead and watching something fall from the sky. As they reached the cemetery, they spotted an American pilot apparently sitting on the ground. When they got close, however, the pilot turned out to be dead, "with his head sunk right into his body, all the way down between the shoulder blades," Moreno said, mimicking the pilot's posture.

Moreno then climbed on top of the near-by bomb because he could not work out what it was. "It looked like a strange and yellowish casket, with a gash on the side," he said. Using a screwdriver, he tried to cut it open, to no avail, because the casing was too hard. The idea that Moreno had been trying to cut his way into a nuclear bomb left me feeling shocked, but also acutely aware of the power of information, whether in the hands of politicians, the military, scientists or journalists. The inhabitants of a remote farming community, in an era when Spain was politically isolated and few people in the countryside even had a television set at home, had no opportunity to work out that American and Spanish officials kept them in the dark about the nuclear dimension of a crash that miraculously spared Palomares, but still claimed the lives of 7 of the 11 crew members on the two American planes.

And while the U.S. Air Force scrambled to remove any evidence of its military failure, the villagers celebrated the fact that Palomares had not suffered a direct hit, and was instead being visited by American servicemen loaded with cigarettes and beers, which they shared with the local population. "This almost became a party atmosphere," González Navarro said.

The Americans decided not to evacuate Palomares and instead told the residents that they had no reason to worry about their health. They were also promised financial compensation for their lost harvests. The villagers, in any case, were just too poor to think about their health rather than their income. "We were told that we should perhaps get rid of what we had been wearing that day, or at least wash it thoroughly, but of course nobody here could afford to throw away clothing," said González Navarro. "We could see some American soldiers walking around with detectors, but nobody realized there was any risk."

The diplomatic effort to draw quickly a line under the Palomares accident is encapsulated in one of the most famous photos of that period, showing Manuel Fraga, Spain's minister of information and tourism, taking a swim in Palomares alongside the American ambassador. Both men waved cheerfully to photographers as if they were enjoying a fun day at the beach. "I think that things were done with the technical knowledge available at the time and the political situation in Spain at the time," Yolanda Benito, an official from Ciemat, told me. "Spain was a dictatorship, so it was not the most transparent government in the world."

But Spain has more recently sought to pressure the U.S. into action, as was demonstrated by the publication by newspaper *El País* of one of the cables contained in the files of WikiLeaks, which was sent in 2009 by the Spanish foreign minister to State Secretary Hilary Clinton warning that Spanish public opinion could turn anti-American if Spain disclosed the content of a Palomares contamination study.

Scientists from Ciemat, the nuclear agency, found about 50,000 cubic meters of radioactive soil — far more than what was removed in 1966 — which prompted the authorities to expropriate some land and cordon it off. Locals however told me that the study was prompted by economic rather than scientific interests, launched after some property developers announced that they wanted to invest in the area.

There is no clear explanation, however, for why the U.S. has been dragging its feet over Palomares. In October 2015, State Secretary John Kerry committed the United States to removing any contamination from the site. During a visit to Madrid, Kerry signed a memorandum of understanding to return Palomares to its pre-1966 normality. The signing came after Spain agreed to allow the U.S. to expand its presence at Spanish military bases. As with the earlier promise made by Clinton, Kerry's promise that "the United States will live up to its responsibilities and do its part" is yet to translate into any action.

In Palomares itself, I have heard different opinions as to why the site remains contaminated and why the U.S. allowed Palomares to remain as a stain on its reputation in Spain. Antonio Fernández

Liria, the mayor of Cuevas del Almanzora, the larger town that has administrative responsibility over Palomares, believed the Americans resist the idea of removing more contaminated soil because "they just don't want to set a precedent, because if they assume full responsibility, there will be plenty of other countries who will ask them to make up for other mistakes." His conclusion was clear: "This is shameful for all involved."

Unlike my colleague in Washington, I got no clear answer about the health of the residents of Palomares and whether some had suffered high cancer rates like the American airmen who cleared the crash site in 1966. Ciemat said their medical checks showed the frequency of cancer in Palomares was in line with that in other towns.

Some inhabitants, in any case, took a more cynical view of why the American and Spanish authorities never evacuated Palomares. "They're just using us as guinea pigs, to see what happens to people who live in a contaminated area," said Francisco Sabiote, a local plumber. "They tell us all is fine, but also that more soil needs to be taken away. So if that is really needed, why all this waiting?"

In 1966, the residents of Palomares were not told what had really happened above their heads. Nowadays, many of the villagers no longer wish to be told. Some have even stopped traveling to Madrid to get their regular test for radioactivity, under the supervision of Ciemat, the nuclear agency. Sabiote, who was 27 years old when we met, said he had last undergone a medical exam in Madrid when he was 12 and had no plans to return. "We all have to die one day of something," he said, shrugging his shoulders.

La larga sombra de Franco
La memoria histórica como asignatura pendiente

Shortly after arriving in Madrid, I visited the city's museum of history, which is filled with impressive displays about the Napoleonic occupation and other wartime events. But to my surprise, I found in it no mention of the civil war.

There are photos of the construction of the Madrid slaughter-houses in 1928. But when I asked a museum supervisor about why there was nothing about the destruction that occurred a decade later, he suggested that I write my question into the visitors' book. I followed his advice, left my contact details, but nobody ever got back to me.

Every country struggles to deal with certain moments in its history. In neighboring France, for instance, there are twisted accounts of the French collaboration with the Nazis, which was long treated as a taboo subject. In 1995, Jacques Chirac, the French president, finally apologized for the role of the French authorities in the mass roundup of Jews in Paris in 1942, a terrible event known as the Rafle du Vel' d'Hiv. It also took the city of Paris six decades to unveil a plaque in 2004 to honor its first "foreign liberators," most of whom were Spanish soldiers who formed a company known as La Nueve, or The Ninth, and who dodged past German soldiers to reach Paris City Hall, on August 24, 1944. Still, the question is how long does it take for a country not only to confront its past, but also to make it known and understandable to most of its people.

In Spain, the government of José Luis Rodríguez Zapatero decided that the time had come in 2007, when it passed its Historical Memory Law, which encouraged the search for mass graves, while calling for the removal of any remaining symbols of Franco from public spaces. The law was introduced 30 years after the amnesty law, a piece of legislation that aimed instead to forgive and forget. In the late 1970s, the politicians were struggling with the difficult task of consolidating Spain's return to democracy. They decided that this transition could not risk renewed feuding over the wrongdoings of the civil war and Franco's dictatorship.

But the law of 2007 was not drawn up by politicians from both sides. It was a Socialist initiative clearly focused on Franco's silenced victims, including the thousands dumped into unmarked graves. As a result, the law immediately became hostage to the bipartisan politics of Spain. Perhaps unsurprisingly, when the Popular Party won a landslide election in late 2011, the law was effectively shelved. The government of Mariano Rajoy not only cut off financing but also closed the Office of Victims of the Civil War and the Dictatorship. In June 2018, a Socialist government abruptly returned to office. One of Pedro Sánchez's first announcements was that he would "immediately" exhume Franco from his Valley of the Fallen underground basilica.

Franco's exhumation proved anything but immediate. Franco's family fought a year-long judicial battle, while a rising ultranationalist party, Vox, led the criticism of Sánchez, even calling him "a scavenger." I joined a radio debate on Cadena Ser the weekend after the Supreme Court suspended Sánchez's attempt to remove Franco's corpse. More than the ruling itself, our discussion centered on its wording, because the Supreme Court had described Franco as head of state from 1 October 1936 until his death on 20 November 1975. In other words, the judges recognized the self-proclaimed legitimacy of Franco more than two years before he won the war. One of the guests on the radio show was a bow-tie-wearing historian and former diplomat, Ángel Viñas. He said the court had failed to remain impartial and instead "chose to add a shocking Francoist interpretation of our history."

It was not the first time that I had been surprised by how institutional Spain defined Franco. In 2011, I wrote an article about how Franco's regime had been portrayed as "authoritarian, not totalitarian" in a biographical dictionary compiled by Spain's Royal History Academy. The dictionary also praised Franco's leadership and bravery in the civil war, without any reference to the killings of civilians and the purge of his opponents. The dictionary required 12 years to elaborate and 6.5 million euros of public funding. It was meant to serve as a work of reference for libraries across the country. Somehow, however, the entry about Franco was entrusted to Luis Suárez, a specialist on medieval rather than twentieth-century history, who was also known as a Franco apologist.

Some historians criticized the Academy's conservative membership and called for the resignation of its president, Gonzalo Anes. But Anes stayed on, explaining that he had not had time to read the section on Franco, which was eventually rewritten. I discussed how the dictionary had described Franco at the time with José Álvarez Junco, a history professor and one of the best experts on Spain's recent past.

"My feeling is that Spaniards are perhaps less comfortable with the legacy of the Civil War today than 20 or 30 years ago," Álvarez Junco told me. "Since about 2000, we have in fact a new generation from the Left who have given much greater impulse to the whole debate, because they really want to know what happened to their grandfathers." I have found that some of these grandfathers also now wanted their story to be told, before their generation disappeared altogether. Over the past decade, I have heard from people who suffered the war in the flesh and still feel hurt by how little recognition is given to the sacrifices that their generation made, or to their own efforts to find missing relatives.

In late 2018, I wrote a profile for the *New York Times* of José Moreno, a Basque who had just celebrated his 100th birthday and enjoyed being known around Bilbao as "the last *gudari*." During the war, Moreno was detained and condemned to death, but somehow his sentence was commuted instead to imprisonment in a work camp. When I visited him, he was spending most of his mornings glued to the television, following Spanish politics and in particular Sánchez's attempt to exhume Franco. Moreno not only wanted Franco removed from the Valley of the Fallen, but also reinterpreted in Spanish history books, so as to get "the same treatment as Hitler and Mussolini, the other Fascist war criminals," he said. Spain, he felt, needed as soon as possible to confront its past and turn the page on its 1977 law of amnesty. "Franco didn't forgive, so don't ask us not only to forgive but also to forget now," he said. Unfortunately for him, Moreno did not get to watch on his television Franco's exhumation, in October 2019. He died a few months after my visit.

In 2015, I visited Valencia, where a new left-wing mayor, Joan Ribó, was trying to remove the last symbols of Franco from his city. I interviewed Alejandra Soler, who was 102 at the time and had just been awarded the honorific title of favorite daughter of Valencia by Ribó's administration.

Soler was a Communist and one of the first women to receive a university degree in Spain, just before the start of the civil war, when she also became a leader of the student movement. When Franco won, she fled to France, then escaped with her husband from one of the internment camps of the Vichy government and finally made her way to the Soviet Union. She became a teacher and found herself in Stalingrad when the German army launched their disastrous offensive. She somehow escaped Stalingrad and led 14 schoolchildren to safety by crossing the Volga River.

Soler was very frail by the time I visited her, but she had this amazing selective memory that I have often found in elderly people, who can recall better the details of their distant past than what they have done in the last week. After sharing with me her gripping account of the civil war, Soler said: "As a former teacher, I really feel sad when I see that the Spanish schoolchildren of today know so little about our history."

Of course, the history of Spain is about more than its civil war and Franco. But should anybody seek to omit altogether the most painful years in the country's modern history? Should Spain not instead make every effort to value the extraordinary accounts of the last survivors of its civil war generation? Thankfully, at least the archive of Soler and her journalist husband, Arnaldo Azzati, found a new home in the University of Valencia, after Soler died in 2017.

More than four decades after Franco's death, no politician has managed to build a museum for the civil war, in a capital city like Madrid that has otherwise assembled some of the world's greatest museums. Anybody visiting Madrid needs to take on the role of detective to find the little evidence that is left of Madrid's key role in the war.

A few buildings around Madrid bear the bullet marks and other physical scars of the war, while the slopes of the Parque del Oeste have military bunkers and gun towers that were built during the battle to control Spain's capital. But there is no information board to explain this dilapidated military infrastructure. Instead, there are detailed instructions on how to use the outdoor gym equipment that stands a few meters away from a former gun tower.

Nearby stands the ancient Debod temple that was given by Egypt in 1968, as a token of gratitude for Spain's contribution to the preservation of some of its Abu Simbel monuments. But in July 1936, this strategic location, overlooking Madrid, was instead occupied by the Montaña barracks. By taking back control over the Montaña barracks from General Fanjul, the Republicans ensured that the coup failed in Madrid, which in effect forced Spain into a three-year war. My personal experience is that relatively few of the Madrid residents who enjoy walking or jogging around this Egyptian temple know that it was once a military stronghold.

David Mathieson, a British amateur historian who is passionate about the civil war, once took me to an unlikely private museum, set up by a resident of Morata de Tajuña, a town outside Madrid that remained under Republican control throughout the war, despite heavy aircraft bombing. Morata is near the Jarama valley, where Franco's troops fought a lengthy battle to cut off the road linking Madrid to Valencia. The mustachioed owner of the museum, Gregorio Salcedo, first combed the Jarama battlefield as a child in search of scrap metal, because "I was hungry and knew that there was money to be made from metal," he recalled.

Eventually, however, Salcedo started to keep whatever he would find, as well as visiting flea markets to buy more battlefield memorabilia. As an amateur curator, Salcedo managed to gather one of the most important collections of civil war artifact in the Madrid region, now exhibited at the back of a family restaurant. "It has required people like Salcedo to do the conservation work that a state would normally be doing," Mathieson told me.

The political feuding over the Valley of the Fallen suggests that Spain might never build a national museum of its civil war. Santos Juliá, who was one of Spain's most respected historians, once told me that Spain should at least have a museum covering its 20th-century history. "I think that to single out the civil war is still too polemical and doesn't really help explain history," he said, "because the civil war cannot be understood without knowing what happened before, while what happened afterward cannot be understood without knowing about the war."

Are foreigners like Mathieson more interested in the civil war than most Spaniards? Perhaps not, but I have received plenty of emails from Americans who are curious about the conflict (and not just because of Hemingway!). Some also have a family connection to events like the battle of Jarama, where the International Brigades, formed by left-wing volunteers from Europe and North America, went on the frontline to prevent Fascism from spreading across Europe.

In 2019, the exhumation of Franco finally took place right between two general elections, which gave the candidates plenty of opportunities to reference the past. On the night of the April election, Sánchez even made a thinly-veiled reference to Franco's Spain in his victory speech, when he told supporters assembled outside his Socialist party headquarters that the election showed that "the future has won and the past has lost."

Franco also continues to cast his shadow beyond Spanish politics. I have also been struck by how little consensus there is over Franco's impact on Spain's economic development. Some right-wing economists defend forcefully Franco's track record as a great modernizer of Spain, like Roberto Centeno, who has written about "the real miracle" that Franco left behind in 1975. Spain was pulled out of its isolationism and backwardness once a group of economists helped Franco's regime introduce its Stabilization Plan in 1959. But not everybody agrees on how much progress was then made, nor of course on whether that should help present Franco as a much more benign dictator than what his earlier track record might suggest.

As I mentioned in the Introduction to this book, I approach any topic that has a link to the civil war and Franco with a sense of foreboding, knowing that I am stepping into an information minefield. Which is also why I am sometimes surprised by how little care is taken by Spanish officialdom when discussing events relating to the civil war.

In August 2019, Dolores Delgado, the Spanish justice minister, joined the anniversary celebrations of the liberation of Paris in 1944. To mark the occasion, the justice ministry put out a Tweet stating that "Spain played a crucial role" in freeing the French capital from the Nazis, in reference to the former Republican soldiers of La Nueve company, who were the first to enter the city. Immediately, Quim Torra, president of the Generalitat, replied to the ministry that it was not Spain but exiled Republican soldiers who helped free Paris. Torra stressed instead that Spain's main contribution in World War II had been to support Hitler and mobilize Franco's Blue Division to help the German war effort.

Torra was once a book publisher, but his own use of words has often been inflammatory. When I first interviewed him in July 2016, I was struck by his references to the censorship practices and ban of the Catalan language under Franco as a "cultural genocide" in Catalonia. Genocide is a frightening term that should be used with far more caution. Thankfully, I have also met plenty of other Catalans who acknowledge the contradictions in Franco's relationship with Catalonia, some of which endure to this day.

In the town of Tortosa, residents voted in 2016 to keep a huge Franco monument, built in the middle of the Ebro river to commemorate Franco's last major battle in the civil war. Tortosa also kept Franco as its honorary mayor until 2016. I visited the town's then mayor, Ferran Bel, who was also deputy head of the Catalan association of pro-independence mayors. But despite his separatist credentials, he told me that some people kept accusing him of being a Fascist for defending Franco's monument. In Tortosa, he explained, residents did not want the authoritarian politicians of Barcelona to tell them what to do with their Franco monument. "People don't like to be lectured, especially not after forty years of nobody showing any interest" in the smaller towns of southern Catalonia, Bel said. The monument, he added, "forms part of our skyline."

Alongside other foreign correspondents, I have received some criticism within Spain for overwriting about Franco. But Franco's death was a watershed moment for Spain that continues to play into its politics, including as ideological fuel for the conflict over Catalonia.

In 2016, I wrote an article about the ceremonies being held in Catalonia to return family documents that were confiscated by Franco's troops and stored in Salamanca, the university city that was turned into his military headquarters. The Salamanca Papers were in themselves a disturbing legacy of the war, but what stunned me about this story is how, decades later, their restitution created more controversy than reconciliation in Spain. Even after the Spanish Congress agreed to return documents to Catalonia in 2005, the process was slowed down by a decade of lawsuits, filed by people determined to keep the documents in Salamanca.

Joan B. Culla, a leading Catalan historian, was among the first academics to gain access to the documents, during the same month of November 1975 when Franco died. Drawing his own comparison, he suggested that returning documents stolen from Republican families was like restituting paintings seized from Jews by the Nazis. "The fact that we're still having such a debate shows that, even forty years later, there is no sense of shame felt in defending the Franco period," he argued. "Could a town in Germany now be saying that something shouldn't leave because Hitler had put it there?"

It seems to me risky to compare dictators, during their lifetime and beyond. Hitler committed suicide, Mussolini was hanged, but Franco died in a Madrid hospital, aged 82. He received a state funeral, with huge lines of people waiting to pay their last respect at his open coffin. "Franco would never have lasted forty years without a very high level of social acceptance," the Catalan politician and lawyer Francesc Homs, once told me. The public grief displayed when Franco died, Homs added, was not "how dictatorships normally end."

In Catalonia, I met a generation of separatist politicians determined to talk about Franco like nowhere else in Spain. Catalonia has also built more civil war museums than any other region. I have visited some in smaller towns, like Gandesa, whose museum is dedicated to the battle of the Ebro. The museum in La Jonquera, opened in 2008, recounts how half a million Spaniards fled Spain after Franco won.

In July 2016, Barcelona commemorated the eightieth anniversary of the start of the civil war. The city authorities held a concert in the sumptuous Palau de la Música and hung anniversary banners from Barcelona's public buildings. "Memory isn't a duty but a civil right that has to be protected," said Ricard Vinyes, a historian and city hall official who had organised the commemoration. Vinyes contrasted Barcelona's efforts with the longstanding silence in Madrid, dating to the Socialist government's attempt in 1986 to ignore the fiftieth anniversary of Franco's uprising. At the time, the Socialist government declared that the civil war "no longer has, and should not have, a living presence in the reality of a country whose moral conscience is based on the principles of freedom and tolerance."

I struggle with this kind of thinking. Today, a majority of Spaniards was born after Franco's dictatorship ended. But if nobody aims to educate children about how a civil war split their country down the middle, it leaves society less prepared to confront future shockwaves. History should be taught not to place blame but instead to help learn from the past.

In November 2016, I wrote about a Franco exhibition in Barcelona that included an outdoors statue of Franco. His equestrian statue was pelted with eggs, splashed with paint and decorated successively with separatist flags, a blow-up doll and a pig's head. It was finally knocked down by vandals four days after being put on display. "It's extraordinary to think that we spent four decades not protesting or disrupting anything to do with Franco, but he then provokes us into destroying his statue four decades after his death," Josep Ramoneda, a philosopher and columnist, told me.

I have several friends in Madrid who tell me they would never visit The Valley of the Fallen. I have been a handful times, each time feeling uncomfortable while watching its statues of angels of death, which seemed to convey "the essence of Francoism," as the historian Álvarez Junco once described the decoration of the Valley to me. Shortly after Sánchez announced he would exhume Franco, I attended Sunday Mass in Franco's basilica, hearing the priest's homily for those who died for God in the civil war. Afterward, a few people walked to the back of the altar, to raise their arm in salute before Franco's tomb. The guard stopped people from taking photos, but he did not object to them making a Fascist salute.

In Seville, I visited another basilica, that of the Macarena, from which some local politicians wanted to exhume Gonzalo Queipo de Llano, one of the main military leaders in the civil war. José Antonio Fernández Cabrero, the head of the Brotherhood of the Macarena, told me how Queipo de Llano had been "a protector of the movement of the Catholic Church," who rebuilt after the war a basilica that is now home to 14,000 brothers, the largest such congregation in Seville. For Fernández Cabrero, no politician should revive debates over the civil war, let alone order an exhumation. Referring to the 1977 law of amnesty, he argued that "if politicians who had played an active part in the civil war managed to negotiate and close this chapter, it surprises me that politicians now tell us we need to reopen all of this." But not everybody in Seville revered Queipo de Llano, or even understood how his family had continued to prosper among the Andalusian establishment. Fernández Cabrero, the head of the brotherhood, said he didn't himself know how Queipo de Llano acquired the land on which his basilica was inaugurated in 1949. A local journalist, Juan Miguel Baquero, also told me about his longstanding failure to access the accounts of the family's foundation, to see exactly what properties and farmlands it inherited from Queipo de Llano.

One of Seville's leading historians, Francisco Espinosa, had even struggled to write a book about Queipo de Llano, because he could not find a local editor willing to publish his text. "My book was full of references to people from Seville who clearly did not want to see their family names in print," Espinosa told me. "There is a very conservative element in the society of Seville who has kept feeding the myth, based on absolutely wrong facts, about how Queipo de Llano bravely conquered this city with just the help of a few people."

The push to exhume Queipo also reflected the changing politics of Spain, particularly after left-wing politicians took charge in 2015 in Madrid, Barcelona and Valencia, Spain's three largest cities, and started renaming squares and streets associated with Franco's regime. In Pamplona, Joseba Asiron, the first mayor representing the separatist EH Bildu (Euskal Herria Bildu) party, orchestrated in 2016 the exhumation of two of the most important participants in the July 1936 coup, Emilio Mola and José Sanjurjo, who had been buried in another imposing structure known as the Monument of the Fallen.

In Barcelona, Ada Colau also targeted some prominent Catalans who had been affiliated with Franco's regime, notably Juan Antonio Samaranch, who was an official in Barcelona at the time of Franco's death. She removed an inscription that had been placed inside Barcelona's city hall to honor Samaranch, who had been the president of the International Olympic Committee who brought the games to his native Barcelona in 1992. As Gonzalo Rodes, a lawyer and president of Barcelona Global, a business association, told me at the time, Colau could remove Franco symbols, but not attack Samaranch, a man who joined Franco's administration because it "was just part of the normal opportunism of those times."

Since the independence movement gained momentum in Catalonia, I have heard many complaints about how its politicians try to whitewash the region's convoluted relationship with Franco.

Laura Freixas, a writer, told me the story of her industrialist grandparents, who were atheists and ardent Catalan patriots who voted for the Regionalist List, the nationalist movement led by Francesc Cambó after 1917. But in 1939, her grandfather joined the crowd that applauded the entrance of Franco's troops into Barcelona. Franco's victory allowed him to get back the factory that had been confiscated by left-wing militants at the start of the war. Under Franco, her family and many other members of the Catalan bourgeoisie "did very well socially and economically," Freixas said. "They were neither revolutionaries nor the martyrs that some of the new Catalan elite now want to pretend they were."

Mercedes Cabrera Calvo-Sotelo, a former Socialist education minister, once talked to me about how she held scant hope that Spanish society could come to terms with its past because of what she described as the unfortunate sequencing of Spain's twentieth-century history. "It would have been a lot easier for Spaniards to digest the past if the dictatorship had come first and had then been followed by a war, as happened in many other countries, but wishful thinking cannot change history," she told me.

In contrast, I have heard in Lisbon about how the "Carnation Revolution" of 25 April 1974 helped Portuguese society draw a line between dictatorship and democracy. Even if Portugal's revolution had started out as a military coup, its enduring image is that of a popular uprising in which ordinary citizens took to the streets to help end decades of authoritarian rule. The Spanish transition was something different. After Franco's death, it then took time for the changeover to get shaped by an elite of politicians and eventually rubber stamped by citizens, first in elections and then with a Constitution that was massively approved in a referendum in 1978.

When I have made a mention of how the modern constitutional order and structures of Spain came into being, my editors have sometimes substituted in my text a reference to "the transition of the late 1970s" with a more specific mention about Franco's 1975 death. For an international readership, their view is that the clearest reference is that to post-Franco Spain, since the concept of "the transition" is not familiar to everybody outside Spain. But even a passing reference to Franco's name in an article unrelated to his dictatorship has infuriated some people in Spain, who have accused me and *The New York Times* of obsessing about Franco. I can sympathize to some degree with them, but I also think that they should acknowledge that mentioning the transition, in whatever terms, is important when discussing a whole range of issues, not least of course the ongoing debate about federalism and a possible reform of the Spanish Constitution. There will no doubt come a point when many Spaniards will themselves also stop referring to their country as "a young democracy," but it is not for me to decide when that will happen.

In the meantime, using Franco as a reference point is not the same as writing about Franco, let alone obsessing about him. Nazism is not on the mind of every German every day, but it remains a reference point when discussing why Germany is the way it is today. The fall of the Berlin Wall was also not the only event that allowed German reunification and eventually the entrance of formerly Communist countries into the European Union, yet it is used as an easy shortcut to talk about another change of era.

More preoccupying, in my view, are the knowledge gaps and misunderstandings of many people in Spain about the events that shaped their country in the past century. I encourage anybody to ask Spanish schoolchildren what they know about the civil war. Like Soler, the former Valencia student who became a Soviet teacher, I have found that this question often draws a blank, or a very confused answer. In Madrid, a friend who teaches history in a state secondary school, Lucía Martín-Retortillo, told me how she put together her own classroom work about the civil war, to complement what her school curriculum did not include. "With hindsight, I think it is possible for anybody to understand that lives were lost on all sides," she told me. "I keep out of the vengeful debate between the left and the right."

In Barcelona, I talked once to a group of children who assured me that their city had led the resistance to Franco in the civil war. When I told them that Franco's troops entered Barcelona two months before Madrid in 1939, they did not believe me.

Nobody can change the course of history, but nor should anybody try to rewrite history to suit a political ideology. Nor, of course, ignore history altogether.

Pequeño pero matón
Cómo el Pequeño Nicolás burló al poder

I came across Francisco Nicolás Gómez Iglesias without knowing or even seeing him. In June 2014, we were among the 3,000 invitees to the royal palace, to witness the coronation of Felipe VI. We offered our congratulations and shook hands with the new monarch and his wife, Queen Letizia. My invitation had been a pleasant surprise, particularly since I had maintained frosty relations with the royal household during the final stage of the reign of King Juan Carlos I, while reporting on some of the scandals that complicated his life.

But for Francisco Nicolás, who had just turned 20, shaking the hand of King Felipe was an event that not only filled him with pride but also cemented his belief that nothing within Spain's establishment was beyond his reach. "Sure, we were 3,000 people invited to the royal palace, but I was clearly the youngest," he told me a few years later, while he showed off a copy of the official invitation that he had received to attend the royal ceremony.

Four months after the coronation, however, Francisco Nicolás was detained by police and accused of a series of crimes ranging from fraud to document falsification. Spaniards suddenly discovered the unlikely life of a young man who had not only met Spain's new king but also rubbed shoulders with several other rich and powerful members of the country's conservative establishment. Soon enough, he became known as "The Little Nicolás," in reference to the famous series of French novels about a mischievous schoolboy, which I had myself loved as a child.

When I told my editor about this strange story, he told me that it sounded as if Spain had found its own and youthful version of Frank Abagnale, the elusive impersonator and conman played by Leonardo Di Caprio in Steven Spielberg's Hollywood blockbuster, *Catch me if you can*. In fact, America has a sizable history of famous imposters, like German-born Christian Karl Gerhartsreiter, who moved to the United States when he was a teenager and eventually renamed himself Clark Rockefeller, a scion of one of America's most wealthy families. His fall from grace was as spectacular as his identify forgery: at the time of writing, Gerhartsreiter was in prison following a 2013 murder conviction.

Shortly after police arrested Francisco Nicolás I wrote an article about how this baby-faced charmer had managed to bamboozle the police while pretending to hold several government and other official posts. Above all, the story of Francisco Nicolás seemed to highlight the importance of personal connections in Spain, which could be strong enough to override any other obvious obstacle. Little Nicolás had repeatedly avoided security checks — with or without the help of actual police officers — in a country with a long history of fighting against the terrorists of ETA, as well as more recently against Islamic fundamentalists.

To cheat his way through life, Abagnale pretended to hold different jobs, from airline pilot and doctor to lawyer and prisons official. To back his claim to be a wealthy Rockefeller, Gerhartsreiter built up an impressive — but fake — art collection.

But Francisco Nicolás never had to fake anything major and only seldom had to use impersonation to open the doors of the establishment. In her initial report, Judge Mercedes Pérez Barrios wrote that she could "not understand how a young person of 20, using only his word and apparently under his own identity, could have access to conferences, places and events without his behavior alarming anybody."

Extraordinarily, nobody seemed to be able to work out just how the Little Nicólas got such access. Even the royal household gave no explanation as to how he had been at King Felipe's coronation. The Spanish media soon zoomed in on Catalina Hoffmann, a businesswoman who had stood alongside Nicólas when he met the king. But she denied adding him to the guest list.

In 2015, I met Francisco Nicolás again by chance, this time when I almost bumped into him at a zebra crossing along Calle Serrano. There stood the young man whose pink cheeks, floppy dark hair and blue eyes had prompted Esperanza Aguirre, one of the most influential politicians in Madrid, to talk about "this sweet-boy face," shortly after Francisco Nicolás was detained.

Even if he had lost his cherubim status, Francisco Nicolás continued to fascinate. In the Spanish media, he triggered a mix of admiration for his bravado and shock and consternation at what his adventures had revealed about the cronyism within Spain's establishment and the shortcomings of its security apparatus.

During our chance street encounter, Francisco Nicolás told me that he had a lot of information to share with me, but that he preferred to wait until he could put an end to the different lawsuits brought against him by the public prosecution. He said that we could then write a book together about his adventures. I responded that we should at least stay in touch. Every now and again Nicolás would send me a WhatsApp message to tell me how he was doing. I also got his Christmas wishes, with a series of colourful emojis of jingle bells and fireworks.

In November 2018, I asked him to meet me again. Much had changed in his life — and mostly for the better, he said. He told me about he had won some lawsuits against the Spanish state, including one that made him particularly proud, after a judge dropped charges brought by the CNI, the secret service. "Can you imagine that a kid beat the CNI in court?" he told me. "I think the CNI does great work in anti-terrorism and outside of Spain, but when it comes to internal affairs, it's pretty terrible. It's just run by old guys and it is so incredibly politicized." I told him that I did not share his views on the CNI, but that I was glad for him that he had managed to come out unscathed from this confrontation.

Our meeting took place in an ice cream parlor opposite the building where Francisco Nicolás then lived, on Santa Engracia Street. His grandfather had received his Madrid apartment, he explained, as a reward for reaching the rank of army colonel. In fact, most of the block of apartments was occupied by high-ranking officers, who had received a home in return for serving Spain. "Four generals have lived in my building," Francisco Nicolás told me. "Franco was good to those who served him well." The story of Francisco Nicólas suggested that this system of rewards stretched far beyond the military and morphed into a different kind of cronyism, once the dictatorship ended. We agreed that at least Franco's award of apartments had something to do with merit, given to those who had climbed up the army ranks. "I don't think everybody who is at the top in Spain now can claim to have done that much for the country," he said, with a wry smile.

Francisco Nicolás started his own social climb at an age when he was not even old enough to shave. In the course of a few hours, he showed me an extraordinary array of photos and documents that helped explain, rather than justify, how he overcame the obstacle of youth. Francisco Nicolás attended secondary school in El Viso, a Madrid neighborhood that has come to symbolize the gentrification of the city. The El Viso colony was first conceived as a housing cooperative, based on a 1925 so-called "Cheap Houses" law, which Spain's then ruler, Primo de Rivera, wanted to use to reward state employees for loyal services to his regime. Nowadays, it is mostly occupied by far wealthier residents, including some of Spain's biggest corporate tycoons, who have hired expensive interior designers to reshape their villas into luxurious dwellings.

Francisco Nicolás struggled at school, but excelled in socializing outside the classroom. He soon understood that his wealthy classmates could benefit from more after-class entertainment. So he convinced the management of some Madrid bars and clubs, like the Macumba and Liberata, to allow him to organize teenage parties in their venues in return for a commission fee. "I could bring between 500 and 1000 school kids to have fun in Liberata on a Saturday afternoon," he recalled. "And many were the children of ministers, local politicians and top businessmen who would then send their chauffeurs to wait for them outside Liberata and drive them home."

Eventually, Francisco Nicolás got friendly not only with the children but also some of their powerful parents and relatives. His pulling power and success didn't go unnoticed among the conservative elite, so that he got invited to the headquarters of the Popular Party to discuss how to form youth clubs for the party. At the same time, he approached Faes, the political foundation set up by José María Aznar, and started moderating debates there. He took his seat next to Spain's former prime minister, with Pablo Casado also at the table, as representatives of the new conservative generation.

Apart from Casado, "almost everybody was over 60 and in a grey suit," he said. "There were some politicians who perhaps didn't take me that seriously, but I think they could still understand that the party needed to attract at least some people younger than them."

As he told me his story, The Little Nicolás kept flicking through the photo album on his smartphone, to show me evidence that he was not exaggerating. He had pictures of himself standing next to the powerful in the most exclusive spots of Madrid. He kept a photo showing him seated behind Florentino Pérez, the president of Real Madrid, in the VIP box of the Santiago Bernabéu stadium. In fact, he talked about the Bernabéu as a second home, where he was regularly invited by friends that included Jaime García-Legaz, who was then a secretary of state. In 2011, The Little Nicolás also occupied a seat in the front row during Pope Benedict XVI's visit to Madrid.

During a business conference titled Spain Investment Forum, Francisco Nicolás shared a table with Ramiro Mato, then president of BNP Paribas Spain bank, Miguel Antoñanzas, then president of th energy supplier E.On Spain, as well as two prominent conservative politicians, Alvaro Nadal and Celia Villalobos. "I actually got to choose who was at my table," he told me. "And I even chose which famous person should give his name to our table: Goya, because he was also called Francisco."

Astoundingly, the climb of Nicolás also became lucrative. His conservative network allowed him to use a house in El Viso, he said, to organize business negotiations there. He said the arrangement included a security detail provided by Spain's security services (who does not have a bodyguard in Spain?). A Filipino couple looked after the house, prepared his food and kept him stocked with alcohol. He showed me another photo, of his kitchen bar overflowing with bottles of gin, rum and Johnny Walker whiskey. "The best part of having this house is that I could party there with my friends," he said. "We would drink and watch the football games together, before going out to a nightclub."

Each and every detail of his life suggested something that needed fixing in Spain, including in its education system. Years before leading politicians like Cristina Cifuentes were found to have been awarded unjustifiable university degrees, Francisco Nicolás turned instead his powerful patrons into his sponsors, in order to help him enter a good university despite his mediocre exam results.

García-Legaz wrote him personal recommendation letters. One of them was sent to Diego del Alcázar, the founder of the IE business school in Madrid, and another to Cunef (*Universidad de Estudios Financieros en Madrid*). Francisco Nicolás told me he was offered a place in both schools, but settled for Cunef rather than the IE because "that's where García-Legaz and many other ministers had studied." In his recommendation letter, García-Legaz highlighted "the accredited academic trajectory and notable talents of leadership" of Francisco Nicolás.

As I read this letter of recommendation, Francisco Nicolás offered his own self-evaluation. "The leadership part is true, I believe, but certainly not the academic, because I never went to class and just somehow managed to do enough to get by," he said. "I would never have got into a place like Cunef without help and if the entrance criteria had only been about my performance at school."

Soon enough, Francisco Nicolás reached the crossroads between politics and business, despite his very limited experience. Among his proudest moments, he claimed to have served as an intermediary in the negotiations between Madrid politicians and Sheldon Adelson, the American gambling tycoon who wanted to build a giant casino complex on the outskirts of Madrid, dubbed EuroVegas. Francisco Nicolás also talked to me at length about his meeting with the chief executive of the Las Vegas Sands company, Michael Levin. But the EuroVegas project was then abandoned in 2013 by Adelson, after a dispute over what tax breaks he could get in Madrid.

As I heard him talk about his past work, I kept remembering that Francisco Nicolás himself used the claim that he was suffering psychiatric problems as part of his legal defense. Along the way, some of his lawyers also abandoned him. But if he was just an impostor and a fabulator, how come he then got cleared in a court case against as powerful an agency as the CNI?

What is clear is that Francisco Nicolás drank heavily from the fountain of Spanish picaresque. One of his most crazy (and true) stories is that of his fake royal trip to the port town of Ribadeo, in the northwestern region of Galicia, whose officialdom had been hoping to receive instead the visit of King Felipe VI. The king never came, but somehow Francisco Nicolás stepped in as an emissary. He was treated to lunch by the town's mayor, after arriving in a convoy of four limousines. Off-duty police officers acted as his bodyguards. At the time of writing, Francisco Nicolás was still due to appear in court for pretending to be a royal representative, with prosecutors seeking a prison sentence of seven years for his Ribadeo escapade.

But when we spoke, his own view was that his downfall was tied to political rather than legal considerations. Francisco Nicolás attributed his downfall to Soraya Saenz de Santamaría, the then deputy head of government. He told me that she got upset to know that an adolescent had befriended some of the most powerful officials in her party.

Francisco Nicolás also ended up on the wrong side of the CNI after working for them, he said, notably on the Nóos fraud case that led Iñaki Urdangarin to prison. His alleged task was to get the lawyers of the Manos Limpias association to drop their pursuit of Urdangarin's wife, Princess Cristina. "They wanted me to convince the prosecution to give up and let her off the hook — and I came within an inch of managing that," Francisco Nicolás claimed. As with some of his other stories, Francisco Nicolás offered me no conclusive proof of his work for the CNI. He is perhaps a delusional young man who could still end up in prison for years, since his own court travails continued at the time of writing. But whatever his own fate, his downfall was also the prelude to one of the biggest scandals in Spain, centering on José Manuel Villarejo, a former police commissioner.

In fact, like most people in Spain, I first heard about Villarejo while following the trail of The Little Nicolás. In July 2016, Villarejo appeared in court after being indicted as part of The Little Nicolás investigation, because of tapes in which members of the police and secret service could be heard discussing him. A year later, Villarejo himself entered jail, after getting charged with crimes ranging from money laundering and bribery. Since then, his secret tapes have opened a window onto a frightening world of political and corporate spying and dirty trick. At the time of writing, Villarejo was the defendant in ten separate fraud investigations that have shaken the Spanish establishment.

Francisco Nicolás told me that he had never met Villarejo. But he somehow played a part in the demise of an over-powerful police inspector whose undercover activities reached into almost every major institution, from BBVA, one of Spain's largest banks, to the energy giant Iberdrola and of course to the political parties and even the finances of the monarchy.

Did money or power motivate Francisco Nicolás? "I wanted the power much more than the money," he replied. "If I had been only after money, I would not have had any of the legal problems that I ended up having. My self-criticism is not that I did anything particularly bad or special for Spain, but that, unlike many other people, I did these things when I was not really old and experienced enough to do them."

Having survived a court confrontation with the CNI, Francisco Nicolás did not decide that it was time to lie low. Instead, he has kept trying to use his past scandals as a springboard to more fame, appearing regularly on television shows including Gran Hermano VIP (a Spanish version of the UK's Big Brother housemates show), from which he was the first candidate to get kicked out of the house. In 2019, he also launched his own political party, Influencia Joven, hoping to win a seat in the European Parliament. He never got close to Strasbourg, but the foray kept Francisco Nicolás a bit longer in the limelight, which is where he has always hoped to be.

Perhaps inevitably given his advanced degree of self-esteem, Francisco Nicolás announced in late 2019 that he would star in a television series about his own life. After all, Spielberg made a Hollywood blockbuster about Abagnale. Rather than a mini-series about the life of a young man who remains in his 20s, I would recommend a two-part Spanish series. The first part could focus on the almost comic and childish adventures of The Little Nicolás. The second would be more somber: about how he helped shed light on the dark state embodied by a much scarier lead character, Inspector Villarejo.

El cuarto poder
Los tejemanejes de la prensa española en época de crisis

Journalism has been undergoing a major and often painful transformation, particularly for newspapers that have struggled to adjust to digital technology and weaker advertising revenues. I get reminders about the fast pace of change in the media world almost every month. There have been many startup publications, but also plenty of established companies that got forced out of business.

Shortly after arriving in Madrid, I met Al Goodman, a correspondent in Spain for CNN, who had found himself on the unpleasant receiving end of the American television network's decision to cut back its presence in Spain. Goodman kindly presented me with a welcome gift: the brass plates that once adorned the office of *The New York Times* in Madrid, which he had somehow inherited. The shiny engraved plates made me think about the life of the correspondent in the not-so-distant past, but before the age of Internet, when it would have been a struggle even to make a phone call to an editor in distant New York. I have nailed the brass plates into a wooden beam that stands in my apartment, which I now also call my office.

The good news, of course, is that *The New York Times* stands out as one of the publications that has gained rather than lost market share during the digital transformation. It has embraced the technological change to add more paying online subscribers. It has built up its international audience and diversified into different languages while maintaining the highest standards of journalism.

As I got to meet more Spanish journalists, however, I found their morale to be mostly poor. More worryingly, many of their complaints went beyond issues of job uncertainty, unsatisfactory pay or excessive workload. Instead, journalists often told me about how hard it was to investigate and write about what they wanted, because their newsroom had been losing editorial independence amid a financial squeeze.

By late 2015, I had heard enough to feel that it was time to alert an international audience to the significant malaise building up within Spanish journalism, particularly since it also seemed to have political and economic implications, highlighted by the circumstances of some firings and high-profile departures from news-rooms. Over the preceding two years, the editors of three major Spanish newspapers had been ousted. Their removal came amid financial losses, but also followed the publication of articles that had ruffled feathers in Spain's political establishment.

The best-known and the most outspoken of these editors, Pedro Jota Ramírez, had publicly blamed his dismissal from his news-paper, *El Mundo*, on his decision to publish embarrassing text messages sent by President Mariano Rajoy to his former party treasurer, Luis Bárcenas, shortly after Bárcenas entered prison. *El Mundo* was one of the newspapers that had investigated whether millions amassed in Swiss offshore accounts by Bárcenas were tied to a slush fund operated by Rajoy's Popular Party. Other news-papers also wrote about this story, but Ramírez insisted that he had been singled out for recrimination by the government.

After leaving *El Mundo*, Ramírez decided to create a new online publication, *El Español*, financed in part by the money from his severance package from *El Mundo*. I soon visited him to hear his views about how the Spanish media was changing. I also spoke to several other prominent reporters and columnists, many of whom agreed to meet on the condition that they should remain anony-mous, often because they feared that they could get fired for criticizing their employer or colleagues. It seemed sad and ironic to think that journalism, a profession that defends freedom of expression, was itself facing a situation where journalists could risk dismissal for speaking out. Some of my meetings were in fact with people who had already been ousted, but they gave me valuable information and even access to some important documents that they had kept as evidence to show that their dismissal had been unfair. In any case, in line with the policy of *The New York Times*, I decided to make sure that I would quote the views of only those people who had agreed to speak on the record.

Published in November 2015, my article discussed broadly the situation of the Spanish media, from the RTVE national broadcaster to different newspapers, in the context of an industry in which about 11,000 journalists had lost their jobs in the seven years since 2008 and the start of the financial crisis. The article also featured criticism from outside Spain, including a report on Spanish media freedom jointly written by the Vienna-based International Press Institute and three other media watchdogs. The report called on Spain to guarantee the independence of the national broadcaster and allocate public advertising money in a more transparent manner. It also said that Spain's freedom of expression and of the press could be threatened by a recent law that quickly became known by its critics as the "gag law," because it allowed the authorities to fine heavily people for offenses like holding unauthorized protests.

I wrote different articles relating to this gag law, including a front-page one in February 2016, after two puppeteers got detained during Madrid's carnival celebrations for staging a show that was considered to have glorified terrorism and promoted hatred. But when it came to the media, I also contacted business people and politicians to hear whether they felt that journalists could work without unfair constraints. Pablo Casado, who was then the spokesman for the Popular Party, told me that "I don't see a problem with the press in Spain," in terms of political interference.

One of my main focus was RTVE, because of the mounting complaints about its bias political coverage, which felt particularly unjustifiable since the public broadcaster was meant to air news that was watched by — and paid for — by all citizens, irrespective of their ideological leanings. Neither RTVE nor any other newspaper responded angrily to my article, with the notable exception of *El País*. At the time, the newsroom of El País was led by Antonio Caño as editor-in-chief, while Juan Luis Cebrián, the co-founder of *El País*, was executive chairman of PRISA (a media conglomerate), the parent company of the newspaper.

In my article, I mentioned some of the internal tensions over editorial independence at *El País*, which seemed odd for a newspaper that established itself as Spain's leading newspaper in the late 1970s when it chronicled Spain's return to democracy. I talked about how Caño had quashed an attempt by members of his newsroom committee to organize a vote of confidence over his leadership. I also mentioned examples of articles that had been either altered or removed from the *El País* website, prompting internal complaints from members of its editorial committee.

Two of these controversial articles concerned Qatar, at a time when PRISA was negotiating an investment from a Qatari company. Another two articles involved Telefónica, a company that was a shareholder of PRISA and that had bought part of its television assets the year before, helping PRISA cut significantly its debt. Following changes made to an article discussing Telefónica's ties to the government, I learnt that two upset journalists had walked out of *El País*. After hearing about the departure of the two journalists, I reached out to Caño and Cebrián to ask their views. But they both declined to meet me, even though I had previously had no major difficulty in interviewing Cebrián about more positive matters, including a much-needed capital increase that PRISA received from an American fund called Liberty.

As a last resort, I decided instead to attend a public presentation by Caño, which allowed me to ask him a question from the audience about the independence of his newspaper from business and political interests. In his answer, Caño said that PRISA's debt burden "in no way" affected his newspaper's editorial content, but he acknowledged that Spanish journalists worked in a country where "the political powers are frankly very far removed from Britain in terms of accepting the fundamental role fulfilled by the media." Cebrián, who was also at the presentation, backed Caño and also stressed newsroom independence. "What gets published is what the editor of *El País* wants to publish," he said.

Once my article was published, *El País* tried to discredit my work. At the same time, the Spanish association of newspaper publishers issued a press release that claimed that my article was a caricature. But then again, the chairman of the association at the time also happened to be the chief executive of PRISA. Caño sent to the management of the *New York Times* a detailed list of what he described as the fallacies in my article, as well as claiming that I had long shown personal hostility toward *El País*. Separately, David Alandete, who was the managing editor of *El País*, called me to complain, saying that my article showed that I was not qualified to work as a correspondent. I saw little point in trying to fight back during what felt like a very unpleasant phone call.

El País next commissioned its correspondents in New York to write an article attacking *The New York Times* for conflicts of interest. The article, published a few days after mine, talked about the expansion of *The Times* in Mexico, at a time when Carlos Slim, the Mexican tycoon, was among its important shareholders. "This link has raised doubts about the difficulty for *The Times* to maintain its independent editorial line with a shareholder of such influence," the article stated, without explaining exactly who had such doubts. In fact, the article didn't quote a single person by name talking about *The New York Times*, nor did anybody offer *The New York*

Times a right of response before its publication, in breach of what is generally seen as a fundamental rule of ethical journalism.

The story could have ended there, but it did not. A few days later, *El País* ousted one of its veteran columnists, Miguel Ángel Aguilar. I had quoted Aguilar warning about the decline of Spanish journalism and saying that some people were leaving *El País* "sometimes even with the feeling that the situation has reached levels of censorship." Aguilar knew much about *El País*, but also the history of journalism in Spain. And he clearly understood the dangers of censorship. During the Franco dictatorship, he was put on trial for promoting public disorder while working at *Diario Madrid*, a newspaper that was then closed down by Franco's regime.

Just before his ouster, Aguilar had founded his own publication, Ahora (which proved short-lived.) But even if he was already engaged in the Ahora project, his unceremonious removal from *El País* still prompted reports in several other publications, which focused on how *El País* had launched what one journalist described as "an open war" with *The New York Times*. I personally did not feel at war with anybody, but I was upset to realize that I had underestimated the reaction to my article. If anything, I had expected *El Mundo* rather than *El País* to get perhaps upset, because I placed the problems at *El Mundo* above those at *El País* in the running order of my article.

Of course, Caño, whom I previously had only briefly met, had every right to defend his management. But I was surprised his newspaper escalated a dispute that was followed by a commercial divorce with *The New York Times*. *El País* severed an agreement to share some printing facilities in Europe with *The New York Times*. It also stopped publishing a weekly supplement of articles from *The Times*, which it had translated for more than a decade. The purpose of my article had been to highlight concerns among journalists about whether the editorial agenda was being taken hostage by their management, shareholders, as well as powerful politicians and businessmen. If anything, I had not included in my article all that I found out about *El País*, partly for lack of space but also because some of my information came from off-the record meetings and internal reports from the newspaper's editorial committee.

For an international readership, my goal had been to write about the broader situation of the Spanish media, rather than only the issues facing one specific newspaper. If anything, the response from the management of *El País* to my article suggested to me that the problem in Spain was at least as serious as I had understood it to be.

In this book, I decided to return at some length to this incident not to revive this controversy, but because I believe the underlying issues remain relevant. Spain, like any other democracy, needs to do everything possible to safeguard the independence of its media. Since my article was published, there have been several more changes within Spanish newsrooms. A new generation of online publications has gained prominence, delivering several scoops that have added to the pressure on more established newspapers. Meanwhile, the abrupt turnovers at the top of the newsroom hierarchy have also continued, including at *El Mundo* and *El País*, where Soledad Gallego-Díaz took over from Caño to become the first woman to run the newsroom, as part of a major reshuffle. She was herself then replaced in 2020.

The debate within Spanish journalism has also become a bit more open. In late 2016, I met for coffee with David Jiménez, who had recently been ousted as director of *El Mundo*. He told me that he was pursuing a lawsuit against *El Mundo*'s management for unfair dismissal. The case, he said, would force into the courtroom several of the most important players in the media industry, as witnesses who could help expose unethical or illegal practices. It sounded like Jiménez would be starting the Spanish media trial of the century.

Instead, Jiménez reached a financial settlement with *El Mundo* and dropped his lawsuit in January 2017, just days before the court case was due to start. Two years later, he published a book in which he presented his year running *El Mundo* as the equivalent of traveling on a fragile raft, against the tide and surrounded by sharks, sometimes disguised as friendly fish. The book also highlighted influence peddling within Spanish journalism that started long before the financial crisis and had nothing to do with a lack of money. In particular, he highlighted systematic plagiarism, defamatory reporting and reliance on unsourced reports. Jiménez wrote that he ended *El Mundo*'s longstanding collaboration with José Manuel Villarejo, the former police commissioner. According to Jiménez's book, Villarejo gave *El Mundo* "most of our scoops" during two decades. It depressed me to think of *El Mundo*, one of the most important newspapers of the country, as a longstanding mouthpiece for Villarejo and his murky schemes. Villarejo was jailed in late 2017 on charges ranging from bribery to money laundering.

Greater media competition can prove very beneficial in Spain or any other democratic society. But there is only an upside if this competition does not turn into a desperate race to the bottom, in which all the participants jump various traffic lights or end up dying from financial asphyxiation. In America and elsewhere, the competition is also intense, forcing media companies to adjust their strategy over and over again. I joined Bloomberg News in 1993, when it was opening an office in Zurich as part of its European expansion. In modern parlance, Bloomberg was then a startup in the news business, treated by some of my competitors at the time from the newspaper establishment as little more than an annoying and over-ambitious younger sister. Even though Bloomberg quickly gained the respect of an important clientele of Zurich bankers, who traded thanks to the trove of information provided by the bulky Bloomberg terminal, the brand was not known to the public at large in Switzerland, nor even sometimes at the highest echelons of government. I remember calling a Swiss official and having to show some patience in order to convince him that my company, Bloomberg, was not in any way related to Bloomingdale's, the American luxury retailer whom he knew very well.

When I left Bloomberg to join the *Financial Times* in 2000, the newspaper was still fine-tuning its online offering. My bureau chief in Paris at the time made it clear to me that he was not interested in writing for the ft.com website and that he would stick to the late afternoon deadline to hand in his articles for the print edition. He was probably part of the last generation of correspondents to enjoy this luxury of time and to consider that what was published online was little more than a draft for what would later go into print.

Over the past decade, I have also seen *The New York Times* change tack. For several decades, *The Times* owned other print publications, including *The International Herald Tribune*, which was first published in France in 1887 under the name of *Paris Herald*. The *Herald* was one of the first publications to be delivered in Europe by plane, to the delight of several generations of readers within my own family. As a child, I often used to get up in order to run to my grandparents' letter box and then deliver the newspaper proudly to their dining room table, just as they were enjoying their breakfast.

But while the *Herald* maintained the unshakable loyalty of my family and many others worldwide, it never developed its own website, so that those searching online for its articles were redirected to the page of *The New York Times*. Slowly but surely, the brand's reliance on print in the age of Internet sealed its fate. In 2016, *The New York Times* announced the closure of its Paris headquarters in Europe, to focus fully on developing a single worldwide brand targeted at digital readers. Dozens of jobs were lost, a few of my Paris editors transferred to London, where they were then joined by others crossing the Atlantic from New York. London took over from Paris as the European hub in what is a 24-hour news operation in which the most important decisions are still taken in New York, but the baton is passed over at regular intervals between senior editors based in New York, London and Hong Kong.

One of the main challengers to *The New York Times* is *The Washington Post*, which was purchased in 2013 for $250 million in cash by Jeff Bezos, the founder of Amazon. The purchase was presented at the time as evidence of media philanthropy, but Bezos was not just handing out charity money. Instead, he has invested enough not only to sustain the newspaper but also to return it to profit within three years of his purchase. As discussed elsewhere in this book, Spain has a deficit when it comes to philanthropy. In terms of helping the media industry, there does not seem to be anybody like Bezos in Spain, who can combine deep pockets, business acumen and a real belief in the turnaround potential of a strong newspaper brand.

The jury is still out to determine who will gain and lose out in Spanish media, but it seems clear that the newspaper industry will remain financially vulnerable as long as some publications continue to offer their online content for free. Hiding articles behind a pay wall can have a painful impact in the short term, as readers look for free news elsewhere. But in the longer term, it seems to me the best and perhaps only way to maintain financial viability. *The New York Times* introduced its paywall in 2011. At the time, I spoke to some Spanish media executives who tried to convince me that the poor habits of the readership had become too deeply entrenched and that it was near-impossible to fight against the "culture of the free" in Spain.

In response, I would draw a parallel for them with the problem of online film piracy, which was very serious when I arrived in Spain in April 2010. Shortly after I settled down, one of my new friends told me about a character called Danko who had become famous among Spain's online movie fans. But nobody actually knew who Danko was, because it was only the pseudonym used by a prolific and enigmatic supplier of downloadable movies and television series, which people watched on websites like Vagos and Series Yonkis. My friend was at the time watching for free a popular American series, *Lost*, on a website managed by Danko.

The problem was so serious that Spain had just been put, for the third year running, on a warning list drawn up by the American government of countries that breach intellectual property rights. Spain was labeled as a country with "particularly significant Internet piracy." My business editor was interested in this issue, which had clear implications for Hollywood. In early 2010, Sony Pictures Entertainment, a leading American movie studio, warned that it was considering halting altogether the sale of its DVDs in Spain because of rampant piracy.

Spanish experts at the time told me that it would be very hard to stop illegal piracy, particularly because most people did not view it as a crime. In fact, Spanish judges had been issuing ambivalent rulings. In 2006, Spain's attorney general advised that peer-to-peer downloading should only be considered criminal if it could be shown that it was done to make a profit.A decade later, piracy has not disappeared, but the situation has clearly improved. Series Yonkis was closed down and its founders were taken to court, although they were eventually absolved of wrongdoing in 2019. Most of my friends now subscribe to watch their entertainment on platforms like Netflix, HBO or Movistar. They enjoy the higher quality and are willing to pay for it. In 2018, Netflix even chose Spain as the location for its first European production hub.

Some media executives might be right that there is no reason to think Spanish readers will pay for their news, just because they are now paying to watch their favorite television series. I might be comparing apples and oranges. But it does seem that Spanish newspapers are finally taking heart from the example set by Netflix and others in Spain. In May 2020, *El País* became the latest major newspaper to set up a paywall. Spurred on by technology developments and better content, I do believe people can change their habits.

La presunción de inocencia
Las acusaciones de pederastia contra un cura granadino

It rarely rains in Granada, but when it does, it can really pour. During a miserably wet week of January 2015, I visited the city to report on what sounded like a miserable story. Together with Laura Léon, the photographer who has worked with me on several reporting trips, we drove around Granada until we found the church of Father Román Martínez. He was the priest at the heart of one of the most serious sexual abuse scandals to emerge in Spain since Pope Francis became the head of the Roman Catholic Church. In fact, the Pope had directly intervened in the scandal, as part of a more hands-on crusade by the Vatican against sexual predators operating within the Church.

In 2014, a former altar boy, David Ramírez Castillo, wrote to Pope Francis, detailing the sexual abuse that he and others allegedly suffered repeatedly when they were teenagers, at the hands of a group formed mainly by priests and led by Father Román. The Pope then phoned him and urged him to pursue his complaints and inform Granada's archbishop. Pope Francis also ordered a Church investigation into the case, demanding complete transparency. The scandal eventually ended up in a criminal court.

By the time I visited Granada, Father Román had been ostracized. After the Pope's intervention, Granada's diocese suspended Father Román and the other main suspects from their public duties as priests. A few months later, four people were briefly detained as part of the judge's inquiry, including Father Román, who was released after posting bail of 10,000 euros. Altogether, 12 people, including 10 priests, faced charges of abusing young boys or covering up for Father Román, who was portrayed as the ring leader.

Although I did not manage to speak to any of the priests, I did not even need to enter the church of San Juan María Vianney to understand how some residents felt betrayed by Father Román. The outside walls of the church had recently been whitewashed, to remove some offensive graffiti. Underneath the fresh paint, however, it was still possible to decipher some very offensive comments, which had been sprayed in red against Father Román and his fellow priests.

The church stood next to a school that was managed by nuns, so I decided to wait outside to talk to parents about the sex scandal. I wanted to know how local families felt about their priests. I could imagine that some were preparing their children for their First Communion. "I don't understand how anybody religious could hurt somebody, let alone a child," a mother called Úrsula Muñoz told me, as she held her young daughter. She said she still wanted her daughter to have her First Communion, but planned to organize the event within her school rather than in a church.

Later that day, we drove up a windy road into the hills of Granada, to a village called Pinos de Genil. On one of its streets, we found the villa where Father Román and other priests often stayed during the summer months.

Most of the information that I had about the scandal came from a summary of the accusations that was released by an investigating judge, Antonio Moreno. It included different witness statements, as well as an account by Ramírez about how Father Román and other priests had turned their hilltop villa into the ideal and secluded spot to host their parties and indulge their sexual fantasies. The priests would cool off in the pool and then shower naked in front of their teenage guests, according to the judge's report. The group would also sometimes watch gay pornography videos while touching one another. Ramírez described the bedside flask of rosemary oil that he claimed Father Román used while receiving full body massages from fellow clerics or other guests. His account went as far as detailing a birthmark on Father Román's penis.

The villa was shuttered when I visited. Given the bad weather, the streets were deserted and only a dog could be heard barking incessantly in one of the neighboring gardens. I found it hard to imagine the place on a hot summer day, with priests sharing the garden pool with their altar boys and other friends. By the time Ramírez wrote to the Pope, he was in his 20s. But he had known Father Román since he was a 7-year-old catechism student. Later, he became one of his altar boys. Step by step, Ramírez said in his court statement, the priest convinced him that to deepen his faith he should spend more time with him and the other priests.

That evening, I met in a bar with Father Román's lawyer, Javier Muriel. I was grateful that Muriel had picked a place located along one of Granada's arcaded streets, so that I did not get soaked on the walk there, as the rain was showing no sign of abating.

As expected, Muriel gave me a very different account. He told me the priest was the victim of a fabrication and that his life had now been ruined by the scandal, even if he hoped to clear his name in court. "Can you imagine what it means for a priest to deal with this?" Muriel said. "I hope that one day we find out why anybody invented such accusations."

I had read enough about pedophilia and other forms of sex abuse within the Catholic Church to find it hard to feel much sympathy. And although much of the case against Father Román and his fellow priests rested on the claims of Ramírez, one other plaintiff had added his name to the case, another former altar boy called Josue Heredia. There were also some witnesses, one of whom I managed to track down, although he only agreed to speak to me on condition that he would not be named. During our interview, he explained how his relationship with Father Román evolved from attending Mass to going regularly to his home to "play cards, chess or watch television." He stopped seeing the priest, he said, after one day going to his apartment to have a shower, after sports. When he stepped out, Father Román tried to touch his genitals, he said.

Ramírez, the main plaintiff against Father Román, did not cut loose from the church after reaching adulthood and leaving Granada. Instead, he eventually joined Opus Dei, the Catholic movement deeply rooted in Spain, where it was founded in 1928. His lawyer, Jorge Aguilera, suggested that his client had felt unable to report the abuse while in Granada but had found it "easier from 1,000 kilometers away," after he moved to Pamplona to complete a doctorate in psychology at the University of Navarra, which has close ties to Opus Dei. Aguilera said that his main worry was that some of the crimes committed by the priests had already prescribed, given how much time had elapsed between the abuses and the start of the court proceedings.

While I could understand why Ramírez, traumatized by the abuse, had not spoken out earlier, I struggled to see why the diocese of Granada had not managed to stop a dozen of its priests from violating its own rules. After all, even though Granada is a sizable city of about 230,000 residents, it seemed likely that more people knew about the villa and the invitations handed out by the priests. In fact, "this story would never have come to light if the Pope hadn't intervened," Amina Nasser, a local journalist, told me. Nasser then detailed her own investigations for her publication, *Andaluces Diario*, into the diocese of Granada, whose reputation had already been tainted by unrelated claims of financial mismanagement after a spending spree by its archbishop.

After the Pope's intervention, the archbishop of Granada, Francisco Javier Martínez Fernández, prostrated himself alongside some other priests in front of the cathedral's altar. "We will pray for a few minutes in silence to God to ask his forgiveness for all the Church's crimes, for all the scandals there have been and for those that may have taken place among us and anywhere in the world," the archbishop said during the service that he delivered that day. When Granada's archbishop then traveled to Rome to visit Pope Francis, there was speculation that he would be asked to resign. Instead, the Pope urged the archbishop to "come down from the cross" and face up to problems within his diocese, according to the account of their meeting given to me by Paqui Pallarés, a spokeswoman for the Granada diocese.

By the time I had finished my reporting, I had enough material to write a story that made the front page of the American edition, under a headline that read "In Spanish abuse scandal, a more open Vatican." What had most interested the editors of the newspaper was not the lurid details of the sex abuse but instead the broader context in which the scandal was unfolding, under a new Pope that seemed keen to differentiate his approach to sex offenders from that of his predecessor, Pope Benedict. After all, America had been gripped by one of the worst sexual abuse scandals, centered on the diocese of Boston, which was eventually turned into an Oscar-winning movie, *Spotlight*.

My story included a section written by one of our correspondents in Rome, about how Pope Francis was bringing "a new sense of personal contact and public outrage to the issue" of sex abuse that contrasted with the image of an unresponsive bureaucracy that the Vatican had previously had. Francis had candidly talked during a plane trip about the Granada sex scandal. "I received this news with great pain, very great pain," the Pope told a Spanish journalist during the flight, "but the truth is the truth and we should not hide it." Still, my Rome colleague also included into the story an important caveat about the Pope's fight against sex abuse within his Church, noting that several victims were left waiting for help after filing claims. At the time, the Vatican was also delaying a long-promised sex abuse trial of its former ambassador to the Dominican Republic, Archbishop Józef Wesołowski.

This Granada story resonated with readers. After its publication, I received some emails from people who wanted to tell me about their own grievances toward the Catholic Church. But the most important email that I got was from Ramírez, the main plaintiff. Far from welcoming the fact that I was talking about the abuses of the Granada clergy, he told me that he was taking me to court for mentioning him by name in my story, unlike the Spanish news media, which had written about the scandal but never exposed his personal identity. Ramírez told me that he was filing a criminal lawsuit against me for violating a Spanish privacy law of 1999 protecting victims of sexual abuse. "You can't do anything you want, Mr. Minder, to sell more," he wrote to me.

My response started with an apology for causing him more pain. But I also explained to him that I had consulted with his lawyer and forewarned that I would be naming him, using the fact that the judge in Granada had decided to lift the secrecy order over the investigation. Anybody who visited the courtroom could find out his name and use the information within the judge's report. I also explained why it was important to give a balanced account that respected the presumption of innocence of priests who were defendants, but whose reputation had already been seriously tarnished. I wanted to stick to the deontology of journalism based as far as possible on facts and information, not rumors and accusations. The reader, I argued, deserved to know that such a major accusation was not anonymous, but coming from an actual victim, who continued to suffer.

Ramírez did not accept my apology and assured me that I would lose the court case he was launching against me. In a separate email, he asked me whether I really believed the Spanish media should have published his name: "Do you think that if no Spanish newspaper has published my name, it is because they are not giving truthful information?" Luckily, no judge ever ordered me to appear in court in Granada. Instead, two years later, I found myself writing again about the case, after another Spanish court cleared Father Román, saying that there was no evidence that he had sexually abused a former altar boy.

In a 81-page ruling, the judge listed several events and details provided by Ramírez that could not be corroborated or proved false. For instance, there was no birthmark on Father Román's penis, contrary to what Ramírez had claimed. The court also found no evidence that the priest lived in any kind of "perverse pedophile atmosphere," as was alleged in Ramírez's version of events.

The priest's lawyer, Javier Muriel, told me on the phone that the verdict showed the case was based on lies. "It is all too easy to denounce pedophilia, a crime that happens in privacy and in which the testimony of the victim is really the only proof," Muriel said. The archdiocese of Granada welcomed the ruling, saying that it put an end to "the suffering that this case has caused, within the diocese but in reality within the whole Church." Ramírez, for his part, did not respond to my request for fresh comment.

Father Román rejoined the Church, after his suspension from office was lifted by the Vatican. He decided not to seek compensation in court for the personal damage suffered, and was instead welcomed to the Vatican by Pope Francis in July 2018. The Pope apologized to him for the personal calvary that he had endured, according to Muriel, the lawyer. That part of the story, however, was barely reported by journalists. "This outcome didn't grab any media attention, only at a very local level," Muriel noted.

By the time the Pope met Father Román, the news spotlight had long left Granada. Beyond the issues raised by this scandal, it crystalized for me a lot of what can go wrong when the media jump onto a story before it reaches a court verdict. In 2015, the government passed a law that changed the terminology used to describe a person in the early stages of a court case, from indicted to under investigation. The justice minister at the time, Rafael Catalá, said that the change was needed because the word "indicted" had "a high level of semantic contamination" and it was important instead to use a word that didn't hurt the defendant unduly.

There are plenty of reasons to continue investigating the Church in Spain, notably over how it has consolidated its wealth through the opaque registration of churches as private property. But there are reasons for the media to be more cautious when dealing with possible scandals, particularly as the pace of the judicial work in Spain means that years can elapse between the opening of an investigation and its conclusion.

How many times have I followed corruption scandals in the Spanish media in which the defendants got dragged through the mud long before they even appeared before a judge? And what to make of the newspapers that have based entire stories on unsourced leaks, some of which proved fake news? As discussed elsewhere in this book, the scandal of José Manuel Villarejo, the police inspector, is also that of the Spanish media that participated in his defamatory work. Without the help of acquiescent journalists, Villarejo could not have spread his damaging reports on behalf of his powerful clients.

In Granada, I had done my best to speak to all the relevant people for an important story that had upset Pope Francis and then made the front page of my newspaper, but which a court later judged to be fundamentally flawed. Sometimes, the best intentions do not yield a perfect result.

Recuperar una herencia
El pasado sefardí de la península

In May 2011, Spain invited the Sephardi Chief Rabbi of Israel, who represents the Jews who fled the Iberian peninsula. He was the first important Jewish religious leader to visit the country in over five centuries. The Chief Rabbi, Shlomo Moshe Amar, landed in Madrid. But the most important and emotional part of his trip was a visit to Granada and its Alhambra palace, in particular to the throne room where one of the expulsion edicts was signed by the Catholic Kings, in 1492.

I was assigned to cover an event that seemed relevant not only for Spain but for Jews worldwide. *The New York Times* covers closely events relating to the Jews and their history, so I did some preparatory work and met with members of the delegation from Israel before the excursion to Granada.

The Madrid meeting took place at Casa Sefarad (Sefarad is the Hebrew word for Spain), an agency of the Spanish foreign ministry set up to promote relations with Spanish Jewry and Israel, as well as a greater understanding of Jewish culture within Spanish society. The evening gathering was also a chance for Spanish and Israeli officials to make a final review of the logistics of the Granada trip, and I listened in on their conversation. One of the Spanish officials explained that the Chief Rabbi would visit Granada's city hall and then the Alhambra, where he would also be the guest of honor at a special luncheon held at the beautiful Parador hotel that is adjacent to the Alhambra palace.

A member of the Israeli delegation asked whether it was possible to look at the menu. His Spanish counterpart told him that he didn't have the details, but that the food would no doubt be varied and delicious. "And of course kosher, right?" the Israeli asked. An embarrassing silence followed that question. The Spanish official then suggested that it would be possible to avoid any problematic dish on the menu, but the Israeli kindly explained that it was not just a question of what was on the table, but how and where the food had been prepared. The search for an alternative kosher venue in Granada proved unfruitful. Even though Granada had about 230,000 inhabitants, it had no establishment where the rabbi could eat. Eventually, the Israelis scrambled to order their own food from back home, and make sure that it could be delivered by plane in time for the Rabbi's lunch. The following day, the official luncheon in the Parador still went ahead, but of course without the Chief Rabbi. I joined him instead for a picnic in the lovely gardens of the Alhambra. The weather was perfect, the trees provided plenty of shade and the Chief Rabbi seemed unfazed by this strange situation, whereby he was a guest of honor sitting on a garden bench, very far from the top table at the official lunch venue.

As he was trying to decide whether to tuck into a plastic tub of humus or a plate of biscuits, I asked the Chief Rabbi what he made of his improvised picnic. "Birds don't eat kosher," he said. "When you have a place that no longer has Jews, you also cannot expect it to have the proper structures to cater to the needs and eating habits of Jews." Overall, the visit was still a success. The Chief Rabbi heard from different officials about the importance of the Jews in Spain, although nobody offered him a direct apology for the expulsion of the Jews in 1492. In return, the Chief Rabbi praised Spain's progress in terms of rekindling the relationship with the Jews.

During the visit to Granada's City Hall, he told the mayor, José Torres Hurtado, that "we now see that this city is full of the light of wisdom, liberty and splendor." Sitting in a salon decorated with religious paintings depicting scenes of the birth and death of Jesus Christ, the Chief Rabbi added: "I consider this visit to be very special because, after centuries, we are erasing the darkness that has covered this relationship." In response, the mayor highlighted "the perfect harmony between cultures" that prevails in modern

Granada. He also shared a joke with the Chief Rabbi: "Let us hope that not so much time goes by until the next visit" by a Jewish religious leader.

But the experience of the garden picnic remained in my mind as a striking example of how a society can easily forget its past — and how hard it is to revive its memory. As the Chief Rabbi had said, it is probably wrong to expect any country to consider the plight of a community that no longer has an important place within its society.

Although there is scant official data, the Jewish community in Spain nowadays is estimated to number between 25,000 and 45,000 members, in a country of 47 million people. This figure is only a fraction of the number of Jews living in Spain before 1492, when the Iberian peninsula was an epicenter of Jewry. Even before getting expelled, Spain's Jewish population started to dwindle, as a result of pogroms, conversions and a devastating plague.

In recent years, Spain has been making important efforts to rebuild its Jewish community. The most significant step has been a 2015 law to grant Spanish citizenship to people who can prove that they descend from the Sephardi Jews who were forced to flee after the order of expulsion of 1492. In the first four years after the law came into force, about 10,000 people with Jewish ancestry managed to claim Spanish citizenship. In the same period, Spain has stood out as one of the countries that has mostly avoided the anti-Semitic violence and abuses that Jews have suffered in other parts of Europe, including countries like France, where several Jewish cemeteries and other buildings have been desecrated.

This is not to say that anti-Semitism is never an issue in Spain. In May 2014, the New York-based Anti Defamation League released its first global survey on anti-Semitism, which found that 29 percent of adult Spanish respondents were judged to harbor prejudicial stereotypes about Jews. A week later, even more alarmingly, I wrote a story about an outburst of Spanish anti-Semitism provoked by a disappointing result in sports. After Real Madrid lost to Maccabi Tel Aviv in the final of Europe's main basketball tournament, almost 18,000 people posted comments on Twitter with a profane and anti-Semitic hashtag. Jewish associations soon filed a lawsuit, citing Spanish legislation against the incitement of hatred. Danny Federman, the general manager of Maccabi, called it "very disappointing to see the rush of anti-Semitism following a well-fought competition."

But overall, in my experience, anti-Jewish feelings in Spain are mostly derived from concerns over the politics of the Middle East, in particular strong sympathy in Spain for the Palestinian cause. I have met some otherwise highly educated people in Spain who really struggle to differentiate between their unhappiness with the politics of Israel, particularly during the long mandate of Prime Minister Benjamin Netanyahu, and other matters that relate to the Jewish religion. When he was appointed by President Barack Obama as U.S. ambassador to Spain, Alan Solomont was disappointed to hear that several Spanish newspapers had presented him as "a Jewish millionaire." "I was coming to represent the United States, so this was not the way I wanted to be described," Solomont told me several years later.

Still, as soon as he reached Madrid, Solomont got a much more positive impression. In January 2010, on the day that he presented his credentials as ambassador to King Juan Carlos I, Solomont also sped across the city in his armored Cadillac limousine to attend a remembrance ceremony for the Shoah (Holocaust), organized by the regional government. "I found that Spanish people had very little familiarity with the Jews, but that they cared about overcoming the distance with their past, including Spanish politicians," Solomont said. Part of his work in Spain, he said, involved "giving a more balanced picture than the bad perception of Spain that exists in some parts of the Jewish American community."

For several years, I have accompanied as a lecturer a group of readers of *The New York Times* on a weeklong tourism visit to Andalusia. The trip is advertised as a visit to a "Center of Judaism, Christianity and Islam," where sites of all three major religions coexist. Each year, it has attracted several American Jews, some of whom are already very familiar with the history of the Jews in the Iberian peninsula. Not being Jewish, I have also found spending time with these Jewish visitors on the roads of Andalusia to be a great learning experience. To cater to this audience, a sizable part of the tour is devoted to showcasing what is left of Spain's Jewish past. The short answer is that not much remains. In Sevilla, for instance, our group walks around the former Jewish quarter, where the local guide mostly asks us to imagine what a former synagogue and some buildings once owned by wealthy and influential Jews must have looked like centuries ago, before they were destroyed, remodeled or turned into a church.

Occasionally, our group also gets to meet officials involved in Jewish affairs in Spain, including from the federation that represents the Jews (*Federación de Comunidades Judías de España.*) Over a dinner in Toledo, I witnessed an embarrassing conversation between a Spanish official and one of the American visitors, who was a woman from New York who had done her doctorate in Jewish history and could read ancient texts in Aramaic. The Spanish official, who was not Jewish, clearly had not expected to be submitted to her precise and detailed questions and struggled to answer any of them.

On the road from Sevilla to Granada, our tour visits the town of Úbeda, one of the lesser known cultural gems of Andalusia. One of our stops is the Synagogue of Water, which was discovered around 2007 and has since become one of the most visited places in Úbeda, drawing about 40,000 tourists a year. Stone steps lead down to its underground ritual bath, or *mikveh*, filled with crystalline water.

The 13th century synagogue has been admired by several travel writers and was described in Fodor's Spain guidebook as one of the "amazing discoveries" of Úbeda, a town that is itself on Unesco's list of World Heritage Sites. So amazing, in fact, that it might not be quite true. Even as the synagogue's promoters continue to publicize the extraordinary circumstances in which the synagogue was discovered, I once received an email from a Spanish expert in Jewish history, who had read about our itinerary. He wanted to forewarn me that our guests would be visiting a place that made a fictitious claim about its Jewish legacy. I looked into this claim and found that some archeologists also questioned the authenticity of the synagogue, noting that the place was excavated by a local property developer who relied exclusively on his own builders rather than experts in ancient history.

Úbeda's water synagogue has been managed as a museum by Andrea Pezzini, a very friendly and welcoming Italian who has contributed significantly to tourism in Úbeda, after he himself decided to settle there 25 years ago. Pezzini has his own tourism company and not only runs the synagogue but also the most famous monument of Úbeda, which is a giant mausoleum, built by one of the main Spanish architects of the Renaissance, that dominates the town's main square.

When I asked him for proof that the synagogue had served as

a Jewish religious site, Pezzini acknowledged that there was no scientific documentation to confirm the *mikveh* and the other features of the synagogue. But he said that any criticism leveled by archeologists and others was probably driven by "envy or unhappiness because they don't control this place." He added: "Are archeologists or historians the holders of the absolute truth? For me, what matters more is that we have had Jewish people pray, sing and even get married here."

Francisca Hornos Mata, the director of the museum in Jaén, the capital city of the province to which Úbeda belongs, said that she didn't want to fuel any controversy over the synagogue, even if its promoters had not respected some rules. "Perhaps the fundamental problem is the absence of any investigation prior to the decisions to restore and recreate" the site as a synagogue, she said.

The synagogue was discovered just before the bursting of Spain's property bubble. Fernando Crespo, a real estate entrepreneur, decided to convert a rundown building into new apartments and shops. In 2007, as his builders started working on what was going to be the building's underground garage, they stumbled upon arches and pillars. Crespo, who also collects antiquities, put a halt to his project and decided instead that his workers should change tack and excavate what has now become the synagogue museum, made up of six different rooms that are also filled with ancient Jewish relics, most of which were actually found elsewhere and then transported to the museum. Pezzini said that there were historic documents showing that Úbeda was an important Jewish town at least until 1391, when Jews suffered a pogrom. The *mikveh* is in an underground chamber that may have already been used thousands of years earlier as a ritual site, he said, particularly as it gets hit every summer solstice by an extraordinary shaft of sunlight.

For me, the debate over the origins of the synagogue raised the broader issue of whether Spain is now doing too much to highlight and earn tourism income from a Jewish heritage that got mostly destroyed. In fact, Jewish tourism has recently become big business in Spain, especially since its government acknowledged the wrongdoing of the past and adopted its citizenship law for descendants of Sephardic Jews. One of the most curious recent examples of Jewish revival in Spain occurred in a tiny village in the region of Castilla y León that I visited in May 2014. At the time, its registered inhabitants — 56 of them — were preparing for a referendum on whether to change the name of their village, which was then called Castrillo Matajudíos. There have been many name changes recently in Spain, mostly related to erasing the footprint of the Franco dictatorship, which I discuss elsewhere in this book.

But when it came to the Jews, I found that the village's mayor, Lorenzo Rodríguez Pérez, was actively campaigning to overcome the conservative reluctance to adopt a change in such a rural area. Some residents doubted that it would be good for their village to end its linkage to the medieval massacre of Jews. "Unfortunately, the truth is that people here had no idea about our history and where we come from," the mayor explained to me. As I walked around the sleepy village looking for people to talk to, I soon understood why the mayor was struggling. People put many other preoccupations ahead of concern about their Jewish past. "We have been living just fine with this name for over 400 years, so why is there suddenly a need to change it?" Anastasio Alonso, a local farmer, told me.

Still, the referendum was approved shortly after my visit, in what proved a relatively tight vote, with 29 residents voting for a new name and 19 against it. The village took on the far less controversial name of Castrillo Mota de Judíos. As part of his referendum campaign, Rodríguez Pérez also called on some history experts and archaeologists to help explain how his village got its unpleasant name in the first place. Nobody got a definitive answer, but one possible explanation is that Christian converts decided to rename their village as a place of Jew killers to protect themselves during the Spanish Inquisition. (The first known document referring to the village as Castrillo Matajudíos is from 1623.)

Since the referendum, the mayor has continued to promote the village's Jewish roots and has worked to highlight the legacy of what was once a thriving Jewish community, founded in the 11th century after Jews were expelled from a nearby town. He launched a search for the remains of the synagogue and other buried evidence of the village's original hilltop settlement. The mayor also decided to build a visitors' center dedicated to the memory and history of Sephardi Jews. Such a project, he told me, would have been "unthinkable" before the name referendum of 2014. Since then, visitor numbers have risen steadily and "we've become for many an example of how to fight anti-Semitism," he said five years after we first met.

All over Spain, travel operators and guides have increasingly been organizing tours to showcase Jewish history, even in cities that have kept only traces of their former Jewish buildings. Some travel guides have argued that, if done carefully, it was possible to put together an itinerary that explained to visitors the difference between the history they can learn and the sites that they can actually see. "Turning the Jewish areas of Spain into a Disneyland does not help at all explain the complex history of Spain and its relation with the Jews," said Moises Hassan-Amselem, who organizes Jewish tours in Sevilla. "We have what we have, as it has been more than 500 years that Jews were expelled from Spain and very little patrimony has been preserved."

This seems to me the right approach. It is best to learn about a fascinating, complicated and enriching past rather than try to rewrite it, or invent it altogether.

Valorar la fiesta
Un mosaico de celebraciones únicas

No American writer has done more to raise Spain's profile than Ernest Hemingway. He covered tragedy and horror during the civil war, but also chronicled the joyful side of Spain and the singular attachment of its people to the "Fiesta," which is how the title of one of his books was translated into Spanish. But by mentioning Hemingway, any correspondent is likely to make some people in Spain cringe. As much as his love of Spain is appreciated, there seems to be just as strong a feeling that Hemingway helped feed some of the biggest stereotypes about the country. In fact, I have sometimes heard people tell me that Hemingway created such a strong image of Spain that he left many of today's visitors expecting to find a country stuck in the groove of the 1930s, and sometimes almost shocked to discover how modern Spain has instead become.

Irene Lozano, who served for 18 months as secretary of state for Global Spain, in the government of Pedro Sánchez, told me once that "the Spain of Hemingway does not exist." Part of her job, she said, consisted in setting the record straight about how far Spain had changed. In one of her speeches, she told her audience that "Spain today is a modern country, at the vanguard in social issues and politically engaged" to such a degree that Hemingway would probably not be able to recognize the nation that he chronicled. Lozano probably had reasons to feel frustrated by the lingering impact of Hemingway's representation of Spain. Nobody visiting Spain should expect to find one of the only European countries to have remained shielded from the convergent forces of globalization and social progress.

But like so many other correspondents, I have been inspired by Hemingway and his search for the uniqueness of a country so strongly defined by its traditions and celebrations. In fact, while many of these fiestas are rooted in ancestral traditions, I have found it fascinating to see how they continue to hold a special place in the Spanish calendar, even as society has changed and people have found new sources of entertainment.

In towns across Spain, children leave their Playstation at home to learn instead how to beat a drum or carry a religious relic. Sometimes, they are even given oversized masks, like Artur Panasiouk, a ten-year old whom I met as he was preparing to adjust an enormous devil's head before taking part in a street parade of giant statues, or Gigants, during the summer fiestas in Gràcia, the neighborhood of Barcelona. At home, Panasiouk collects miniature versions of the giant statues, his mother explained to me. "Some kids play video games, but Artur much prefers our giants," she said.

Many adults, of course, also set aside much of their free time to maintain Spanish traditions. In Seville, I once wrote a story about the *costaleros*, who are the human pillars of the Semana Santa procession and practice for weeks how to carry a massive altar through narrow streets with right-angled corners, walking together at the same pace and with the kind of precision normally displayed in a military parade. One of the many striking features that I learnt about this community of *costaleros* is that many of them never go to Mass. Another was that they got no money for their hard work and sweat, unlike in older times when the *costalero* job was normally held by a dockworker who received an extra pay for carrying the altars during the Semana Santa. "It's a unique chance to achieve something special together and also build real friendships," Juan José Gómez Sánchez, the man charged with leading the float of the Carretería Brotherhood, told me. "You start as *costaleros* and end up going to each other's birthdays and weddings."

Upholding the fiesta is part of what gives Spain its deep-rooted and exceptional sense of community. At the same time, it can provide a much-needed and light-hearted break from the worries and troubles of daily life. Take the example of the feast held every December in the town of Ibi, on the Day of the Holy Innocents, when a group of citizens stage a dawn military coup, take control of the town hall and then spend the rest of the day rewriting the laws and fighting their opponents on the streets, with rotten eggs and flour. The concept of this fiesta probably dates as far back as the role reversal of Ancient Rome's festival of Saturnalia, when masters provided table service for their servants, according to José Vicente Verdú, a lawyer who has researched Ibi's history.

But when I made my way to Ibi in December 2014, I had to add a stopover in Alicante, the provincial capital and the arrival station of my AVE train. Only four days earlier, Alicante had witnessed a real political coup, as its mayor was forced to resign after being charged in two corruption investigations relating to the city's once-booming construction sector. Adding to the sense that reality can sometimes outshine fiction, I then learnt in Ibi that the town's own mayor had also resigned, in 2013, after members of her administration were charged with fraud relating to public work contracts.

The night before the feast, the conspirators, known as *Els Enfarinats* (The Flour Men), drove around the town in a truck, reciting diatribes mostly targeting local politicians and businessmen. At sunrise on December 28, I met them in their makeshift headquarters, and watched as they put on their makeup and uniforms and gathered their ammunition — flour bags, egg boxes, fire extinguishers and firecrackers. Around 9 a.m., they assaulted the town hall and ousted the mayor, amid much shouting.

Soon enough, the rebels found themselves in a pitched battle against a group of residents who had stayed loyal to their elected mayor. The fighting ended with a cease-fire declaration, allowing everybody to enjoy a well-deserved beer in one of the surrounding bars. Under the new town rules, however, I was denied entrance to a bar because I was deemed to be "too tall." I argued my case, but the result was that I was fined instead 10 euros. Other unlucky offenders were told that they would be heading for prison after they finished their drink.

The mock fines, which are noted in a ledger in purposefully illegible writing, provide much laughter, but they also serve a social purpose, as the collected money then becomes a donation to a local residence for the elderly. "I prefer to pay this fine than my normal taxes, which are just too high," said Elena Otych, owner of the Maseros bar, after she was fined by the rebels because her bar counter was also found to be too high.

The jokes continued to flow throughout the afternoon almost as fast as the beer. But there were also a lot of bittersweet moments and sarcastic comments as residents looked back upon what had been a period of great frustration and economic hardship for some of them. Nobody seemed to have a fond word for the real politicians running Spain.

"These people should be in power not just for one day but for the whole year, because we have reached a point where anything is better than what we have had in our real politics," said Isabel Romero, a factory employee. "These people are collecting money for the elderly, rather than robbing public money like what our politicians have been doing."

Ibi was not the only place where I found ancestral celebrations influenced by modern political tensions. A festival, called La Patum, is celebrated each year in Berga, a town that has become the heartland of the Catalan independence movement.

As in Ibi, I arrived in Berga long before the official start of the Sunday celebration that closes in spectacular fashion the weeklong La Patum festival. But while the rebels of Ibi got prepared in the early hours, I found Berga fast asleep. Somebody finally opened the door to the town hall, but only to inform me that there was no way the mayor would arrive on time for our appointment, so it would be best for me to have a coffee nearby.

When she finally arrived, Montserrat Venturós, the mayor, looked worse for wear. The previous night, she explained, had already been one of heavy celebrations, apparently also involving plenty of drinking. "You have to understand that this is the moment of the year everybody here looks forward to, so we all do our best to celebrate until our energy really runs dry," she said. But however tired, Venturós sounded determined to use the main day of La Patum to showcase Berga as a symbol of the Catalan independence movement, as well as a rare bastion of the far-left politics of her small but influential party, the CUP.

For the following 12 hours or so, I noticed plenty of ways — some subtle, others less — in which modern politics had waded into a celebration that dates back to medieval times and is inscribed on the list of "Oral and Immaterial Heritage of Mankind" drawn up by Unesco. It was particularly striking to see how the mayor had carefully shifted the focus onto the strong pagan elements within the Patum and away from its Catholic dimension, as an event celebrated during the Feast of Corpus Christi.

In fact, Venturós watched La Patum from the town hall's balcony alongside other officials, but she was not accompanied by any representative from the Church, nor by anyone from the Spanish military. For the first time in La Patum's ancestral history, neither institution had been invited. That morning, Venturós was also the first mayor who did not attend the festival's Sunday Mass. "That things have always been done a certain way doesn't mean you should never adapt to how we live and feel, in a secular country," Venturós told me. "In the 21st century, I see no need for the Church to keep the same role in this feast."

After the congregation left, I walked down the aisle to talk to the priest about how he viewed the impact of Berga's recent politics on his Church. The priest, Marc Majà, sounded despondent about how Catholicism was getting eclipsed from La Patum, but he showed no desire to join the debate over independence. "The fact is that the roots of La Patum are religious, so it makes every sense to continue to invite each other," he said. "But I'm not here to promote a new conflict between church and state when we have so many more serious problems to deal with."

La Patum is celebrated on an asymmetrical town square that is overlooked by the balcony of the town hall and surrounded by residential homes. The Estelada flag (an unofficial symbol of Catalan independence) was hanging from dozens of balconies, but was also wrapped for the first time around the neck of the eagle and dragons that are among the central characters in the traditional representation of the fight of good against evil. While many of the performers sported beautiful and colorful costumes, it looked as if the politicians also wanted to make a statement with their choice of clothing. Venturós wore a sleeveless top and sandals. Some of her fellow left-wing councilors were similarly casually dressed. One of them, Francesc Ribera, better known under his musician name of Titot, looked as if he had just stepped off a concert stage. But the town councilor representing the Convergencia party, Ramon Minoves Pujols, wore a dark suit and a tie. Whatever her views on religion and society, he said, the mayor should have stuck to the usual format of La Patum, as well as gone to Mass. "It's just a lack of respect," he grumbled to me.

Amid a secessionist conflict, I found in Catalonia plenty of other examples of how modern politics influenced traditions. *Castells* (human towers), which are also listed by Unesco, have been erected at pro-independence rallies, not only in Catalonia but also in cities like Brussels, Rome and Paris, in front of the Eiffel Tower. In Valls, the town that is considered the birthplace of the *castells*, I watched the competition between the two oldest teams from the balcony of the town hall, next to the mayor, Albert Batet, who enjoyed talking about the official slogan of the *castells* — "*força, equilibri, valor i seny*" (strength, balance, courage and common sense). Batet drew a comparison between the values required to create a state and a human tower. "Both are proof that we can build great things if we come together," he told me.

As in many other countries, I have also found in Spain plenty of lovers of a tradition who are deeply ignorant about its origins. While researching my book on Catalonia, I heard about the convoluted history of the *sardana*, before it became recognized as the favorite folkloric dance of Catalonia. When the *sardana* finally moved from the countryside to the cities, during a wave of Catalan romanticism in the late nineteenth century, it did not generate unanimous enthusiasm. The newspaper *La Vanguardia* called it "a strange dance," performed by some people during the city's 1892 celebrations of the discovery of America. Narcís Serra, a former mayor of Barcelona whose career also included serving almost a decade as Spain's defense minister, once gave me a good summary of "political dancing" around the *sardana*: "I love the *sardana* and everything it represents. But even if all Catalans seem to think of it as a thousand years old, we should acknowledge that it rose as part of a nationalistic drive."

Don't let the facts get in the way of a great tradition, Jordi Pujol, the former president of Catalonia, once explained to me. "Every country creates its mythology and symbols, the only question is whether they work and serve good or bad purposes," he said.

Not all of the feasts of Spain have been updated to fit modern times, of course. The festivals showcasing the historic struggle between black-painted Moors and white Christian knights, which are particularly celebrated in the region of Valencia, are not exactly symbols of political correctness. Within Spain, the same event can also be celebrated very differently in different cities, particularly the feast of Epiphany, with its traditional parade of The Three Kings.

When he was mayor of Madrid, Alberto Ruiz-Gallardón followed the example set by his conservative predecessors and took part in the parade of the Three Kings as a black-faced Baltasar. Spain was clearly not Canada, where Justin Trudeau nearly lost a national election in 2019 after photos and videos were published of him with black face in costume from decades earlier. Trudeau apologized often and profusely.

But Madrid's parade changed after Manuela Carmena became mayor in 2015. This far-left politician and retired judge enraged the city's establishment by allowing drag queens into the parade and having the Three Kings dressed in funky costumes. The camels disappeared, as did VIP seats that had long been reserved for the governing conservative politicians of Madrid, as well as their relatives and friends.

Is Spain changing? Yes, but not everywhere. In the town of Alcoy, the municipality has so far resisted complaints from anti-racism groups and instead has been pushing since 2011 for its special Epiphany parade to get a Unesco listing, on top of already being ranked as a national tourism treasure. But Alcoy's parade includes about 200 pages, known locally as *els negrets*, who get fully dressed in black and use bright red lipstick to contrast with the blackness of their painted faces. The negrets climb up ladders to deliver gifts to the children who are watching from street balconies.

The fiestas enrich Spain and add to its diversity, as well as showcase the historical roots of the country. Alcoy's *Cabalgata de los Reyes Magos* (The Three Kings Parade) is in fact considered the oldest in Spain. But I would be surprised if it can withstand the test of time much longer. For all its intensity, any such celebration should respect modern principles of tolerance and inclusivity, so that it can be enjoyed by everybody irrespective of race or gender.

Proteger al denunciante
Los peligros de destapar la corrupción

Working as a correspondent involves a fair share of trial and error. The important part is recognizing an error early, before too much time is wasted in reporting and, of course, before it turns into printed misinformation. Every journalist faces this challenge. An added difficulty for the correspondent is that, as a foreigner, it can take more time to establish the reliability of a source, or the relevance of an issue. My workflow follows a pattern that sounds obvious, but that I find myself explaining regularly, because some people seem to forget that the correspondent does not decide what goes into print.

First, somebody tells me something interesting, or I read something intriguing, which convinces me that it is worth digging deeper. Once I know enough to feel that this story could also interest international readers, I propose an article to the editor of the relevant section (politics, business, culture, etc.). Although sometimes the editor rejects the proposal outright, I often get instead the green light to start my reporting in earnest. Once I have filed my article, it goes through two rounds of editing by separate people, sitting either in London or New York. In the first round, the editor focuses on the subject matter, tries to improve the text and often asks questions that require me to make some additional reporting, if not a complete rewrite. The second round is focused on copy editing and fact checking, although often the editor comes up with a new set of questions and suggestions, which can force me to do again some more reporting. Some bigger articles are subjected to a broader debate among the top editors, during their daily news conference, led from New York. And at any stage during this editing process, the foreign editor in New York or another senior editor can step in to force another change or review. As a result, I have seen some of what I considered to be completed articles then change shape several times. The alterations can feel overdone, especially if the text relates to events that are changing by the day, and my natural impatience as a reporter takes over. But like a chameleon that can make several adjustments on the way to reaching the desired color, the extra time spent on editing ends up producing some major improvements.

The whistle-blower's protection

Sadly, during the past decades, many publications have cut their newsroom costs by stripping their editing process down to the bare bone. The result has been a flurry of errors in what gets published, from misspelt names to more serious factual inaccuracies that can also leave publications open to very serious accusations like defamation. But there is also another underlying problem with such job cuts: by offering early retirement and other incentives to long-standing copy editors, publications have also risked losing part of their quality control and identity. Copy editors can have quirky personalities, often working late shifts when others are out for dinner or already tucked in bed, but in my experience they have always been among the most meticulous and dedicated people in the newsroom, as well as proud wordsmiths. They sometimes remind me of the librarian in the college of my university, who would know on which shelf to find a text without needed to check in the card catalog (yes, I went to university when students still borrowed reference books and did not have mobile phones!). Of course, the times have changed and publications now have added video editors, graphics designers and data specialists who have considerably enriched their online offering. But laying off veteran editors still feels to me like a decision to abandon part of the collective memory of a publication.

Thankfully, my newspaper has been among those that have managed to maintain the principle of a second round of editing, ensuring that at least two pairs of eyes get to read what a journalist has sent, and thereby help avoid some crass mistakes. In fact, I am among those readers who lose interest in an article if the opening paragraph starts by calling a famous person Jane rather than Julie.

I have sometimes hit a major roadblock as soon as I have started reporting a story, which I of course then try to overcome. But occasionally, it seems best to abandon the article project, swallow the moment of disappointment and the embarrassment of telling the editor about this failure, and move on to the next story.

As in the other countries from which I have reported, Spain has yielded instances in which I have pursued the wrong story, or failed to follow up on a good lead. Stories have come my way relatively easily and quickly in part because, as mentioned at the start of this book, I arrived in Spain at the same time as the financial crisis. But soon enough, I also found myself struggling to establish the veracity of a flood of stories that involved lost or missing money, particularly about companies in the property and banking sectors.

I was lucky to reach Spain with several years of experience as a financial journalist, during which time I covered some major corporate scandals, like the bankruptcy of Parmalat in Italy in 2003 or the overstating by Shell of its oil and gas reserves, which resulted in a landmark fine in 2004. I had also done a semester of accounting at Columbia Business School in New York. But this didn't give me the skills and confidence to audit myself the books of a troubled Spanish company.

As Spain was sinking into financial trouble, I started receiving more phone calls and emails from people who wanted me to pursue specific stories about economic scandals, which often involved fraud that they claimed executives were ignoring or covering up. (The crisis eventually ended, but the calls continued even after Spain emerged from recession in 2013.)

Often, I tried to politely turn down such story proposals, urging my informers to offer them instead to the Spanish media. I explained to them that what might seem like big news in Madrid or Valencia might not fascinate a reader in New York, let alone one of my editors who gets to decide whether the newspaper would publish such a story. After all, if I am myself not entirely convinced about a story, how can I then hope to convince an editor, who is already sitting on a pile of story proposals from all over Europe? (I am always amazed to meet some people working in corporate sales and marketing who manage to sell products they admit in private that they would never want to own themselves.)

But at the same time, I was often hearing from people who claimed that it was very difficult to blow the whistle on corruption or other forms of wrongdoing in Spain. Several people explained that they wanted to tell me about a problem after failing to get a fair hearing within their workplace.

Not everybody knows how to present their worries well. I have received many emails that I have dismissed out of hand (whether rightly or wrongly) because the way they were written simply sounded too emotional, vengeful or personal to warrant giving it much attention. I am particularly wary of emails that contain words written in red, bold or capital letters, that are filled with exclamation marks or that conjure a degree of desperation that seems exaggerated: "You must write URGENTLY about this." It is also a red flag when an email contains an obvious factual error, or a gross spelling mistake. If the plaintiff has not taken the time to explain a problem properly or even work out that I now no longer work for the *Financial Times*, how can this person expect a correspondent to devote time and energy to what is often a local issue?

But there is one good reason not to dismiss all such complaints, even if badly worded, which is that I have come to learn how hard and lonely the life of the whistle-blower can be. In fact, despite all the political talk about fighting corruption, some people who have actively exposed corruption in Spain have then themselves been ostracized, prosecuted and left jobless.

Take the case of Ana Garrido, who became one of Spain's most famous whistle-blowers during the financial crisis. For two decades, Garrido held one of the most secure jobs in Spain, as an employee on a fixed contract working within her town hall, Boadilla del Monte, on the outskirts of Madrid. But in 2008, after she questioned how Boadilla awarded public contracts, Garrido's life descended into what she later described to me as a calvary. Her downward path took her from office mobbing to depression to sick leave to unemployment to costly lawsuits and even death threats, while also forcing her into a fight for economic survival.

By the time I visited her in 2016, Garrido was 50 years old and making handmade bracelets to stay financially afloat. She was also relying on crowdfunding money to help cover her legal expenses, which had by then reached 20,000 euros. Forced to rent out her own home to continue paying the mortgage, she sold most of her clothes and furniture and then moved instead into an apartment with peeling orange walls that was abandoned by friends who were unable to pay their own mortgage. She had, in her own words, become an *"okupa"* (squatter).

Still, Garrido was getting belated recognition, particularly from Spain's emerging parties. A month before I went to her home, she was invited to Congress by the lawmakers of Ciudadanos. Luis Garicano, the main economic adviser of Ciudadanos, told reporters that day that if Spain could not protect whistle-blowers like Garrido, "we don't have a country that is worth it." He added: "I don't want to live in such a country."

Spain emerged from the financial crisis as part of a handful of European nations without any legislation to help whistle-blowers, according to a 2013 study by Transparency International, a nongovernmental organization. Their report lambasted Spain for not even giving public servants protection from "retaliation when reporting suspected crimes." "There are a lot of corruption cases that don't come to light because the whole system is designed to hurt rather than to protect those who denounce corruption," Pedro Arancón, the president of an association called Platform for Honesty, told me around the same time.

Blowing the whistle could even mean risking prison, as I found out from Roberto Macías, who went on trial in Seville, accused of revealing secret information after copying computer files, even though his actions had helped uncover fraud within the Andalusian chapter of the UGT (Unión General de Trabajadores) labor union. Prosecutors wanted Macías to spend three years in prison, as well as pay 60,000 euros in moral damages claimed by his former union. The trial started just as UGT itself stood accused by the Andalusian government of misspending at least 1.8 million euros in public money allocated for unemployed workers, but used instead to pay for parties and gifts to union officials.

Macías lost his own UGT job in 2012. Even so, he told me how he then continued to suffer harassment for snitching on union bosses. "I've faced a witch hunt from an organization far more interested in punishing those who leaked documents than in trying to recover millions of wasted public funds and pursuing the officials who misspent that money," Macías said.

I used an interview with Carmen Castilla, the secretary general of the UGT in Andalusia, to raise the issue of Macías, but she showed little interest in discussing his case. If anything, she argued, both the alleged theft of documents and public money fraud should be prosecuted. "If any presumed crime has happened, it should be dealt with by the judiciary — and presumed theft is a crime," Castilla told me. The court case of Macías only reached a verdict in 2020, eight years after he was dismissed from his union and switched instead to a precarious life oscillating between temporary jobs and unemployment benefits. He was sentenced to two years in prison, although the ruling was being appealed at the time of writing this book. In the meantime, politicians have continued to investigate several millions of unaccounted UGT money, while the public prosecution requested in June of 2019 archiving the case against Manuel Pastrana, the historic leader of the union in Andalusia, who was by then considered to be too ill to take part in a trial.

While working in the town hall of Boadilla, Garrido also fell ill, but she used her sick leave to compile a 300-page dossier on how Boadilla awarded fraudulent contracts. Her findings were the starting point of an investigation that then spread to other towns and politicians and became the far-reaching Gürtel case, the most serious fraud scandal faced by Mariano Rajoy's Popular Party. Garrido said she risked more than just her job to expose fraud. When she briefly returned to work in 2011, she told me about how Boadilla's new mayor and administration were "simply determined to make me pay for being a snitch." The harassment went as far as "death threats and trying to drive me off the road," she claimed. She also told me in detail about returning home to find a man wearing black waiting near the front door of her building. She had seen the same man before, following her on the street.

Eventually, she left and took the town hall to court for harassment, winning her case before a Madrid court. Boadilla's new town hall administration, however, told me that Garrido had built up a case of "inexistent harassment" and that she had left her job of her own accord. Garrido said that the new mayor's denial of any wrongdoing only confirmed that she should never have expected any institutional support. "I once had a normal job and life, but once you denounce, you should get ready for a nightmare," she said. "It's a situation that I could never have endured if I also had children to look after."

Garrido and Macías are probably not perfect role models. Some of their claims are near-impossible to verify, including Garrido's about getting physically threatened. But when meeting them or any other whistle-blower, I have mostly felt that fighting corruption in Spain can come at a significant and unwarranted personal cost. Sometimes, however, I have wasted time and energy on pursuing a story that led into a cul-de-sac. And in a few cases, I came to regret ignoring what turned out to be a major story for Spain. Here are some examples.

In 2013, a French friend moved to Madrid with her husband, an Israeli engineer, and their daughter, because he had got a job at a Spanish technology company. A few months later, we met for dinner and I asked him how the new job was going. He bluntly told me that it was a mess, because he could not understand how the company was being managed and also doubted its technology, which provided WiFi on public transport. "Start checking it out for yourself," he recommended. "Take a bus in Madrid and try to connect to the WiFi network to see if it works." I took several buses, but never tested the WiFi. Meanwhile, frustrated by his job, this Israeli engineer resigned in May 2014.

His company, Gowex, declared bankruptcy two months later, after being found to have falsified its accounts during four years. By then, Gowex was also operating in other major cities like New York, after receiving millions in funding from Banco Santander and other financial institutions to help it expand faster. This major fraud scandal hurt the reputation of Spain's technology sector, since Gowex had been one of its international success stories. I might never have discovered that Gowex was fraudulent. But I was sorry not to have listened better to a trustworthy friend who was seriously concerned about how his company was operating.

Spain has an open society that makes the job of the reporter much easier than in several other countries, including some with a longer democratic track record. I believe this great media access reflects a very positive aspect of Spanish society, which has grown distrustful about the quality of its journalism (like in the rest of the Western world), but has maintained an environment in which communication flows freely and in which there are few social barriers.

I have asked myriad questions to random people on the street, even in complicated situations like in the midst of street protests. I have almost never drawn suspicion, let alone been asked to show my press card. People have also shared with me their personal details, including their age and political ideology, far more openly than in countries like my own, Switzerland. Sometimes, people have even spontaneously pulled out their own DNI (*documento nacional de identidad* — identity card) to help a foreign journalist like myself spell their names correctly.

Over the past decade, I have also managed to use the calling card of *The New York Times* to get an interview with almost anybody whom I wanted to speak to. Writing for *The New York Times* is an invaluable asset. It generates excitement and interest, but also sometimes anxiety in those whom I try to get information from. In some rare cases, however, it has not proved possible for me to sit down with somebody whom I really hoped to meet. I repeatedly failed to get an interview with Mariano Rajoy during the many years in which he ran Spain. Whenever I exchanged a few words with Rajoy, on the sidelines of a conference or at a reception, I found him to be far more jovial and charming than I had anticipated. But I never climbed over the wall erected between us by his press team.

There are also some solid walls protecting the leaders of corporate Spain. As the financial crisis deepened, I got intrigued by how some banking chairmen ran their companies as if they owned them. One striking example was that of Banco Santander, believed by many people in Spain to be owned rather than just controlled by the Botín family, when the truth is that the family's shareholding is a tiny fraction of what it was a century ago, when the bank was still firmly anchored in Santander. At the time of writing, the Botín family owns less than 0.5 percent of "its" bank.

In 2011, together with a colleague who specialized in the banking sector, I spent several days shuttling between Madrid and Santander to try to understand how the Botín family had managed to keep their control over a bank that they helped transform from a mid-ranking Spanish player into a global financial powerhouse. Our research was prompted by some bad news for the Botín family, whose name had appeared on the long list of tax evaders leaked to the authorities by Hervé Falciani, a former employee of HSBC in Geneva. As a result, the Botíns paid Spain about 200 million euros in back taxes to avoid criminal evasion charges related to money that the family started hiding in Switzerland around the time of the civil war.

The tax investigation prompted a brief flurry of articles in the Spanish media, but nothing that could put into question the integrity of the current family members or undermine Chairman Emilio Botín's grip on the bank. As Salvador Arancibia, a business journalist who had covered Santander since 1980 and had also worked for the bank, told us at the time: "Santander spends massively on advertising and this influences the news treatment that they receive." Botín died unexpectedly in September 2014, a few weeks before turning 80. He was succeeded by his daughter, Ana Botín, who had long been groomed for the top job. Her appointment was rubber-stamped unanimously by members of an internal committee, a few hours after Botín's death, in the most perfect tradition of family handovers.

There were several other interesting examples of all-powerful banking bosses in Spain, from BBVA to La Caixa. But in the autumn of 2015, I decided to look instead at the management structure outside the financial sector, to see how many bosses had managed to survive the crisis and stay in office even past Spain's official retirement age.

I decided to make Telefónica the test case for my story because its chairman, César Alierta, had just turned 70 and held his government-appointed job since 2000. When I discussed this story with my business editor, he asked me whether Alierta had strong technology credentials, and whether Telefónica had done particularly well for its shareholders. The answer to both questions was negative. Alierta came from the world of finance, was appointed in 1996 by the government to run the state-owned tobacco company, Tabacalera, and was then moved by President José María Aznar to take charge of Telefónica and replace Juan Villalonga. Alierta had proved himself a savvy financier and astute executive, but he was not the Steve Jobs of Spain.

Alierta had brought a more conservative management style to Telefónica than his predecessor, but the company's share price was down significantly compared with 2000, when Alierta took charge. My editor's final question was harder to answer: since Telefónica was no longer government-controlled, was nobody asking for a management change?

I started talking to institutional investors and fund managers about Alierta. I found a friend whose portfolio included shares in Telefónica. He agreed to help me, as long as I didn't make him part of my article. We met for coffee and he carefully took me through the list of Telefónica's directors, which he had printed out. The nexus that he drew was one in which the board owed a very strong allegiance to Alierta. Some board members who were listed as independent directors had not only political backgrounds, but even a personal connection to Alierta that dated back several decades, to the time when Alierta worked at Banco Urquijo and then set up Beta Capital, the finance company that he eventually sold in the 1990s. How could such people be described as having full independence from Alierta?

I requested an interview with Alierta. In response, two members of Telefónica's press team offered to set up a preliminary meeting to discuss what I wanted. Over lunch, I told them that I was fascinated by his outstanding capacity to survive in turbulent times and in a fast-changing industry like telecommunications. They politely told me that, whenever an interview could be arranged, Alierta would no doubt be happy to discuss his resilience and track record.

A month later, I wrote to them to see whether we could finally agree on an interview date. I was told that Alierta was preparing for a very busy month, but that I would hear back as soon as he had more time. I next heard from Telefónica almost two months later, but in a press release that announced that Alierta was stepping down as chairman (although he remained both as board director and president of Telefónica's foundation.) Alierta's withdrawal from the top position made my preparatory work seem outdated and pointless. I was left with the feeling that the press office had done a good stalling job, making me believe for long enough that he would give me the interview. My editor was also not interested in an alternative story about how Alierta got replaced by his long-standing heir apparent.

I have occasionally given up on stories because I got uncomfortable during my reporting. In 2013, I read an article about graphene, a revolutionary material that was starting to be used in Spain. I knew nothing about graphene, which was not entirely surprising as it was in its infancy. In 2010, the Nobel Prize was awarded to two British physicists for their work on graphene, which is both extraordinarily thin and strong. But at a time when smaller Spanish corporations were still struggling to raise financing, I was also surprised to read that graphene was gaining traction in Spain. I called a European Commission official in Brussels, who told me that Spanish companies had got a significant share of a fund, worth one billion euros, which the European Union created to help develop graphene.

I convinced my business editor that this could be an intriguing story about a possible industrial breakthrough not only for Spain, but also for the EU, which was trying to challenge the United States in technology. I got the editor's blessing to visit companies working with graphene, several of which were located in the province of Alicante.

In Alicante, I teamed up again with Samuel Aranda, a photographer whose work I discuss elsewhere in this book. We spent a full day driving around the province, visiting companies that used graphene to make products ranging from cycling helmets to bed mattresses. Outside Elda, Spain's shoemaking town, we visited a research laboratory in which graphene was being added to the soles of footwear. It was one the most basic labs that I had ever visited, completely out of sync with what I imagined to be advanced industrial research. I ended the visit without a clear understanding of how the process worked and how graphene could become financially profitable, given the difficulties in scaling up production.

I took the train back from Alicante to Madrid with a queasy stomach, not because I had eaten anything difficult to digest but because this whole story suddenly felt like an incomplete puzzle. The executives who had shown us around the different companies had been extremely warm and welcoming, but I could not always understand clearly their answers. A couple of days later, I phoned my editor to tell him that I would abandon the story, because I had not been able to understand just how graphene would become the Spanish industrial miracle story that some of its developers claimed it would be.

In 2012, I traveled to the Catalan seaside resort of Lloret de Mar because of a corruption scandal. It involved very little money compared to some of the other fraud cases of Spain, but it interested *The New York Times* because it had an unexpected international dimension, involving Russian money. A century ago, Lloret was the playground of the bourgeoisie of Barcelona. But during the Spanish construction boom, Lloret became one of the most heavily-built stretches of the Catalan coast, popular with foreign tourists, including Russians. In 2013, Lloret's mayor, Xavier Crespo, was accused of using Russian money to boost the finances of his city hall, while allowing Russians to launder their money in property investments around Lloret.

The reporting trip to Lloret went well. The mayor denied wrongdoing, but answered most questions, including about a paid trip that he took to Russia. We then visited several real estate projects, including a sports stadium financed with Russian money. One of the Russian sponsors of Lloret, Andrey Petrov, was at the time sitting in prison in Spain. Coincidentally, Aranda lived in a village near Lloret. Since it was close to home, he told me that he would return to Lloret on another day, to take advantage of better natural light and take more photos of the town.

Aranda called me a few days later to share a worrying piece of information. Back in Lloret, he had spotted one of the activists who blew the whistle on the mayor's property deals. The activist was driving a brand-new Porsche car that was completely out of tune with the image he had given us, of a humble citizen fighting against

Lloret's corrupt officialdom. I could not understand this apparent contradiction, so I gave up on the story.

In November 2015, Crespo, the former mayor, was convicted. He got suspended from politics for nine-and-a-half years and received a fine, as well as being forced to reimburse the cost of the trip and the luxury watch that he received in Russia. A year later, Crespo's political suspension got cut down to two years.

In retrospect, the ruling against Crespo showed that I could have gone ahead with my article. But I was still left with the feeling that, even if the mayor had been singled out for wrongdoing, his misdeeds mostly showed that too much money had been earned too fast by too many people in Lloret. Including possibly by the city's own whistle-blowers.

EPILOGUE

El desafío de la Covid-19
Una crisis sin precedente

On 24 March 2020, Isabel Muñoz, a doctor, was found lying dead on the floor of her kitchen in Salamanca by the police. The door of the fridge was open and water was spilt around her, showing she had been struggling to get a drink. She was reported to be the first Spanish health care professional to die of Covid-19.

Ten days earlier, Dr. Muñoz had felt fever and started coughing, so she immediately decided to self-isolate. She told her husband that she could look after herself and asked him to move out of their apartment because "she was obsessed with not getting anybody else infected," her brother, Jesús Muñoz, told me weeks later by phone. Like so many others, Dr. Muñoz, who was 59, died after trying to save others. She got infected while attending patients in her medical center, in the village of La Fuente de San Esteban to which she would drive to work from Salamanca.

In her final days on the job, she regularly complained to her family about not receiving from the authorities enough protection gear and not getting tested for Covid-19. "I unfortunately consider that she engaged in this battle like a soldier sent to the frontline without a helmet and a shield," her brother told me. "She was a real fighter, who kept telling us that she would overcome this disease as quickly as possible so as to get back to the job she loved."

Spain owes a huge debt to those who fought against Covid-19, often in desperate conditions that shocked a nation that had long considered its public health care system to be among the most robust in Europe. Many of these health care workers showed the kind of courage that only comes from doing a job that is actually a lifetime vocation.

When Dr. Muñoz was only six years old, her father had to undergo two surgeries to overcome bone tuberculosis. During his lengthy hospital stay, she decided to become a doctor, showing such interest in how the hospital functioned that a nun who was looking after her father told him that his young daughter clearly had "the passion for medicine running in her blood," her brother, Jesús Muñoz, recalled.

As I write the Epilogue to this book, it it too early to draw firm conclusions about Covid-19's impact on Spain. In particular, the jury is still out (literally since there are several lawsuits) on whether the Spanish authorities could have done more to avoid the death of Dr. Muñoz and so many others. Spain was among the nations worst hit when Covid-19 first spread across Europe, but obviously not the only one. The pandemic left a trail of death and sorrow across the world, as well as an economic recession whose scale and duration are yet to be established. Some countries that had been left relatively unscathed in early 2020 then got devastated in the later waves of the pandemic.

On 1 April 2020, I marked a decade of writing for *The New York Times* from Madrid. There was no celebration to be had, in the midst of a very strict lockdown and just as the epidemic was at its peak in Madrid, killing more than 300 people a day and pushing hospitals to the brink of collapse, with some patients forced to sleep in the corridors. That evening, like on so on many others, I joined the 8 p.m. round of applause for the health care professionals. Some of the faces on the other side of my one-way street had by then already become familiar. It felt weird not to know their names, but to still get tempted to invent something about their life story, having been able to observe for weeks my neighbors in a way that I had never done before. The lockdown had made physical contact impossible, but yet had also made us much more aware of each other's presence, or lack thereof.

I marveled particularly at a family who lived in the block opposite me and who would always dress smartly their children as if they were about to go to Church. Instead, they would regularly play mini-golf together in their living room. Like others, this family had hung from their balcony the Spanish flag that they first floated in 2017, to show Spain's unity in the face of Catalan secessionism. This time, however, the flag was adorned with the black ribbon of mourning. On my street, however, most of the balconies had stayed empty since mid-March. It was clear that several wealthy neighbors had used the state of emergency decreed by the government as their signal to flee Madrid for the safe haven of a more isolated countryside or seaside vacation home.

In 2010, I had arrived in Madrid at the onset of the financial crisis, only a month before the government of José Luís Rodríguez Zapatero made its first budgetary cuts, including the removal of one of its own trademark pieces of legislation, the "baby check" that had been promoted as an answer to Spain's falling birth rate.

I was now in the epicenter of another crisis, but one that was all about death. It was unfolding under the watch of another Socialist prime minister, who was again facing fierce accusations of having underestimated the risk and then mishandled the onset of the crisis.

I believe that a crisis generally brings to the surface extreme behavior in people, for the better and the worse. Covid-19 produced extraordinary gestures of solidarity in Spain, from famous chefs elaborating instead menus for food banks to health workers returning to the job as soon as they came out of quarantine, as Dr. Muñoz had hoped to do. During the epidemic, much was written and spoken about the soaring death toll in Spain, including the muddle over how the government counted the dead. Unfortunately, not so much was written about the very high recovery rate from Covid-19, which showed just how hard doctors and nurses worked to keep Spain's health care system performing.

By and large, the citizens of Spain rose remarkably to the challenge of the crisis. Unfortunately, once the immediate health threat started to fade, economic and social feuding resurfaced. There were complaints about greedy landlords, as well as companies more interested in protecting their shareholders rather than the jobs of factory workers. And while tens of millions of people followed diligently the rules of the lockdown, a few also showed the kind of disdain and recklessness that can put the lives of others at risk.

Worse still, the politicians of Spain did not unite in the face of adversity and instead displayed a volume of discord as soon as the death toll started to rise that was particularly remarkable when contrasted with the political harmony in neighboring Portugal, which also faced Covid-19 under a minority left-wing government.

In Spain, not a single opportunity was wasted to trade accusations. Speaking before a parliamentary commission in June 2020, Luis Garicano, who had become a member of the European Parliament, gave a good summary of political debating in Spain in the midst of a pandemic. The goal of Spanish politicians, he argued, was now "to look, among all the issues under the debate, for the one that is going to irritate everybody the most, so as to make it more newsworthy."

The coronavirus crisis gave right-wing politicians plenty of fresh ammunition against the fragile coalition government of Pedro Sánchez, whom they notably accused of criminal negligence and of lying about the data. The government responded with criticism that even turned into an ugly feud with the military police, adding institutional tensions at a time when citizens were being asked to respect law and order. Sánchez poured more oil on the fire in Congress by raising the ghost of the "patriotic police" allegedly used by the previous conservative government against political opponents. Tensions also mounted between regional politicians and the central government, not least over whether strict lockdown measures risked instead doing more damage by destroying the economy. In the capital region of Madrid, Isabel Díaz Ayuso very successfully ran for re-election in May 2021, on a simple "Freedom" slogan and in open defiance of the central government's call for more lockdown restrictions. The blame game was in full flow.

If this was the kind of "new normalcy" that Sánchez was expecting Spain to enter after overcoming Covid-19, it looked unfortunately remarkably similar to the old one, at least in terms of politics.

About the Author

Raphael Minder has been a correspondent for *The New York Times* since April 2010, based in Madrid and covering Spain and Portugal. He has written extensively on the impact of the financial crisis and the resulting political tensions, including the secessionist drive in Catalonia. He has also covered the abdication of King Juan Carlos I, as well as social issues, like migration from Africa and domestic violence in Spain. He also writes about sports and culture, including the rivalry between Real Madrid and F.C. Barcelona, and efforts to complete Gaudí's Sagrada Família basilica.

Born in Geneva in 1971, Raphael has been a journalist since 1993, when he started working in Switzerland for Bloomberg News. He spent 10 years as a staff correspondent for the *Financial Times*, working in Paris, Brussels, Sydney and finally Hong Kong as the newspaper's Asia regional correspondent.

Raphael holds a Bachelor's degree from Oxford University, where he studied politics, philosophy and economics. He also has a Master's degree from Columbia University's School of Journalism in New York.

Raphael has always worked in English, but also speaks French, German and Spanish.

Printed and bound by CPI Group (UK) Ltd, Croydon, CR0 4YY

16/04/2025

14658575-0002